Protections of Tenure and Academic Freedom
in the United States

Matthew J. Hertzog

Protections of Tenure and Academic Freedom in the United States

Evolution and Interpretation

Matthew J. Hertzog
UnityPoint Health Methodist College
Peoria, IL
USA

ISBN 978-3-319-85871-5   ISBN 978-3-319-56270-4 (eBook)
DOI 10.1007/978-3-319-56270-4

© The Editor(s) (if applicable) and The Author(s) 2017
Softcover reprint of the hardcover 1st edition 2017
This work is subject to copyright. All rights are solely and exclusively licensed by the Publisher, whether the whole or part of the material is concerned, specifically the rights of translation, reprinting, reuse of illustrations, recitation, broadcasting, reproduction on microfilms or in any other physical way, and transmission or information storage and retrieval, electronic adaptation, computer software, or by similar or dissimilar methodology now known or hereafter developed.
The use of general descriptive names, registered names, trademarks, service marks, etc. in this publication does not imply, even in the absence of a specific statement, that such names are exempt from the relevant protective laws and regulations and therefore free for general use.
The publisher, the authors and the editors are safe to assume that the advice and information in this book are believed to be true and accurate at the date of publication. Neither the publisher nor the authors or the editors give a warranty, express or implied, with respect to the material contained herein or for any errors or omissions that may have been made. The publisher remains neutral with regard to jurisdictional claims in published maps and institutional affiliations.

Cover image © Image Source / Alamy Stock Photo

Printed on acid-free paper

This Palgrave Macmillan imprint is published by Springer Nature
The registered company is Springer International Publishing AG
The registered company address is: Gewerbestrasse 11, 6330 Cham, Switzerland

Contents

1 Introduction 1

2 History of Tenure and Academic Freedom in the USA 23

3 Tenure-Related Issues in the Lower Courts: Decisions and Ramifications 83

4 Landmark Cases in Higher Education on Academic Freedom and Tenure 139

5 Conclusion: Summary and Recommendations 181

Glossary 197

Index 199

LIST OF TABLES

Table 2.1 Expansion of Universities and Colleges
          between 1939 and 1969   56
Table 2.2 Total number of US Supreme Court Cases 1930–1969 58
Table 2.3 Percent of full-time instructional staff
          with tenure: 1980–2010   59

CHAPTER 1

Introduction

The origins of higher education date back to the time of Plato as it was he who put forth that intellectual liberty existed between teachers and their students. As noted in his work, The Republic, a format must be established to permit students to be educated in a manner where they are free to ask and answer questions.[1] Centuries later, during medieval times, this concept of the academy as put forth by Plato was further enhanced and developed as universities were founded and expanded throughout Europe. As these institutions matured, the concept of tenure and the retaining of faculty long term also evolved. By the early nineteenth century, German universities began offering a system that focused on an instructor's freedom of speech, known as Lehrfreiheit as well as a contract-based employment system.[2] This contract-based system, established in Germany, eventually led to the American system today known as tenure.

Tenure, as implemented in today's colleges and universities throughout America, provides academics a high degree of job security; however, over the past few decades, with the financial restraints placed on public institutions by the lack of state and federal funding and the declining of enrollment in certain disciplines, the value of tenure in today's institutions of higher education is being raised by university administrators, the media, the public at large, and politicians. These discussions on tenure commonly focus on faculty productivity and accountability when institutions remove a tenured faculty member. In addition, tenure has the tendency to create a two-class faculty system (i.e., tenured

© The Author(s) 2017
M.J. Hertzog, *Protections of Tenure and Academic Freedom in the United States*, DOI 10.1007/978-3-319-56270-4_1

track and non-tenured track) which may impact the faculty members' freedom of teaching, learning, and research. Although there are various approaches to higher education in the USA (e.g., junior colleges, private 4-year institutions, research institutions, and typical 4-year institutions to name a few), higher education in the US has established itself as a system focused on providing a faculty member with protection from wrongful termination, or more so, termination without due process, as well as the academic freedom to discuss controversial topics in the classroom.[3] Similarly, the same rights that are awarded to faculty through the protection of tenure and academic freedom also provide students an opportunity to question theories presented to them in their classrooms.

The rights and freedoms afforded by tenure and academic freedom did not coalesce until, in 1915, a group was formed (American Association of University Professors) which put forth the goals of what has become known as tenure. In a document drafted by this association, the goals of tenure and academic freedom were defined as: (1) to protect a faculty member's academic freedom in the classroom; and (2) for the faculty member to be able to perform other job duties without the fear of termination.[4] However, within the review of relevant literature on tenure, a topic that is not addressed is the relevance of tenure in the twenty-first-century academy. Trends in higher education have shown that simply having tenure does not provide the willingness of faculty to speak freely or to publish and/or teach about controversial topics.[5]

Review of Resources

Brief History of the Rise of Tenure in Higher Education

In the early to mid-nineteenth century, faculty in higher education served at the pleasure of the governing board of trustees of their universities. Because state or federal funding did not exist then as it does now, many institutions of higher education relied on donors of large sums of money to keep the schools operating.[6] However, since the donors knew they were the sole support for the university remaining open, they felt they could remove professors from the faculty or prohibit the university from hiring someone whose religious and/or political beliefs differed from those of the institution or donor.[7] While the rise of science and research in various disciplines at times came into conflict with religiously based institutions during the mid-1800s, professors throughout the country were coming into higher education from a wide assortment of backgrounds. Many of these newly hired faculty members had recently returned from studying in Europe and had observed the freedoms held by European counterparts. This diversity in the faculty led to confrontations as professors and administration clashed over social, religious, and political issues. In addition, with the passage of the Morrill Act (1862)[8] faculty members were now focusing on areas other than religion and were engaged in research in various disciplines. Nonetheless, a de facto tenure system did exist since faculty members typically only were terminated for interfering with the religious teachings of the university.[9]

The goal of tenure was, and is, to establish a contractual system between higher education faculty and administration to provide continuous employment for faculty.[10] Although academic tenure was loosely in place at universities in the USA during the nineteenth century, tenure itself remained more or less a de facto system at these institutions that warranted term appointments for instructors rather than the lifelong commitment that tenure is today.[11] Furthermore, the early forms of tenure provided no explicit rights for professors and made no guarantees about the concept of academic freedom within the classroom.[12]

Around the turn of the nineteenth century, contractual agreements between faculty and universities were rare because gentlemen's agreements between governing boards and instructors were the norm.[13] During the late nineteenth and early twentieth century, however, the higher education system in the USA went through a period where a handful of universities were established through large donations made by the elitist class. These contributions enabled university faculty to continue research that provided opportunities for them to contribute to the industrial expansion to the West. The faculty made these advancements which, in turn, financially benefited their university through the university's ability to place patents on these advancements, but no provisions were made that guaranteed the individual faculty member's employment once the research was completed. When it was deemed that their services were no longer required at the university, faculty had no claim on the research they conducted because the university claimed that the work was done on the university's time.

Although tenure was initially thought of in terms of job security for higher education faculty, instances can be found where faculty members were dismissed because of their views or speech. Issues such as these prompted educational leaders to discuss tenure as an issue of academic freedom as well as an issue of job security. An early example of a faculty member being scrutinized for his political views occurred in 1894 when the press and the Wisconsin State Legislature demanded that Richard Ely, an economist at the University of Wisconsin, be terminated for his public views on labor strikes and boycotts. Ely supported the rights of laborers to strike and boycott their current employers if working conditions were not improved. Uncommon for the time, the governing board for the University of Wisconsin released a statement indicating that they supported Ely's academic freedom and no action was taken against Ely by the university.[14]

A similar example of a faculty member's employment being jeopardized by a community leader is seen in the case of Edward Ross. In 1900, Ross, a Stanford University professor, spoke out publicly against several controversial topics of the time: (1) municipal ownership of public utilities; (2) his public support for railway union strikes; and (3) how the use of Asian laborers instead of the European-American working class was destructive for the US working classes' well-being.[15] Ross's statements went directly against the business practices of Leland Stanford, the founder of Stanford University. When Stanford's widow learned of his statements, she demanded Ross's immediate termination.[16] The university president adhered to her demand and Ross was terminated because of his views on immigrant labor and train monopolies.

Administration within higher education in the late nineteenth and early twentieth centuries ruled universities with a firm hand and tightly controlled the research and conduct of their faculty.[17] Recognizing the lack of job security awarded to faculty across the nation, in 1915 two professors, Arthur Lovejoy and John Dewey organized a meeting for university professors with the stated goal of defining academics as professionals and not simply as employees.[18] Dewey and Lovejoy sent invitations to 867 faculty members known for their prominence in their respective fields across the country; 650 attended.[19] The final act of this meeting was the establishment of the American Association of University Professors (AAUP), an organization designed to protect academic freedom and provide tenure for all faculty members.[20]

This concept of tenure and its issuance to faculty members was defined when the AAUP released its Declaration of Principles of Academic Freedom and Tenure in 1915. Prior to this document, the notion of prolonged employment for university faculty was based on a gentlemen's agreement and solely at the discretion of the governing board for the university.[21] This document described the rights and freedoms that all faculty members should have for safeguarding their freedom of expression in the classroom and their guarantee of job security. The document also recommended that there be probationary period of 10 years for a faculty member prior to receiving tenure.[22] Since the release of this document, the terms academic freedom and tenure have been entwined and inseparable.[23]

Following the publication of the 1915 AAUP document, universities, and in some instances state departments of education, gradually began to recognize tenure as a right of faculty, but the recommendation of a probationary period to acquire tenure was not widely accepted. Up until 1940, universities used variations of the recommended probationary period for awarding tenure and did not follow the AAUP's recommended 10-year probationary period for faculty tenure.[24] In 1940, however, the AAUP released their Statement of Principles on Academic Freedom and Tenure which altered their recommendation for the probationary period by reducing the timeframe from 10 to 7 years. They further stated that during this probationary period the instructor had to meet the university and/or state requirements for academic tenure or he/she could be terminated without cause. Within this statement, the organization identified that tenured professors could not be dismissed without adequate cause except for extraordinary reasons related to financial emergencies.[25] Furthermore, the 1940 document stated that if a tenure-track faculty member did not receive tenure by the end of the identified probationary period, he/she could then be terminated without cause if, through a peer review process, the individual demonstrated a lack of professional progress in scholarship.[26]

Shortly after the AAUP statement was made public, World War II broke out and college enrollments declined as the country went to war. However, with the end of World War II, returning war veterans were given opportunities from the federal government through the passage of the Montgomery GI Bill (1944) to attend college for little or no cost.[27] Because the number of students applying to and attending college far surpassed the number of faculty employed at that time, many of universities began to offer faculty members and those they recruited tenure as a benefit in hopes of attracting new faculty to their institutions.[28]

With returning veterans now in college and the influx of additional faculty within colleges to meet this educational demand, a growing fear of Communism raced through the country as the Soviet Union and the

US became embroiled in an ideological war of governmental systems. It was during this time (late 1940s and early 1950s) that the American public feared the spread of the Communism growing in Eastern Europe and China. This fear caused turmoil throughout the country and gave rise to what became known as the Red Scare.[29] This era, known as the McCarthy era (after Republican Senator Joseph McCarthy—WI) became the first test for AAUP's tenure document. During his Senate investigations, Senator McCarthy accused many academics of contributing financially to the Communist Party citing that their support to that Party was a conduit for Soviet espionage efforts within the USA.[30] McCarthy, through his hearings, demanded that those he accused of being Communist sympathizers identify the political party they supported and answer questions concerning their loyalty to the USA. These accusations amounted to overt political intrusion into higher education and threatened to jeopardize the scholarly dialogue within universities. However, because universities had utilized tenure as a benefit in the retention and recruitment of faculty immediately following World War II, academic tenure provided faculty a shield that prohibited university administrators from dismissing faculty who refused to cooperate with McCarthy.[31]

A few years later, in the late 1950s and 1960s, the USA was under duress again as the rights of African-Americans and the animosity toward a publicly unsupported war in Vietnam were brought to the forefront of the political debate. The rise of the Civil Rights Movement and the public outcry against the Vietnam War was influenced, and supported, by a strong following from higher education faculty members who sought equal rights among all races and an end to the war in Southeast Asia. Although protection was provided to higher education faculty members through tenure, it did not provide safeguards to faculty for their actions outside the classroom. Many instructors who supported the Civil Rights Movement and the Anti-War Movement were jailed for their involvement in protests across the campuses of their universities.[32] Even though the faculty members' freedom of speech was in question by The House Committee on Un-American Activities (HCUA) for their participation in various activities related to these movements, tenure provided them a shield which enabled them to retain their jobs even after being incarcerated.[33] With the protections provided to faculty during this era, many felt they were able to voice their expressions concerning the issues of the time (Civil Rights Movement and Vietnam War) without retribution from university administrators.

Despite the fact that tenure was in place at universities and colleges across the nation during the mid- to late 1960s, university officials continued to challenge the legality of faculty retaining employment based on the tenure system. The number of litigation cases related to tenure, or the right of continued employment of faculty, in the 1960s increased dramatically from previous decades. Because the Civil Rights Act of 1964, more commonly referred to as Title VII, deals with breach of employment contracts, this increase in lawsuits during the 1960s was linked to the passage of Title VII.[34] In recent years, tenure continues to be under attack as student enrollments are on the rise (a 34% increase from 2000 to 2009).[35] in many disciplines while declines are faced in other, more traditional areas.[36] However, universities and colleges are still faced with financial burdens incurred from a reduction in state and federal funding which inevitably leads to legal battles over institutional layoffs of tenured faculty members. In addressing this issue as it relates to tenure, in 2015, Scott Walker, Governor of Wisconsin, proposed a policy that his state legislature approved permitting state university administrators to reduce faculty compliment without regard to academic tenure status due to declining enrollment in programs or financial exigencies.[37]

Examples of Tenure-Related Cases in Higher Education

Legal precedent has been established in support of tenure when the loss of property can be associated with the denial of tenure. In 1972 the US Supreme Court ruled on the legality of continuous employment granted to faculty through tenure. This issue is seen in the case of *Perry vs. Sindermann* (1972). In this case, the US Supreme Court identified that the denial of tenure is the same as a loss of property. Sindermann had been a faculty member within the University System of Texas for 10 years. During his last 4 years of employment, he taught classes at Odessa Junior College. In May 1969, the Texas Board of Regents decided not to renew Sindermann's contract based on allegations of his acts of insubordination. Upon receiving his notice of contract non-renewal, Sindermann filed suit against the Board of Regents stating that their decision was based on his public criticism of the policies and procedures of the college. His case eventually wound its way to the US Supreme Court which ruled that: (1) although there was a lack of a contractual right or tenure of re-employment, the plaintiff's claims could not be dismissed; (2) a teacher employed for multiple years at an institution should be permitted to show that, while no explicit tenure system existed, a de facto tenure system was in place; (3) proof of such a system would not guarantee re-employment, but provided the plaintiff with the opportunity to receive a hearing; and (4) at such a hearing the grounds for his non-renewal of contract should be given to him.[38] Because of the de facto state of tenure in place at the college that had been awarded to Sindermann, the Supreme Court decision gave him the right to due process and essentially awarded him the right to retain his position at the college. In its ruling the Court stated that although there may be no contractual form of tenure offered within a university, if a professor has held employment within that educational establishment for multiple years, he/she must be provided the opportunity to participate in a hearing so that the reasons for non-renewal can be presented to him/her.[39]

A different outcome was reached when the US Supreme Court reached its ruling in *Board of Regents of State Colleges v. Roth* (1972). In this landmark case, Roth was employed by the Wisconsin State University's Oshkosh campus. After not having his yearly contract renewed, his contention the fact of his speaking was that he had not been rehired based on out against university administration. Roth alleged that by the lack of university officials providing him written notice of his non-renewal and the lack of his receiving due process, his Fourteenth Amendment rights had been violated.[40] The US Supreme Court in its decision stated that since his contract was based on a year-to-year basis, and along with the lack of an expectation of continual renewal of his contract, he lacked a property interest in his claim and thus there was no reasonable expectation for continued employment with the university.[41]

Another example of tenure and its relation to property is found in the late 1980s when Ernest Dube, a former assistant professor at the State University of New York, Stony Brook, filed suit against the university claiming that he was denied tenure and that this denial violated his First Amendment rights under the US Constitution (*Dube v. The State University of New York* (1990)). He claimed that his denial of tenure was a direct result of his use of controversial topics during his classroom lectures and presentations. In addition, he further claimed that he was denied due process which violated his rights under the Fourteenth Amendment of the Constitution as well. The university officials asked for a summary judgment in the case based on the fact that they qualified for immunity granted under the Eleventh Amendment of the United

States Constitution which states that states, and state employees working in their official capacity, have sovereign immunity protecting them from legal recourse. After hearing Dube's case, the US Court of Appeals for the Second Circuit ruled that: (1) the plaintiff failed to prove that a protectable liberty or property was denied to him when he was denied tenure; (2) the plaintiff was not entitled to any relief from the university when university officials were acting in their official role; and (3) the plaintiff's First Amendment claim shall be referred to a jury since there were appropriate questions raised by the defendant regarding his freedom of speech being denied in the classroom by university officials. The Court also ruled that even though officials were acting in their official capacity, university officials were not protected against claims filed against them in their personal capacity.[42] With this ruling by the Second Circuit, the right of tenure, or the denial thereof, was disassociated with the value of property or liberty since the plaintiff was unable to clearly prove how his denial of tenure was the cause of his loss of property.

For tenure to be awarded to a faculty member, he/she must first meet the criteria identified by the institution and/or state for attaining tenure. In the case of *Fairchild vs. Vermont State Colleges* (1982), the professor did not meet the criteria established by the state university system and was therefore denied tenure. Fairchild was a physical education professor and athletic coach at Johnston State College, a member of the Vermont State Colleges' Board and therefore required to follow state guidelines for the awarding of tenure to faculty members. In 1982, Fairchild was notified by the president of the college that, because she did not meet the state criteria to be awarded tenure, her contract of employment would be terminated. The state requirements for tenure to be awarded to a non-tenured faculty member were explicit and stated that the faculty member must meet the following: (1) demonstrate superior teaching within the classroom; (2) ability to demonstrate significant personal growth; (3) display a balance between college and community service; and 4) attain a terminal degree within their field of expertise. Fairchild was denied tenure on the grounds that she had failed to complete a terminal degree in her field. Upon notification of her denial of tenure, she filed a grievance with the Vermont Labor Relations Board (VLRB) on the grounds that the criteria used for awarding tenure were based on an arbitrary process that did not set a standard for the achievement of receiving tenure. After reviewing her case, the VLRB dismissed Fairchild's claim stating that it was the place of the institution to grant or deny tenure, not the Boards. Furthermore, the Board stated that it did not have the authority to determine if an applicant for tenure was qualified or not; their role was one of determining if the reasons offered in support, or denial, of tenure represented an arbitrary or discriminatory procedure within the application process of the tenure criteria.

During the review of Fairchild's case, the VLRB also identified that the determination for her denial of tenure was based on the state-mandated criteria for receiving tenure implemented at the state level and applied at each state institution as the qualifying criteria for the awarding of tenure. The VLRB also found that, although Fairchild received multiple warnings from the university's president concerning her lack of a terminal degree, she made no effort to obtain the advanced degree which inevitably was the issue upon which she was denied tenure. Following the ruling of the VLRB, Fairchild filed suit with the Supreme Court of Vermont alleging that the Board's, as well as the college's, decision was based upon her gender and not the credentials she possessed. Throughout her testimony, she attempted to support her case by commenting about a male colleague, who was similarly qualified, but who recently had received tenure. The Court ruled that it was not the Court's role to determine if someone met the qualifications for tenure, but rather to decide upon the legality of the criteria used to determine the granting of tenure. In the Court's opinion, the requirement of a faculty member attaining a terminal degree prior to being granted tenure was not erroneous in its nature.[43]

A final and more recent example of the denial of tenure is that of *Omosegbon v. Wells* (2003). In this case, Omosegbon was employed at Indiana State University as an untenured faculty member from 1998 to 2000. During his time there, he received two yearly performance appraisals which identified concerns related to his teaching ability and performance at the university. Following his second unsatisfactory evaluation, his college dean recommended to the university provost, who concurred with the dean, that Omosegbon not be brought back for the following fall semester. Upon receiving the decision of the dean and provost, Omosegbon requested a hearing with a committee of faculty members concerning the decision made for his termination as per university policy. His request was granted and a committee of four faculty members met to consider his denial of tenure. The faculty committee recommended that Omosegbon be reinstated with two members voting for conditional reappointment and two members for voting for unconditional reappointment. However, because the committee had no binding authority, the dean and provost stood by their decision. Omosegbon filed suit in the US Court of Appeals for the Seventh Circuit for monetary damages from the university for wrongful termination. The Court ruled that since Indiana was not a person it was protected by the Eleventh Amendment (no state can be sued by an individual—sovereign immunity). Additionally, the plaintiff accused the university of depriving him of his protected property in continued employment and negatively impacted his right of liberty by tarnishing his reputation. To these issues, the Court ruled that the university had discretion in offering reappointments to faculty and that Omosegbon had no property interest in his denial of employment since an opportunity for due process was granted by the university. Likewise, since his dismissal was not disseminated to the public, the Court ruled that his reputation had not been negatively impacted. Because Omosegbon had received unenthusiastic yearly evaluations at best, the Court stated that he had no expectancy for tenure and thus no right to liberty or property claim.[44]

Summary

According to Metzger, the original purpose of tenure in higher education was to provide economic stability and job security for faculty members.[45] However, over the years tenure has become associated with the right for faculty to present and discuss controversial topics in the classroom and conduct research without the fear of repercussions from college administration.[46] This change in purpose has linked tenure with academic freedom and the two have become synonymous.[47] With academic freedom receiving this protective benefit from tenure, campuses have realized institutional stability.[48]

The American Association of University Professors (AAUP) has identified that for academic freedom to be present in today's higher education environment, tenure is required to safeguard that right. However, when asked about the relevance of tenure in higher education and its relationship to academic freedom, Steven Levitt, professor of economics at the University of Chicago stated, "What does tenure do? It distorts people's effort so that they face strong incentives early in their career and very weak incentives forever after."[49] From a social and economic standpoint, providing a system that guarantees lifetime employment, but does not promote continued learning or excellence in the classroom, appears to lessen the quality of instruction within the classroom.[50]

Rudolph points out that by offering tenure to incoming faculty members, a responsibility is placed on the university to commit to the excellence that the faculty member is presenting in the classroom, serving on academic committees, and conducting research,[51] the three recognized job functions of faculty in higher education and the cornerstone of the tenure review process. If, in view of the departmental committee or chair, a newly hired individual is deficient in one or more of these areas, it is his/her responsibility to provide mentoring to assist the faculty member in remediating these shortcomings. Within the context of the tenure review process, it is the university's responsibility to develop a guide to help establish the standards in these three areas for the awarding of faculty tenure.[52] With set guidelines in place for the awarding of tenure, academic departments and college administrators can effectively evaluate the collegiate contributions made by each faculty member applying for tenure and compare individual productivity campus-wide to determine a person's acceptability for receiving tenure. However, if after a period of time (generally 7 years as per the AAUP document of 1940) the individual has not made sufficient progress, the committee and/or chair must take the initiative to non-renew the person.[53] If this initiative is not taken, institutions get weighed down with employees who are unproductive or at least not doing what they were hired to do but who are protected by tenure.[54]

Universities and their administrators are sometimes reluctant to pursue the non-renewal of non-tenured and, in some instances the termination of tenured faculty members who do not measure up using the review process because of the possibility of litigation.[55] These cases can last for several months and even years with no assurance of the outcomes. Given this uncertainty of the Court's decisions in these cases, this book will examine and review cases from the state and federal court systems as they pertain to the First and Fourteenth Amendment of the US Constitution and the protection these amendments offer faculty who have been non-renewed or terminated.

NOTES

1. Plato, "The Republic," bk.VII (360 B.C.), http://classics.mit.edu/Plato/republic.8.vii.html.
   Plato was a Greek philosopher born in 428 B.C. His thesis was that a social structure existed within society that could be separated into three separate classes: the governing class, the warrior class, and the working class. He stated that the human soul was comprised of reason, spirit, and an appetite for knowledge. Plato has been credited for the establishment of the Academy, a place in Athens where professors and learned individuals (including Plato) gave lectures to those who sought to broaden themselves through the pursuit of knowledge.
2. Richard Hofstadter and Walter Metzger, "The Development of Academic Freedom in the United States," New York: Columbia University Press, 1955 (Hofstadter and Metzger 1955).
   During the 1800s, the concept of tenure remained a matter of term-based employment, but was not the lifelong guarantee as provided today.
3. Walter Metzger, "Academic Tenure in America: A Historical Essay," in Committee on Academic Tenure in Higher Education, "Faculty Tenure: A Report and Recommendations by the Commission on Academic Tenure in Higher Education," London: GB: Jossey-Bass, Ltd., Publishers (1973) (Metzger 1973).
4. American Association of College Professors, "History of the AAUP," http://www.aaup.org/AAUP/about/history.
   The American Association for University Professors (AAUP) was established in 1915 when Arthur Lovejoy and John Dewey organized a meeting to address academic freedom for professors working in higher education. The concept of academic freedom came to light during the late 1800s but was not a national topic until 1900 when Edward Ross, an economist at Stanford University, was terminated from his position at the university for his position on immigrant labor and railroad monopolies.
5. Wendy Williams and Stephen Ceci, "Does Tenure Really Work?" Chronicle of Higher Education (March 9, 2007), http://chronicle.com/free/v53/i27/27b01601.htm (Williams and Ceci 2007).
   Williams and Ceci discuss how financial restraints have impacted the issuance of tenure within higher education. At the time of the article, less than 40% of all faculty members across the nation were on tenure track. The authors of the article also raised the question of how effective tenure is and if it still addresses its original goal, i.e., the safeguarding of academic freedom. In the opinion of the authors, academic tenure falls short in upholding its original concept of safeguarding freedom of speech, writing, and action.

6. Edward St. John and Michael Parsons, "Public Funding of Higher Education," Baltimore: The Johns Hopkins University Press (2004) (John and Parsons 2004).
   Although the royal and colonial governments had an obligation to fund colonial colleges, the colleges gained financial stability with endowments made by alumni and college supporters.
7. Ryan Amacher and Roger Meiners, "Faulty Towers: Tenure and the Structure of Higher Education," Oakland: The Independent Institute (2004) (Amacher and Meiners 2004).
   Before the twentieth century, faculty employed by a university were expected to follow the beliefs of the institution, donors, and governing boards.
8. Morrill Act of 1862 7 U.S.C., § 301.
9. Amacher and Meiners, supra, at 7.
   An example of a university employee being terminated for their different religious view to that of the institution can be found when Harvard University's first president, Henry Dunster, denounced the institutions stance on baptizing infants. According to Dunster, only adult baptism should be allowed in the church. Since his beliefs were different from that of the university, Dunster was forced to resign from his position in 1654.
10. Id.
11. David Loope, "Academic Tenure: It's Origins, Administration, and Importance," South Carolina Commission on Higher Education Staff Position Paper, South Carolina Commission on Higher Education (May 1995), http://www.eric.ed.gov/ERICWebPortal/contentdelivery/servlet/ERICServlet?accno=ED382149 (Loope 1995).
    As the British colonized America, they brought along with them the concept of higher education. At the first three universities in the colonized states (William and Mary, Harvard, and Yale), faculty were hired under contractual agreements with the university's governing board for a fixed period of time. However, these agreements did not provide lifelong job security.
12. Kathryn Moore, "Introduction; Academic Tenure in the United States," Journal of the College and University Personnel Association (1980) (Moore 1980).
    In the 1800s, tenure remained a concept of where term agreements existed between university governing boards and college professors. Although this form of gentlemen's agreement was common in the USA during this period of time, there were no policies, or practices, that provided safeguards to college instructors from governing boards terminating their employment for religious beliefs different from that of the institution.

13. Melanie Peterson, "Academic Tenure and Higher Education in the United States: Implications for the Dental Education Workforce in the twenty-first century," Journal of Dental Education 71, no. 3 (2007), www.jdentaled.org/cgi/reprint/71/3/354.pdf (Peterson 2007).
Peterson addresses the history of academic tenure within higher education and how it has impacted the dental field across the nation. The author was able to summarize the effect that academic tenure has had in dental schools across the nation and that the institution of tenure itself is in great need of reform. The question of significance raised by the author is if the quest for tenure directly impacts the quality of instruction and research. The author also raised the question of does tenure inhibit an academic's ability to devote adequate time to his/her students and research in his/her field of study. To address these concerns, Peterson identifies four recommendations: review the tenure policies at all universities and colleges; establish faculty tracks that will permit an individual to select a track that best fits their professional strengths; academic freedom; and job security be safeguarded without tenure being present, and execute a follow-up survey to identify the progress of each institution.
14. Amacher Meiners, supra, 7.
During the late nineteenth and early twentieth century, college presidents, as well as governing boards of universities, did not like university professors to publicly speak on controversial topics of the day. However, the college presidents of several of the top universities in the nation took the stance that no donor should be allowed to interfere with the academic freedom of university professors.
15. William Tierney and Estela Bensimon, "Promotion and Tenure: Community and Socialization in Academe," State University of New York (1996) (Tierney and Bensimon 1996).
Prior to the 1870s, academic pursuit was focused on theology and religion. However, from 1870 on intellectual investigation focused more on the social and economic issues of the day. Leland Stanford had utilized business principles that were publically denounced by professor Ross.
16. William Tierney and Estela Bensimon, "Promotion and Tenure: Community and Socialization in Academe," State University of New York (1996).
In his tenure at Stanford University, Ross always promoted the right for academics to safely voice their opinions publically. The president of the university at the time, Dr. David Jordan, felt that it was his responsibility to ensure that the faculty at the university follow the wishes of Governor of California, Leland Stanford, and stay clear of all political activities and debate.

17. Karen Nelson, "Historical Origins of the Linkage of Academic Freedom and Faculty Tenure," PhD diss., University of Denver (1984) (Nelson 1984).
    During the time that the AAUP was created, faculty members across the nation had typically been controlled by the firm hand of university administration. There was also a concern within academia over the quality of research and instruction going on at the university. Many academics feared what they had identified as "a diminishing status of the academic profession." Professors such as Arthur Lovejoy and John Dewey believed that academic governance should be in the hands of academics and not that of the university administration.
18. Tierney and Bensimon, supra, 16.
    Prior to the first meeting of the AAUP faculty worked at the leisure of the governing board for the university. Faculty members were viewed as a common employee who could be found at any other employer.
19. Walter Metzger, "Origins of the Association: An Anniversary Address," AAUP Bulletin (Summer 1965), under "History of the AAUP," http://www.aaup.org/NR/rdonlyres/165DDCF2-6391-488F-824E-9E57BF919046/0/OriginsoftheAssociation.pdf (Metzger 1965).
20. American Association of College Professors, supra, 4.
    The main goal of this meeting was to identify safeguards for academic freedom. Six hundred and fifty faculty members attended the first meeting of the AAUP. These individuals represented the top research universities of the time.
21. Peterson, supra, 13.
    Prior to the turn of the twentieth century, contractual agreements were in the form of verbal agreements. These agreements did not have a set duration for employment.
22. American Association of College Professors, "1915 Declaration of Principles on Academic Freedom and Academic Tenure," http://www.aaup.org/AAUPAAUP/pubsres/policydocs/contents/1915htm (American Association of College Professors 1915).
23. Id.
24. Amacher and Meiners, supra, 7.
    Most universities in the early twentieth century which had a tenure track only had a 2- to 3-year probation period.
25. American Association of College Professors, "1940 Statement of Principles on Academic Freedom and Tenure," http://www.aaup.org/AAUPAAUP/pubsres/policydocs/contents/1940statement.htm.
26. Id.
27. Servicemen's Readjustment Act of 1944, P.L. 78–346, 58 Stat. 284 m.

The Servicemen's Readjustment Act of 1944, more commonly known as the Montgomery GI Bill, was the federal government's attempt to provide training, both college and vocational, to World War II veterans.
28. Moore, supra, 12.
29. Arthur Miller, "McCarthyism," Public Broadcast System. http://www.pbs.org/wnet/americanmasters/episodes/arthur-miller/mccarthyism/484/.
30. Loope, supra, 11.
Throughout the 1940s and 1950s, the American government was concerned with the spread of Communism within Eastern Europe and China. Taking advantage of the American public's paranoia, Senator Joseph McCarthy made accusations indicating that over 200 Communists had infiltrated the US government and the nation's universities and colleges.
31. Id.
In 1948 the state of Washington's Un-American Activities Committee questioned a handful of University of Washington faculty members concerning their involvement with the Communist Party. Two of the faculty members questioned admitted to belonging to the Communist Party and were denied tenure and ultimately terminated. Following the publicized case of the University of Washington, academia established a consensus that any "card carrying" Communist member had no place in the university system.
32. Id.
33. Loope, supra, 11.
Although the AAUP's 1940 Statement of Principles on Academic Freedom and Tenure provided job security to tenured faculty members, junior faculty members who had not attained tenure at that time, and who were accused of belonging to the Communist Party, were often released from their service to the university.
34. Peterson, supra, 13.
The legal meaning of tenure is the guarantee to a job after a defined probationary period is completed.
35. US Department of Education, "Digest of Education Statistics: 2010."
36. US Department of Education, "Digest of Education Statistics: 2004" and US Department of Education, "Digest of Education Statistics: 2010."
37. Nico Savidge, "Changes to tenure, budget and Regents show extent of Scott Walker's impact on UW", Wisconsin State Journal (Mar 27, 2016), http://host.madison.com/wsj/news/local/education/university/changes-to-tenure-budget-and-regents-show-extent-of-scott/article_90954155-df31-5fdb-bb93-dd93a0f81225.html (Savidge 2016).
38. Perry v. Sindermann, 408 U.S. 593 (1972).

Robert Sindermann had been employed in the Social Science Department at Odessa Junior College from 1959 to 1969. During the 1968–1969 academic term, Mr. Sindermann had been elected president of the Texas Junior College Teachers Association. Various times throughout the academic year Mr. Sindermann was required to leave his teaching duties to testify before the state legislature in his capacity as president for the teachers association. Likewise, while serving as the president of the Texas Junior College Teachers Association, Mr. Sindermann became involved in public arguments with the college's governing board. At the end of the academic year, Mr. Sindermann was not offered a contract for the upcoming academic term. Furthermore, the governing board released a public statement identifying acts of insubordination against Mr. Sindermann.

39. Id.
40. Board of Regents of State Colleges v. Roth, 408 U.S. 564 (1972).
41. Id.

Dr. Roth was hired by the Wisconsin State University, Oshkosh branch as an assistant professor of political science. Roth worked under a year-to-year contract that specified his employment would be for the academic year that started on September 1, 1968, and which would end on June 30, 1969. Under Wisconsin statutory law, a university professor can attain tenure only after successfully completing 4 years of year-to-year employment at the university. While employed at the university, Roth had been critical of policies and procedures utilized by the college administration. On February 1, 1969, the university president notified Dr. Roth that he would not be offered a faculty contract for the 1969–1970 academic year; however, no reason for the non-renewal of contract was provided to the professor. Wisconsin statutory law states that a tenured, and non-tenured, faculty member cannot be terminated without first being presented the reason(s) for the termination; however, no protection is offered to a non-tenured faculty member from not having their contract renewed at the end of an academic year.

42. Dube v. The State University of New York, 900 F.2d 587 (2d Cir. 1990).

Professor Dube had been employed by the State University of New York's Stony Brook campus in the African Studies Department from 1977–1987. In fall, 1983, Dube was scheduled to teach a new course titled AFS/POL 319: The Politics of Race. In the course description, the instructor identified that there would be open discussion that focused on three main types of racism: Nazism, the Apartheid, and Zionism. A visiting professor, Dr. Selwyn Troen, took offense to Dube's reference to Zionism as being a form of racism and subsequently wrote a letter to the university's Dean for the College of Arts and Sciences. Troen's complaint was investigated by the Executive Committee of the Stony Brook

Senate. The outcome of this investigation was that Dube's instruction for AFS/POL 319 fell under the realm of Academic Freedom and that no further action was required by the university. Troen then elicited the help of Jewish community leaders for the removal of AFS/POL 319. Prior to the start of the 1983 fall semester, AFS/POL 319 was removed from the college's course offerings. In the 1984–1985 academic year, Dube became available for tenure and promotion. Even though the tenure ad hoc committee confirmed Dube's approval for tenure, the college dean, university provost, and university president all denied the instructor's request for tenure citing Dube's record for professional research and publication were insufficient for a research university. The Court found that there had been evidence supporting Dube's First Amendment claims where university officials responded to state and community officials' outcry for action against the Dube's instruction which denied him the rights awarded to him under the First Amendment. However, the Court ruled that for Dube's Fourteenth Amendment claim failed since it did not show an entitlement to lifelong employment. A claim for tenure constitutes a protected property interest only if it supports a legitimate claim of entitlement, which Dube was unable to prove.
43. Fairchild v. Vermont State Colleges, 141 Vt. 362 (1982).
    Diane Fairchild was a PE instructor and a coach at Johnson State College in Vermont. In 1980 professor Fairchild was informed by the college's president that she had been denied tenure. The president of the college identified that Ms. Fairchild's failure to attain a terminal degree was the primary reason for her denial of tenure. According to the criteria set by the Vermont State Colleges Board, for a faculty member to attain tenure the person must: (1) demonstrate superior teaching; (2) have significant professional growth; (3) balance college and community service; and (4) attain a terminal degree within their area of expertise, or have significant professional or scholarly accomplishment. According to the college president, Fairchild had been given several warnings indicating that her lack of completing a terminal degree could affect her chances of being granted tenure. Ms. Fairchild indicated that although she did not possess a terminal degree she had ample examples of scholarly achievements in her field of expertise which could be used to meet the criteria for her attaining tenure.
44. Omosegbon v. Wells, 335 F.3d 668 (7th Cir. 2003).
    Professor Oladele Omosegbon was employed with Indiana State University's African and African American Studies Department from 1998 to 2000. Each of his annual evaluations was conducted by a personnel committee of four professors from the same department as Professor Omosegbon. After the first evaluation, the committee recommended to

offer Dr. Omosegbon conditional reappointment for an additional academic year. In a letter from the Dean of the College of Arts and Science to the University Provost, to which Omosegbon received a copy of, it was outlined that there were various problems with this instructor's teaching duties and his scholarly work. For any additional reappointments to occur after the second year, each of these concerns needed to be improved upon by Dr. Omosegbon. The following academic year the personnel committee split their vote with two members voting for conditional reappointment and two members voting for unconditional appointment. The Dean of the College for Arts and Science decided to not offer Omosegbon a third contract to which the Provost concurred.

45. Metzger, supra, 3.

Tenure is considered the cornerstone for academic freedom by many, if not all, academics, tenure providing faculty members with the freedom to teach and research in a manner that they select. In addition, tenure provides economic security to those seeking to enter into the field of higher education.

46. James Fishman, "Tenure: Endangered or Evolutionary Species," 38 Akron L. Rev. 771 (2005) (Fishman 2005).
47. American Association of College Professors, supra, 22.
48. William Cotter, "Why Tenure Works," Colby College Magazine (April 1995) (Cotter 1995).
49. Steven Levitt, "Let's Just Get Rid of Tenure: Including Mine," Freakanomics (March 3, 2007), http://freakonomics.blogs.nytimes.com/2007/03/03/lets-just-get-rid-of-tenureTenure (Levitt 2007).
50. Metzger, supra, 3.
51. Fredrick Rudolph, "The American College & University," Athens: The University of Georgia Press (1990) (Rudolph 1990).
52. Thomas Diamantes, June Ovington, Douglas Roby, and Charles Ryan, "An Analysis of Prevailing Myths Regarding Tenure and Promotion," CBS Interactive Business Network (Spring, 2003), http://findarticles.com/p/articles/mi_qa3673/is_3_123/ai_n28998163 (Diamantes et al. 2003).

Academic tenure and how it's offered to a faculty member is under the watchful eye of non-academics. For tenure to be successful in this and any future decades, university administrators need to re-investigate the current concepts of tenure and make changes to the system based on current research and studies on academic tenure and academic freedom. Focus should be moved away from the traditional practice of evaluating someone's scholarly research solely and lean towards a more centered approach on an individual's teaching ability and community service.

53. American Association of College Professors, supra, 25.

54. Levitt, supra, 49.
55. Elizabeth Ellis, "Is Tenured a Synonym for Lazy?," *The Muleskinner*, University of Central Missouri (September 9, 2010) (Ellis 2010).

References

Amacher, Ryan, and Roger Meiners. 2004. *Faulty Towers: Tenure and the Structure of Higher Education*. Oakland, CA: The Independent Institute.

American Association of College Professors. 1915. *Declaration of Principles on Academic Freedom and Academic Tenure*. http://www.aaup.org/AAUPAAUP/pubsres/policydocs/contents/1915.htm.

Cotter, William. 1995. Why Tenure Works. *Colby College Magazine*, April.

Diamantes, Thomas, June Ovington, Douglas Roby, and Charles Ryan. 2003. *An Analysis of Prevailing Myths Regarding Tenure and Promotion*. CBS Interactive Business Network. http://findarticles.com/p/articles/mi_qa3673/is_3_123/ai_n28998163.

Ellis, Elizabeth. 2010. Is Tenured a Synonym for Lazy? *The Muleskinner*, University of Central Missouri, September 9.

Fishman, James. 2005. Tenure: Endangered or Evolutionary Species. *Akron Law Review* 38: 771.

Hofstadter, Richard, and Walter Metzger. 1955. *The Development of Academic Freedom in the United States*. New York: Columbia University Press.

John, Edward St., and Michael Parsons. 2004. *Public Funding of Higher Education*. Baltimore, MD: The Johns Hopkins University Press.

Levitt, Steven. 2007. Let's Just Get Rid of Tenure: Including Mine. *Freakonomics*, March 3. http://freakonomics.blogs.nytimes.com/2007/03/03/lets-just-get-rid-of-tenure.

Loope, David. 1995. Academic Tenure: Its Origins, Administration, and Importance. South Carolina Commission on Higher Education Staff Position Paper, South Carolina Commission on Higher Education, May 1995. http://www.eric.ed.gov/ERICWebPortal/contentdelivery/servlet/ERICServlet?accno=ED382149.

Metzger, Walter. 1965. Origins of the Association: An Anniversary Address. *AAUP Bulletin under History of the AAUP*. http://www.aaup.org/NR/rdonlyres/165DDCF2-6391-488F-824E-9E57BF919046/0/OriginsoftheAssociation.pdf.

Metzger, Walter. 1973. Academic Tenure in America: A Historical Essay. In *Committee on Academic Tenure in Higher Education, Faculty Tenure: A Report and Recommendations by the Commission on Academic Tenure in Higher Education*. London: Jossey-Bass.

Moore, Kathryn M. 1980. Introduction: Academic Tenure in the United States. *Journal of the College and University Personnel Association*, 31 (3–4): 1–17.

Nelson, Karen. 1984. Historical Origins of the Linkage of Academic Freedom and Faculty Tenure. PhD dissertation, University of Denver.
Peterson, Melanie. 2007. Academic Tenure and Higher Education in the United States: Implications for the Dental Education Workforce in the Twenty-First Century. *Journal of Dental Education* 71 (3). www.jdentaled.org/cgi/reprint/71/3/354.pdf.
Rudolph, Fredrick. 1990. *The American College & University*. Athens: The University of Georgia Press.
Savidge, Nico. 2016. Changes to Tenure, Budget and Regents Show Extent of Scott Walker's impact on UW. *Wisconsin State Journal*, March 27. http://host.madison.com/wsj/news/local/education/university/changes-to-tenure-budget-and-regents-show-extent-of-scott/article_90954155-df31-5fdb-bb93-dd93a0f81225.html.
Tierney, William, and Estela Bensimon. 1996. Promotion and Tenure: Community and Socialization in Academe, State University of New York.
Williams, Wendy, and Stephen Ceci. 2007. Does Tenure Really Work? *Chronicle of Higher Education,* March 9. http://chronicle.com/free/v53/i27/27b01601.htm.

CHAPTER 2

History of Tenure and Academic Freedom in the USA

While the concept of tenure is rather new in the academic world, providing faculty protection from loss of employment dates back to the days of the Holy Roman Empire and its Emperor, Frederick I Barbarossa, King of Germany (1155–1190). Throughout the Middle Ages, European university "masters" enjoyed safeguards that were put in place by territorial monarchs and, with the Great Western Schism of 1378, these masters experienced the initial stages of a university without any linkage to the Papacy. With the rise of the non-religiously affiliated university also came issues of faculty self-governance and job security.

Centuries later, higher education began to establish itself in the New World during a historical period referred to as the Colonial Period. The universities of this period were greatly influenced by the structure of their European counterparts and, when the American Federal Government began its westward expansion, universities began to develop in the newly acquired territories. As these newly developed institutions came into being, faculty became increasingly interested in issues related to their job protection; an interest which ultimately lead to the formation of the American Association of University Professors.

© The Author(s) 2017
M.J. Hertzog, *Protections of Tenure and Academic Freedom in the United States*, DOI 10.1007/978-3-319-56270-4_2

Development of the European Higher Education System and Its Influence on American Higher Education

The history of tenure can be traced back to the *studium generale*, the universities of the middle ages. Those who taught in these institutions were known as "masters" (the common term for those teaching in higher education during this time). The subjects taught by these individuals did not include the traditional subjects of arts, canon law, medicine, and theology as these subjects were taught in the *universitas facultatum*. Rather, in these settings the primary subject of arts was taught along with at least one of the other higher faculties of theology, medicine, or law.[1] Students who attended the *studium generale* came from across the catchment of the region (i.e., students from Italy would attend the University of Bologna and students from France would attend the University of Paris). After completing their studies, these students were thought to have great promise and were often considered for the distinct privilege of teaching in these institutions.

To assure that the scholars who taught in the *studium generale* were able to move freely throughout the empire, Emperor Fredrick I Barbarossa of Germany and the Holy Roman Empire provided the masters a form of job security with his decree known as *Authentica Habita*. This decree guaranteed that any scholar traveling within the Holy Roman Empire would receive safe passage during his journey. If any unlawful injury were to befall masters during their travels, they then would be reimbursed for the loss of their wages by the person committing the unlawful act.[2]

As Barbarossa's *Authentica Habita* became more widely known throughout Europe, rulers of the surrounding nations, as well as the Roman Papacy, began to offer similar protection to scholars within their lands. However, the influence of the Roman Papacy, especially with the link between the Catholic Church and the Cathedral School of which the *studium generale* originated,[3] began to use their vast financial influence to support academies that focused on the development of the clergy.[4] In hopes of enticing scholars to educate students at these clerical academies, the popes permitted a master to continue to receive the benefit of longevity of employment even while he was traveling to other regions across the empire.[5] Along with the assurance provided to scholars by the Roman Church, monarchs awarded additional benefits (e.g., freedom from paying local tolls and duties, provisions so that scholars would receive good housing at a fair price, etc....) to the masters in hopes of enticing them to stay within their regional *studium generale*.[6]

However, the masters at a regional *studium generale* not only sought the rewards of lengthened employment, they also desired immunity from the outside influence of regional tribunals and the right to govern themselves from within. Issues such as these by medieval scholars led to the formation of education guilds. As these guilds gained in strength, additional issues were addressed. These issues included: (1) the right to elect their own officers, (2) the ability to be legally represented as a single legal entity, and (3) the freedom to develop a set of codified rules and policies that each member was accountable to follow.[7] However, one ability that medieval universities, and in essence the guilds to which the masters belonged, did not possess was the ability to award the *licentia docendi* (a licensure credential awarded to a "to be" master permitting him to lecture to students). This power, for those in the field to name others to their field, was a right reserved solely for the Chancellor of the Cathedral, an individual who was the appointed head of the institution and to whom the masters had to swear an oath of allegiance.[8]

Along with the turn of the thirteenth century came changes within the *universitas facultatum*. Masters at the *universitas facultatum* began to question the criteria used to award the *licentia docendi*. By the early twelve hundreds, the *licentia docendi* became a priority issue among the masters in the medieval university. To the masters within the faculty of the arts, the concept of an outside agent awarding this credential endangered the quality of students entering their guild.[9] By foregoing the input of the guild on the admittance of students to the university, the masters contended that the quality of their instruction was being weakened by the Church. Likewise, the masters expressed concern that because the awarding of licensure and, in essence, the ability to revoke licensure rested with an external agent, masters could be displaced even though they had successfully completed guild instruction.[10]

The struggle which ensued (the issuance of the *licentia docendi* being beyond the control of the guild as well as the requirement that guild masters swear an allegiance to the Chancellor of the Cathedral) between the guilds and the external forces threatened the existence of the medieval university. These issues caused the guilds to be concerned that their scholars might migrate to a different region and form new universities.[11] Along with this perceived threat of relocation, the guild masters sent numerous appeals to the Roman hierarchy urging them to enlist changes within the governance of universities, suggesting that the determination of awarding the *licentia docendi* should be in the hands of the guild masters. Responding to the concern made by the guild masters on the issuance of the *licentia docendi*, Pope Gregory IX issued the *Parens Scientiarum* (a form of charter issued by a pope) in 1231 granting the right of licensure to the guild masters at the University of Paris where he had studied theology.[12] Furthermore, Pope Gregory's charter removed the requirement that masters had to swear allegiance to the Chancellor of the Cathedral. In its place, the Pope stated that masters were required to take an oath of allegiance to their university instead of the Chancellor.[13]

Although there were examples of employment protection in the medieval university, job security guarantees within either the *studium generale* or the *universitas facultatum* were not a facet of position, but that of papal or monarch decree.[14] However, to receive the decree of a governmental body (either a governing monarch or the Catholic Church) a master had to meet certain conditional thresholds. These thresholds ranged from university to university, but commonly focused on the areas of advancement of degrees and the acquisition of guild specific *licentia docendi*.[15]

Traditions within *universitas facultatum* began to change during the thirteenth century as the Holy Roman Empire saw the development of sovereign states outside of their realm as well as the rise of Christian denominations other than that of Catholicism. With these changes the previous separation between the *studium generale* and the *universitas facultatum* began to disappear as the *studium generale* began to change from a single trade school to that of a *universitas facultatum*, providing instruction in canon law, medicine, and theology as well as the inclusion of the social sciences and the arts into the curriculum which was spurred by the start of the Renaissance.[16] This change in higher education structure gave rise to the *universitas magistrorum*, an educational design that separated masters into four *facultates* (law, medicine, philosophy, and theology) and permitted these instructors the autonomy to determine the content of their lectures.[17] As this new educational design gained popularity, it soon became the de facto pattern for the establishment of new universities throughout Europe.[18]

Throughout the fourteenth century, there was limited growth of universities throughout Europe. The major universities at the time were located in the cities of Oxford, Paris, and Bologna, and although other cities had universities during this timeframe, they did not have the same prestige as those in these three cities. Then, in 1386, Germany established its first university in Heidelberg. Researchers have identified that the establishment of this university (the University of Heidelberg) was in response to the Great Western Schism caused when Pope Gregory XI returned the Papacy from Avignon to Rome in 1378.[19]

This Schism occurred when, in 1309, the newly appointed Pope Clement V (appointed in 1305), a Frenchmen, decided to move the papacy from Rome to Avignon, France.[20] For the next 68 years, a time known as the Avignon Papacy, the papacy remained in Avignon.[21] However, in 1377, Catherine of Sienna contacted then Pope Gregory XI stressing that, with the threat of a Muslim invasion in Eastern Europe and with the financial tolls coming from the 100 Year War between England and France, restoring the papacy to Rome and launching a Crusade against the Muslim nation Pope Gregory XI could unite Christians and stop the Muslim invasion.[22] The Pope agreed and the papacy returned to Rome.

Upon Pope Gregory XI's death in 1378, Bartolomeo Prignano (who would become Pope Urban VI), Archbishop of Bari, was named the papal successor. However, almost immediately, the legitimacy of Pope Urban VI's election was questioned by the French and Spanish Cardinals and, a few months after his inauguration, the only Cardinals that remained in Rome were those from Italy.[23] The defecting Cardinals claimed that the election of Urban VI had been negatively influenced by the Roman crowd that had gathered during the conclave demanding a Roman pope and that those incidents supposedly influenced the election process.[24] In response to these claims, on August 9, 1378, the College of Cardinals, who had originally elected Urban VI as their pope, denounced Urban VI'S election and within several months appointed Robert of Geneva as Pope Clement VII.[25] The election of this second pope now meant that there were two claiming leadership over Catholicism. This second election, which provided for two sitting popes, had come to be known as the Great Western Schism, and, according to religious scholars, led to the weakening of the influence of the Catholic Church during the years from 1378 to 1417.[26] It was during this weakened position of the Papacy that Germany seized the opportunity to establish its first university—the University of Heidelberg.

Prior to the Great Western Schism, German students and masters traveled great distances to attend the *universitas magistrorums* in Paris or one of lesser status in Orleans. Rashdall cites that the reason students and masters left Germany to study and teach was that German nobles feared an increase in the power and influence of the clergy and decided against establishing a *universitas magistrorum* that was commonly influenced by the papacy.[27] However, at the time of the Great Western Schism, the University of Paris, under the influence of the French Catholic Cardinals, did not accept anyone, either as an employee or student, who supported the Roman pope, which effectively locked out German students and masters who followed the Pope in Rome.[28]

The Roman popes during this time, however, were known to be interested in offering the necessary papal bulls or decrees to establish a *universitas magistrorum* in hopes of weakening the influence of French universities. This division within the Catholic Church and availability of papal decrees allowing for the creation of a *universitas magistrorum*, provided the impetus for Germany to move forward and establish its first university in Heidelberg (1386).[29] In its establishment, Elector Palatine Ruprecht (the founder of the University of Heidelberg) stated that the university would be ruled, disposed, and regulated in the same manner as that of the University of Paris.[30]

By the fifteenth century, the onetime broad lecture in canon law, medicine, theology, and the arts began to become a more specialized concentration within the *facultates* of the *universitas magistrorum*. Prior to the Protestant Reformation (1517), only students and masters of the Catholic faith were allowed to enroll in, or be employed by, the *universitas magistrorum*.[31] However, Sanz and Bergan note that along with the Protestant Reformation came the demise of papal supremacy as well as a weakened Roman influence over the *universitas magistrorum*.[32] This reduction in the role played by the Catholic Church in higher education led to a greater financial commitment and denominational preference of other Christian religions of the regional nobility for the institution. However, this form of logic, where a *universitas magistrorum* identified itself as the same Christian denomination as the territorial noble, established a belief system where only one form of religion could be prevalent within an institution while all other denominations were shunned.[33]

During the seventeenth and eighteenth centuries, European universities began to move away from their denominational views toward a more philosophical view that focused on human progress through knowledge and reason.[34] As philosophical reasoning began to replace theology in the curriculum, the concept of conducting research enhanced the self-directed motivation of improving one's self through the understanding that knowledge was a social good.³⁵ This philosophical leaning, known as the European Enlightenment, brought with it the belief that if something was to be acquired through the process of research, then that research must be conducted without outside influence.³⁶ Germany was no exception to the influence of the Enlightenment in its universities. The approach supported by the German leaders promoted the belief that a university is a place where an individual should be able to have the freedom to accomplish his own educational development by selecting subjects to study (*Bildung*).³⁷

As the Age of Enlightenment gave rise to the nineteenth century, the face of German education changed drastically when philosopher Wilhelm von Humboldt became the Minister of Education in Prussia from 1809 to 1810. Although he only held this position briefly, his impact was tremendous as it was under his leadership that three important reforms were initiated in German education. These reforms were: (1) all secondary school teachers must receive university-level training; (2) the establishment of the *Abitur*, an entrance exam used as an instrument to determine an individual's qualification for admission to a university; and (3) the need for freedom in teaching and learning.³⁸ His reforms gave rise to the introduction of three principles that guided German universities in the areas of academic freedom (*Lehrfreiheit*), the unity of teaching and research (*Einheit von Forschung und Lehre*), and self-governance (*Selbstverwaltung*) by professors.³⁹

It was at this time that German universities evolved from the control of territorial governing agencies (i.e., territorial nobility and governing boards of trustees) to that of self-governance.⁴⁰ With the influence of Humboldt's principles (the place of the government in relation to university governance should be simplistic; the role of the government should be to protect *Lehrfreiheit* and appoint qualified faculty.⁴¹) began to gain acceptance throughout Germany and eventually spread throughout Europe. As the nineteenth century drew to a close, it was evident that Germany was moving away from the medieval design of a university as an avenue to pass on recognized knowledge to its students and onto an enlightened model whereby knowledge could be utilized toward a more faculty-driven belief and that the university was a place where students learned how that knowledge had been discovered.⁴²

Humboldt's theories and principles spurred growth in academia throughout Germany bringing about advancements in science and university research. Seeing the impact of these advancements encouraged

Humboldt to strengthen his resolve for research. He later stated that all subjects should be held accountable to scrutiny under scientific research and discovery and that this discovery was an ongoing process, one that never ended.[43] His focus on individual growth and the ability of the professoriate to conduct unbiased scientific research provided the momentum for German universities to become the focal point for scientific advancement within the nation.[44] The scientific advancements made in nineteenth century Germany, which were spurred by university research, led to the strengthening of industry which, during the later part of the nineteenth century, was starting to surpass its surrounding European counterparts.[45] With its emphasis on scientific research and faculty security, the German universities of the nineteenth century became the model sought out by academics in the USA as their universities were starting to separate from religious orientations.

THE RISE OF HIGHER EDUCATION IN THE USA

The beginning of higher education in the USA can be traced back to the British colonization of North America.[46] During this time in history, universities such as Harvard, William and Mary, and Yale, all of which had ties to various religious denominations, allowed masters to stay on staff as long as they shared the same religious beliefs as those of the university.[47] Furthermore, the professors of the colonial universities were individuals who had hoped to become clergymen; however, due to reasons of health, had chosen the profession of educator, one viewed as less demanding in those days than that of a clergyman.[48]

HIGHER EDUCATION IN THE COLONIAL PERIOD

The foundations of higher education in the USA date back to 1636 when the General Court of the Massachusetts Bay Colony passed legislation that laid the groundwork for the founding of a new college which would later be named in honor of the college's first benefactor, Charlestown minister John Harvard, in 1639.[49] However, due to the General Court's questioning of the legality in the creation of a corporation (Harvard College) by another corporation (the Board of Overseers who had been established in 1642 by the General Court of the Massachusetts Bay Colony as the legal controlling entity of Harvard College), it was not until 1650 that, with the urging of Harvard's president (Henry Dunster), that the General Court awarded a corporate charter to the college which supported the college's mission of educating the youth of the colony in the Puritan life of godliness.[50] With its charter now in place, the university formed a governing board to establish governance of the college and the creation of the institution's bylaws.

In the General Court's charter for Harvard, the college was created as a corporation composed of a president, treasurer, and five fellows (or tutors as faculty were called in those days) giving it the customary rights of a colonial corporation. These rights awarded by the charter placed the president and fellows of Harvard as the possessors of all the college's properties, the governing agent with the right to elect the college's officers, and awarded the corporation with the ability to establish the college's internal operating policies.[51] By including the tutors (the American equivalent of the European masters) of the college as fellows in the corporate charter, the General Court of the Massachusetts Bay Colony established that academics were self-governing and thus needed to be established as such in the college's policies.[52] However, due to the poor financial status of the college at the time, the original tutors of Harvard College left the institution shortly after their appointment as fellows to the corporation. The vacancies created by their departure allowed for their seats in the corporation to be filled by non-academics leaving the president of the college as the only academic member of the corporation.[53]

Similarly, in 1693 the College of William and Mary was established and became the second institution of higher education in the colonies. This college was constituted to educate and prepare young men for the clergy within the Colony of Virginia.[54] However, in its charter (issued by the King William III of England), William and Mary trustees (similar to the Overseers at Harvard) were appointed solely to establish the college and appoint its tutors. Once this task was completed, the trustees were instructed to transfer the properties of the college to the institution's president and tutors[55]; however, this did not occur. Instead, the trustees of the college, known as Visitors and Governors, viewed their appointments as having an unidentified term of longevity with the authority to remove the president and the college's tutors as they saw fit.

Governance of the College of William and Mary went well until 1768 when the Board of Visitors and Governors terminated half of the teaching faculty for reasons based on the ability of the faculty to marry at will and/or the faculty's ability to pursue positions as pastors elsewhere.[56] In response to the Board of Visitors' actions, the president of the college (James Horrocks), along with the institution's tutors, demonstrated against the termination of their colleagues and declared that the tutors and president of the college did not serve at the leisure of the college's governing board and that with the creation of the college's charter the institution was an incorporated entity and self-governing.[57] The principle behind the dispute over the governance of the College of William and Mary was based on the Board of Visitors and Governors' interpretation of the charter that the tutors and president of the college were ministers of the Crown and, as such, were governed by the ministers of the King of England. However, the agents of the college contended that since the King had awarded a charter to the college stating that the Board of Visitors and Governors was to be comprised of the president and five fellows, they contended that they had the same rights as a corporation, something a minister of the King did not possess.[58]

In response to the declaration of incorporation by the tutors and president, two of the terminated faculty members were reappointed to the college.[59] Then, in 1779, the Board of Visitors and Governors sided against academic freedom when they awarded themselves authority over the teaching methodologies used within the classroom, as well as authorizing themselves with the ability to identify which areas of learning would be offered in the college.[60] In its decision regarding these areas of learning, the Board of Visitors and Governors, on a recommendation from Thomas Jefferson, chose to dispose of the college's grammar school by declaring that a grammar school belonged in the public-school system, not within a college.[61]

This move on the part of the Board of Visitors led directly to an issue regarding the terms of employment at the College of William and Mary when, in 1780, the Reverend John Bracken (Master of the College's Grammar School and Professor of Humanity) was removed from his positions at the college. Following his termination, Reverend Bracken filed suit against the college claiming that the Board of Visitors did not have the authority to eliminate any tutor, nor did they have the authority to determine the subject matter taught within the college. Bracken's attorney, John Taylor, claimed that, because the college had been awarded a charter during its inception, it was established as a corporation giving it all the rights and responsibilities as such an entity which included the hiring and termination of academics.[62] In addition, Taylor claimed that within the college's charter the transferring of all rights to property and governance were to be awarded to the faculty and president of the college; however, the Board of Visitors and Governors failed to follow these guidelines and attempted to retain the powers awarded to the agents of the college, thus exceeding their own powers.[63] Bracken's attorney issued a writ of mandamus against the college's Board of Visitors and Governors directing them to restore his position at the college.

The attorney for the College of William and Mary, John Marshall (later to become the fourth Chief Justice of the US Supreme Court), responded to the claims made by Bracken and his attorney claiming that the fundamental issue raised by the plaintiff was with the issuance of the college's 1779 reform and not with the authority of the charter itself (originally issued in 1693), although the interpretation of the charter differed between the defendants and the plaintiff.[64] In Marshall's presentation of the facts of the case, he claimed that within the college's charter, the Board of Visitors and Governors was given broad powers over the university. With these powers the Board was directed to appoint the college president and the tutors of the college and was given the authority to identify the subjects to be taught at the college, namely divinity, philosophy, and languages. Marshall further claimed that since there had been no mention of a grammar school in the college's charter, and recognizing that the removal of the grammar school was under the jurisdiction of the board, that the grammar school's removal was then lawful. Finally, the Board's attorney claimed that because the grammar school's removal was lawful, the position for Reverend Bracken had been eliminated and therefore the plaintiff's claims were unjustified and unwarranted against the Board of Visitors and Governors for the College of William and Mary.[65]

The resolution of this case (*Bracken v Board of Visitors and Governors of the College of William and Mary*) occurred in 1790 when the Court of Appeals of Virginia sided with the Board of Visitors and Governors. In its verdict, the Court identified that, within the legal system, there were two types of corporations: one being a civil corporation; the other being a charitable corporation. The Court further stated that if a corporation fell under the realm of civil identification, it was not subject to its founder or board, but to the general law of the land.[66] Furthermore, if a corporation was designated as a charitable corporation, it was subject to its founder and the board appointed by the entities' founder.[67] Therefore, because the College of William and Mary was identified as a charitable organization, the Court ruled on behalf of the College's governing board. This case established the initial determination of the power possessed by a college's governing board with regards to its ability to terminate faculty.

In the eighteenth century, the founding of additional colleges and universities within the American Colonies followed their predecessors with the formation of lay boards for the governance of the schools.[68] During this Colonial Period, the establishment of a college was commonly initiated by the formation of a lay board comprised of local community leaders and clergy from the local parish.[69] These lay boards were tasked with the establishment of the college, the hiring of the college's president and tutors, and the identification of the subject matter to be taught within the classrooms of the institution. Once these tasks were completed, the lay board was to relinquish its control to the president and fellows of the college (as seen in the College of William and Mary's Charter). However, as previously mentioned, the lay boards rarely relinquished the power they had been temporarily awarded and commonly ended up becoming the ruling board of the institution.[70] According to Wayland, many of the members of these lay boards were appointed to a college's governing board as a way to demonstrate to the surrounding community the college's financial stability and level of political importance.[71] However, since many of the members of these governing boards did not receive training in the operation of a college or university, by today's standards, they would be considered unfit to deal with matters of education.[72]

Terms of Faculty Employment

It was not until the eighteenth century that the topic "term of employment" was discussed within the American collegiate setting. With the establishment of the first colleges in the Colonies, the term of employment for faculty had not been considered in their founding charters. This lack of inclusion in the college charters regarding faculty employment gave many scholars the impression that their employment term was unlimited and never ending.[73] However, as with the Board of Visitors and Governors for the College of William and Mary, college lay boards viewed their authority as being all encompassing giving them the right to remove college presidents and tutors (faculty) of the college as they saw fit. This difference of opinion between the tutors and the lay boards of colleges regarding the issue of employment led to a clash between the tutors and their college's lay boards.[74] The result of this conflict was the creation of a contractual system for faculty employment.

The initial venture into limiting the term of faculty employment through the implementation of a contract in American higher education occurred in 1700 when Harvard College's president, Increase Mather, proposed a limit of 7 years of employment for college tutors.[75] Although his proposal was not adopted, the question of term of employment remained a topic for discussion. Then, in 1716, the Corporation for Harvard College passed the Triennial Act, an act which limited all tutor appointments to 3-year terms with an option for renewal.[76] The impetus behind the Corporation's decision to include a term of employment for faculty was based on the fact that, although the Corporation could dismiss a tutor as defined within the college's charter, there was no formal way for the board to remove a tutor without cause. Because members of the board made their case that the Corporation needed such authority, it was deemed necessary for them to possess such power so employment decisions could be made and viewed as being final and without question.[77]

Although previous provisions were made to address the terms of employment for incoming tutors, no wording had been added to the charter to address the issue of existing faculty who had been grandfathered into the new employment system at Harvard College. Without specific wording in the college charter mandating a retirement pension for tutors employed by Harvard College prior to the passage of the Triennial Act, these individuals were able to work at the college for an unspecified amount of time. Therefore, according to Metzger, the reason for the Corporation of Harvard College including a retirement pension in its charter was to prevent termed appointments from being lengthened out of sympathy toward the aging educator or neglect/oversight of the institution.[78]

Additional language regarding faculty employment was added to the Harvard's Charter by the Corporation in 1760 when the Corporation defined a specific amount of time (maximum of 8 years) that a tutor could spend within a specific academic rank.[79] However, consistency in terms of employment within the confines of Harvard College was not experienced as the college implemented, with finances provided by its benefactors, the position of endowed chairs at the institution. Those faculty appointed to an endowed chair position (called professorship), unlike their academic brethren, did not suffer the limitation of defined term employment.[80] This inconsistency in employment standards among the faculty led to discord between the masters and governing boards of Harvard College. In contrast to the term limitations imposed on college masters by the Board of Overseers, the unspecified employment status of an endowed chair was seen as self-defeating because of the inconsistency in employment standards between the two groups and was viewed as a deterrent for qualified applicants in applying for a tutor's position at Harvard College.[81]

During the mid-eighteenth century, professional rank faculty, or individuals hired as full-time tutors at a university, had a form of employment security where they were allowed to continue in their jobs provided they exhibited good behavior.[82] Although the term "tenure" was not used during this time, contractual agreements between faculty members and college trustee boards were introduced at the three major universities in eighteenth-century America—Harvard, Yale, and William and Mary. These agreements introduced the concept of faculty retention based on duration of time served in the profession rather than collegial consensus.[83] However, a written contractual agreement between a faculty member and a college trustee board was rare and only provided a time frame for employment of the faculty member; it did not provide any form of job security.[84] Additionally, during the eighteenth century the common practice for college governing boards when hiring a faculty member was to offer the individual a 1-year contract that automatically renewed at the end of the year.[85] According to White, the view of the university in using this approach was to free faculty from the obligation of applying for reappointment at periodic intervals, allowing them to focus on the responsibilities of their positions.[86]

As American colleges entered the nineteenth century, the manner in which faculty were appointed to their positions changed markedly. With the development of additional colleges in the country, tutors were being replaced by professorships which were granted unlimited term appointments. It was also during this time that the theory of "up or out" came to the forefront within the American higher education system. According to Metzger, the term "up or out," which originated at Harvard, was in reference to the requirement of a tutor to advance to the next academic rank or be dismissed from service.[87]

In the nineteenth century at colleges and universities across the nation, the tutor system was being replaced with professorships that consisted of various levels of employment. This change in status from tutor to professorial rank introduced a new hierarchy in American colleges. The ranks developed, from lowest to highest were: instructor, assistant professor, associate professor, and professor.[88] Within this hierarchical system, one that developed from the system utilized at Harvard University during the mid-eighteenth century as a way to solicit financial support from college benefactors,[89] tutors were now viewed as the lowest form of educator, below that of an instructor, and their years teaching as a tutor were not even recognized as an apprenticeship.[90] This type of hierarchy created a two-class system where a non-promoted tutor could be reappointed after a 3-year term; however, the tutor wouldn't receive the benefit of job security that was awarded to his academically ranked colleagues.[91]

The Rise of the Concept of Tenure in American Universities

As the eighteenth century ended and the nineteenth century dawned, three events took place that would lead to the development of the current concept of tenure in the USA. These events were: (1) The German influence on American academics; (2) the involvement of the federal government in higher education through the passage of the Morrill Act of 1862[92]; and (3) a series of court cases known as the "Economic" cases.[93] These court cases take on a level of significance within higher education as it was because of the issues they addressed which gave rise to the formation of an association (American Association of University Professors) designed to protect the rights of higher education faculty.

The German Influence

Up until the late 1800s, the mission of American universities was similar to that of the early European universities—to produce clergymen for the church with little emphasis placed on collegial research or continued learning for faculty. However, during the nineteenth century, American students who wanted to study fields other than religion began traveling to Germany to receive their education from the leading non-sectarian universities of the time. According to White, upon graduating from these institutions, students had not only gained valuable knowledge that would enable them to fill academic positions in the USA when they returned home, but also were introduced to the philosophical distinctions between colleges and universities underway in Europe, especially in Germany (the European distinction between colleges and universities was that colleges attracted fewer students than a university, offered fewer choices of subjects for students, and focused on teaching rather than research while a university focused less on teaching and placed an emphasis on scholarly research and graduate studies[94]). This change of thought in the roles of a university and college contributed to the rise of men to administrative positions who had received their formal educational training at German universities[95] where the focus was on graduate studies and utilized seminars and lectures to present specialized topics of instruction to advanced students who were seeking graduate degrees.[96]

A second area of German influence on American higher education was the principles of *Lernfreiheit* (a student's right to determine an individual course of study)[97] and *Lehrfreiheit* (faculty granted the freedom to teach or communicate ideas or facts without being targeted for repression, job loss, or imprisonment).[98] Although these concepts provided a form of freedom in higher education, *Lehrfreiheit,* a term that first appeared in 1850 when Prussia adopted its Constitution with Title II, Article 20 stating that "Science and its teachings shall be free,"[99] was the one that had influence on academic freedom in America.

With the Prussian Constitution of 1850 in place, as well as the unification of the Prussian territories into one state (Germany), German universities experienced the freedom of self-governance without the influence of public opinion.[100] However, the universities were now considered part of the state, much like the country's military forces and, as such, were subject to state control of the institutional budget, appointment of professors, and the general establishment of subjects offered within the university. Although the Prussian/German Government maintained control over various areas of institutional governance, the faculty members of the universities were given the power to appoint academic officials, appoint lecturers, and nominate individuals for the coveted role of professor.[101] Furthermore, although the German concept of *Lehrfreiheit* did not prescribe unconditional employment for faculty, it did institute the belief of freedom of speech within the classroom, as well as establishing a professional environment that promoted research and instruction as the responsibilities of a faculty member without fear of recrimination.[102]

Upon the introduction of *lehrfreiheit* in the USA by returning academics, it also was seen as an approach to provide academic professionals the freedom to research and present their findings without the fear of retribution from the administration.[103] The understanding of this term was influential in establishing the preliminary beliefs of tenure and employment options as it was implemented in the American higher education system. Implementation of this concept led to an approach for academic freedom and the protection of faculty employment.

In addition to their concern for academic freedom and employment protection, these returning academics found that employment methodologies to which they were accustomed in Germany while doing graduate studies were in conflict with American universities where university administrators were adopting a form of term employment based on a 1-year contracts with every appointment being vacated at the end of the academic year. American administrators in public institutions claimed that the use of this form of 1-year term employment was justified because their yearly budgets were based on the allocation of funds received from the state in which they were located or from their benefactors and were subject to change each year. Therefore, a 1-year term of employment for faculty did not commit the institution to a term that might not be funded the following year.[104]

Because of their lack of scholarship, these existing American educators were viewed as low-status teachers by their administrators, served at the will of their college presidents and were treated as scholars in the same sense as their European counterparts.[105] During this time in history, state and/or federal funding of education did not exist for all practical purposes and many institutions of higher education (state-supported and private) relied heavily on individual philanthropy to keep the universities operating.[106] These donors knew that their contributions were a significant reason for the university remaining financially solvent and felt that they had the authority to remove professors or prohibit the university from hiring specific individuals who differed in religious or political beliefs from the individual donor or that of the institution.[107] Furthermore, faculty members holding lower academic ranks were commonly awarded varying term contracts while faculty members holding higher ranks received indefinite appointments for term employment.[108] However, as Metzger points out, typically governing boards that terminated a faculty member at the end of his 1-year contract did not do so out of necessity, but out of desire.[109] Nonetheless, even though faculty served at the discretion of the donors and/or institutional administration, a de facto tenure system did exist as faculty members were typically non-renewed only for interfering with the religious teachings of the university.[110] However, as advances in science and technology were made, colleges sprang up with little or no regard for the individual professor's political or religious beliefs. These new colleges altered the higher education scene in the USA as they provided students an alternative to the religious-oriented institutions of the past and posed no belief requirements for student admission or faculty employment.[111]

As American higher education faculty continued to gain status and security in the nineteenth century, two employment-related questions were prevalent. These questions were: (1) if a professor had been awarded indefinite employment, could he still be discharged for reasons outside the realm of incompetence or misconduct; and (2) what, if any, safeguards were present to protect a professor from unreasonable discharge? The answer to these questions came from two presidents from prestigious institutions. The first was William Harper, President of the University of Chicago who provided an answer to these questions when, during the late nineteenth century, he stated that a pre-dismissal trial was unwarranted for faculty who were non-renewed and that non-renewed faculty should leave their positions if the university administration found that the professor demonstrated characteristics deemed immoral and/or incompetent.[112] Similarly, President Nicholas Butler of Columbia University concurred and added that the university had the right to dismiss a faculty member without bringing charges against the individual.[113]

Administrative actions such as these provided little, if any, protection for faculty from wrongful termination. Furthermore, such claims by college presidents were grounded in legal rulings awarding governing boards the authority to dismiss faculty for any sign of misconduct. Therefore, with the absence of a minister of education similar to that in Germany to rule on such issues, academic matters in the USA were handled by each individual university and thus there was no form of consistency from one institution to the next.[114]

An example of an early court case that dealt with the permanency of faculty employment and the authority of a governing board as it relates to faculty job security is found in the *Board of Regents of the Kansas State Agricultural College v. B. F. Mudge* (1878). In this case, Professor Mudge became the chair of Natural Sciences at Kansas State Agricultural College in 1865. During his tenure at the college, a question in back pay was raised by the professor which inevitably led to his discharge in 1873. Mudge filed suit against the college stating that he was not given a 3-month notice of dismissal as defined in the college's bylaws.

The case was eventually heard by the Supreme Court of Kansas which ruled that the governing board of the college had the right to employ a faculty member, a teacher, or even a president for any period of time. However, even though the board had those powers, the right to discharge, as identified within the college bylaws, was to occur only when there was an indication of misconduct. The Court further explained that, even though a governing board's authority was vast, it must follow the bylaws of the institution. Therefore, in the verdict of the Court, Mudge was awarded 3 months back pay upon his dismissal.[115]

However, the ability of a governing board to remove an employee after identifying that the employee was no longer working toward the same values and standards of the university came under scrutiny when the Supreme Court of Arizona ruled on the case of William Stowe Devol. Devol, employed by the University of Arizona as a professor of agriculture, brought suit against the university when he was terminated from his position without being awarded a 3-month notice of dismissal as defined by the faculty contract.[116] In the ruling issued by the Supreme Court of Arizona, the Court identified that the governing board of the University of Arizona had the authority to remove any employee or officer from their employment if they deemed such an action as being necessary. However, the Court further defined that the board had no authority to enter into a contract where employment could only be terminated after a fixed amount of time and that any agreement made for such a term for dismissal was not recognized by the law.[117] Therefore, the Court ruled that the board was not required to provide a termination notice or offer a promise of a specified employment term.[118]

The Involvement of the Federal Government and the Rise of Tenure

With the dominance of the church in higher education during the seventeenth and eighteenth centuries, the mission of American universities was devoted to the moral and intellectual development of its students.[119] However, in 1862 the Federal Government enacted three laws that spurred the westward expansion of the country and, in turn, established the creation of state universities. The first of these laws was passed on May 15, 1862, when President Lincoln signed the Department of Agriculture Organic Act establishing the US Department of Agriculture.[120] This new federal agency had, as its mission, the acquisition of any and all information concerning agriculture through the use of education and scientific research.[121] Furthermore, given that, in 1862, the USA was a country in transition from an agricultural-based economy to one based on industry, the passage of this Act signaled that the country would continue to maintain its agricultural roots, but that these roots would be enhanced by the latest scientific advances and education to assure that those engaged in agriculture had the benefit of the latest technological developments to enhance their crops and livestock.

Then, 5 days after signing the Organic Act, on May 20, 1862, President Lincoln signed into law the Homestead Act. This Act marked the first time that the Federal Government officially encouraged the westward expansion of the country by providing settlers the opportunity to acquire 160 acres of public land for a $10 filing fee.[122] However, this Act also included a provision whereby those who agreed to reside on their recently acquired property for at least 5 years would be given the opportunity to purchase their land from the government for $1.25 per acre after only residing on the property for 6 months.[123] Although this Act was signed into law during the Civil War, the effect of this Act on inexpensive land was felt 3 years later when the War ended as it gave veterans and their families an opportunity to move west and put behind them the devastation, physical and emotional, left at the end of the fighting.[124]

The last of the three laws that impacted the country's westward expansion was the Morrill Act, signed into law on July 2, 1862, by President Lincoln. This Act provided each Union state 30,000 acres of public land for each federal senator and representative the state had in Congress to be allocated for the development of state universities whose missions were to focus on the advancement of agriculture and the mechanical arts, a direct response to the Industrial Revolution that was sweeping the country.[125] The Act was seen as a boon to advancing industry and agriculture as prior to its passage, there were only four states that had agricultural colleges; however, just 10 years later, 1872, 26 additional states had introduced state agricultural colleges bringing the total to 63 the number of universities throughout thirty states that were established under the Morrill Act,[126] making it one of the most significant and influential pieces of federal legislation to impact American higher education up to that time. Additionally, this Act linked the Organic Act (technology and scientific advancement of agriculture) and the Homestead Act (available land for inexpensive settlement) with establishing state universities and acknowledging the expansion of the west and the Industrial Revolution.

Background of the Morrill Act of 1862 and Federal Involvement in Education

The history of the Morrill Act of 1862 can be traced to the eighteenth century when the newly formed Continental Congress passed the first of a series of land-grant acts designed to help in the development of the western territory of the newly formed USA. During the Revolutionary War there were debates between colonial representatives on how to support the war effort financially. These representatives recognized that there were no provisions in the Articles of Confederation for funding the war associated with the separation from England by the colonies, and acknowledged the inability of Congress to tax the citizenry or to establish any programs to support the war efforts.[127]

A debate ensued among the representatives to determine an approach to increase the nation's revenue and decrease its looming financial shortfall. During this debate, the representatives came to realize that western lands (at that time, lands that had a western boundary at the Mississippi River) could be incorporated into the newly independent nation leading the Continental Congress to pass the Land Ordinance of 1785.[128] This Ordinance, passed in 1785, laid the foundation for the Homestead Act and Morrill Act of 1862 by setting guidelines for the establishment and surveying of the western territory.[129] These guidelines served to instruct surveyors working for the government to develop the land into townships (land that is six square miles with 36 parcels contained therein) and lots (36 parcels per township with each lot being one mile square). In addition to the specifics identified for the parceling of land, the Ordinance also provided direction and implementation of education within the township such that each township reserved one lot (lot number 16) of the 36 for the development and construction of a public school.[130] This inclusion for the establishment of public schools in the western expansion serves as an indication of the Colonials' view toward education and the mission for the development of the western territories. The pervasive view for education in these territories was not only for those settling the land, but also was viewed as essential to civilize the indigenous natives. Furthermore, by placing emphasis on education in designating which numbered lot was to be set aside for a public school, the passage of this Ordinance also set a precedent for the federal funding for education.[131]

Then, in 1787 with the adoption of The Northwest Ordinance, the federal government became further involved in the support of education when it was deemed legal for public land to be sold for the support of and founding of a public school.[132] Although vague in many of its policies, this Ordinance was significant in its support for education and the creation of states by standardizing a geographical baseline that ran from the western territory to the Ohio River. In addition, support for education was mentioned in Article III of the Ordinance where it stated that "Religion, morality, and knowledge, being necessary to good government and the happiness of mankind, schools and the means of education shall forever be encouraged."[133] While the Ordinance only provided encouragement for education, it marked the first significant effort of the Continental Congress to address the importance of education across the nation.[134] However, even though there was no direct statement of action for education within the Ordinance, its mention was indicative of the Congress's desire to provide provisions within land contracts for financial resources to be dedicated to education at all educational levels.[135]

During the nineteenth century, a majority of Americans continued to remain on the eastern coast of the USA, not taking advantage of the opportunity provided to them through the Land Ordinance of 1785. However, as word got back east that individuals were becoming wealthy because of the California Gold Rush (1848–1855), individuals and families began taking the government's offer to move westward. This westward migration took on added importance as these groups benefitted from the provisions afforded them by the Land Ordinance of 1785 and began to populate the west coast of the country.[136] While the east and west coasts experienced an increase in population, the area between the two coasts, the Midwest, remained a sparsely populated region of the country. Agricultural economics also contributed to the sparse population in the Midwest during the 1830s and 1840s as the cost of corn, wheat, and cotton had increased significantly allowing for larger Southern farms to take control of the market and force out their smaller Midwest competitors.[137]

In the 1850s, the federal government, on several occasions, attempted to pass legislation to permit the development of railroads to connect the western and eastern coasts which, in turn, would serve to open the Midwest to commerce and population. However, the Southern States, who supported the use of slavery for the maintenance of their farms, opposed the idealism of mid-western expansion fearing a reduction in the number of slaves willing to work in the southern farmlands when they could obtain agricultural employment in non-slave Midwestern territories and states.[138] Furthermore, the Southern States feared that if the federal government promoted westward expansion by the issuance of drastically reduced, or even free land, the government would eventually need to raise money through other means including increased taxation or the inclusion of tariffs on trade to pay for the giveaways.[139] Although the Land Ordinance of 1785 and the Northwest Ordinance of 1787 laid the groundwork for the establishment of states from western territorial claims, it was not until the passage of the Homestead Act of 1862 that Americans began to benefit from the provisions allotted them for the development of homesteads in the Midwest.[140]

Government policies that promoted the western expansion of the country changed drastically with the start of the Civil War (April 12, 1861). The onetime separation between the east and west coast was overcome when the federal government authorized funding for a transcontinental railroad which permitted travel and communication to occur across the country.[141] With the onetime opponents of westward expansion, the Southern States, no longer in the Union, the Northern-controlled Congress passed the Homestead Act of 1862. The significance of this Act was that with its passage federal lands acquired through treaties between the US Government and Native Americans (i.e., Agreement with the Rogue River 1853 and the Quinault River Treaty of 1855) or the purchasing of territorial land from foreign powers (i.e., Louisiana Purchase in 1803 and the Gadsden Purchase of 1853) were now available for settlers looking to establish homesteads in the west.[142] Farmers who earlier had been displaced by the larger Southern plantations were now able to look westward for land that could be acquired for no upfront cost, or for a minimal fee of $1.25 per acre (up to 160 acres) if the settler decided to purchase the land after a 6-month grace period rather than waiting the required 5-year period of continuous residence to receive the land for free as stated in the Act.[143] Likewise, many new immigrants took advantage of the Act's provisions and as they left their homelands and headed westward to the New World to establish a home for themselves and their families with the promise of economic prosperity and the financial provisions made available through the Homestead Act.

Prior to passage of the Morrill Act, the US Government had taken active measures to populate the western territories but had offered few incentives to would-be settlers as seen in the provisions of the Land Ordinance of 1785 and the Northwest Ordinance of 1787. While these Ordinances mentioned education (land for public school—Ordinance of

1785; encouragement for education—Ordinance of 1787), they focused on land development and westward expansion with no mention of funding for schools, colleges, or universities. Then, with the passage of the Homestead Act, settlers of the western territories were provided financial incentives to acquire land for settlement, but still, financial support for education in the western territories was missing. This previous lack of financial support for education all changed with the passage of the Morrill Act of 1862, which, at that time, made the USA the first nation in the world to commit federal funding for the support of higher education.[144]

In the 1850s there were numerous debates over federal support for colleges and universities in the nation. The first of these debates about federal support for higher education occurred in Illinois when, in 1850, Professor Jonathan Baldwin Turner promoted a new type of university that would help prepare industrial workers in the advancements of science and technology. Turner, who received his formal training in classical studies at Yale College, accepted a position at Illinois College (1833–1847) upon his graduation.[145] While at Illinois College, Turner became an abolitionist and spoke out against slavery in his classroom. After being forced out of the college because of his views on slavery, he led the movement for an industrial education designed for the education of the working classes.[146] Turner's focus was on providing a liberal education to the vast majority of the country's citizens, namely farmers and employees of manufacturers, rather than the elitist 1% of the nation.[147] To gain support for his view, he encouraged farmers to pressure their federal representatives to assure that each state received an appropriation of public land designated for the development of a university that focused on industrial education.[148] In 1853 Turner's model for educating the working class passed the Illinois legislature who then sent a set of policies calling for the Federal Government to provide financial support ($500,000 per state) to all states for the state development of an industrial college.[149] However, no action was taken on this proposal as Congress allowed the recommendation to die.

Although the recommendations of the Illinois Legislature died at the federal level in 1853, the topic of Federal support of an agriculturally based state university was kept alive when Representative Justin Morrill (later Senator) of Vermont introduced similar legislation into Congress. Morrill, a self-educated man who regretted his lack of opportunity to attend college as a young man, became well versed in agriculture and manufacturing through his life experiences as an experimental farmer and blacksmith. His dream was to have America provide educational opportunities for children from working class families.

Morrill's first attempt at legislation to provide federal support for higher education (1857) called for Congress to provide each state with public land for the development of a state-supported agricultural college. Using the data from the federal census of 1850, Morrill's proposal called for each state to receive 20,000 acres of land for each congressional representative and senator.[150] One disadvantage to his proposal, however, as seen by western representatives, was that because the eastern states were more populated than the rest of the country and had little or no public land to sell for the development of a state agricultural college; they feared that their lands would be sold so eastern states could raise money for the development of these universities.[151]

Following the standard procedure for such a proposal being introduced into Congress (directed to the House Committee on Public Lands—a committee controlled by the Southern states who were also opposed to such a proposal) and sensing that such a proposal would be denied by the Committee, Morrill requested that his proposal be directed to a committee of his peers for review in an effort to receive a more favorable examination than what he feared from the House Committee.[152] When his request was denied, Morrill called for parliamentary rules that forced his proposal to receive a floor vote bypassing the House Committee on Public Lands. This move proved successful; however, the legislation only narrowly passed both houses of Congress.[153] Although the legislation passed both chambers of Congress, when it arrived on President Buchanan's desk, he vetoed it arguing that it was unconstitutional and would award the federal government unnecessary powers that would interfere with constitutionally guaranteed state rights.[154] Buchanan further explained that if the land-grant bill were to pass, the viability of exiting colleges and universities would be threatened. With the passage of the bill so close in both chambers, Buchanan's veto was sustained.

Although Morrill's first land-grant bill was vetoed by President Buchanan, he did not allow his dream for a federally supported state agriculture universities to die. Realizing that his proposal had received widespread support from the American people, he urged voters to influence their representatives and senators to support his bill the next time it came up for a vote in Congress.[155] Therefore, shortly after Lincoln became President in 1861, Morrill presented a modified version of his land-grant bill. The first modification called for 30,000 acres of public land (10,000 more acres than his original proposal) to be awarded to states for each representative and senator they had in Congress, based on the 1860 census rather than the 1850 national census of the first bill.[156] The third difference between the original bill and the modified bill was made because, at the time, the country was fighting the Civil War. Therefore, to address the needs of the military and to garner additional support for his legislation, he added that each land-grant institution must include military science and tactics within its curriculum.[157] Even though the Southern states had seceded from the Union, Morrill's land-grant bill still met opposition, this time from the western delegates who feared that if his bill became law, the more heavily populated eastern states would receive a greater benefit from the sale of western lands than they would.[158]

As Morrill awaited the decision from the House Committee on Public Lands, which came as a recommendation for non-passage, he asked Senator Benjamin Wade of Ohio to present the bill to the Senate's Committee on Public Lands. The Senate Committee approved Morrill's bill and moved it forward to the entire Senate where, on June 10, 1862, it passed by a vote of 32 to 9. With Morrill's land-grant bill clearing the Senate, it then went back to the House of Representatives where it was presented before the entire House without the recommendation of the Committee on Public Lands. With the full House voting, the bill passed on June 17, 1862, by a vote of 90 to 25.[159] Finally, after a 5-year battle between Congress and two presidents, the Morrill Act became law on July 2, 1862, with President Lincoln's signature.

Twenty-five years later, in 1887, a supplement to the Morrill Act of 1862 was created when Congress passed the Hatch Act. This Act enabled the federal government to provide federal matching grant funding, in the amount of $15,000, for each state to establish agricultural experimental stations in connection with the state's land-grant institution.[160] In addition, the funds awarded to each state land-grant institution through this bill were determined by the use of a formula based on the number of small farms found within the state. To receive these funds, states had to match the amount they received from the federal government.[161]

At the end of the Civil War (1865), and with advancements in science and technology, American educators began to realize that the standardized curriculum being taught in colleges and universities was outdated and irrelevant for educating the next generation of students.[162] In addition, after the War ended, colleges and universities began to see an increase in the enrollment of African-American students. Prior to 1865, few African-Americans were given the opportunity to attend college; however, with the end of the slavery and the Civil War, several private colleges were established with the sole purpose of providing the children of freed slaves a college education.[163] However, the ability of African-Americans to attend the land-grant universities created by the Morrill Act of 1862, especially those in the southern states, was not evident after the Civil War as many of the former Confederate States enacted laws that legally separated the races. In an attempt to address this issue in higher education, Congress passed the Second Morrill Act on August 30, 1890.[164] This new Act specified that for states to receive the federal funds awarded by the Morrill Act of 1862, each state had to either show that race was not a criterion for admissions or that the state maintained separate colleges for different races so that there would be an equitable division of the federal funds.[165] With this law in place, sixteen black land-grant colleges were established throughout the South and became known as the 1890 Land-Grant Institutions.[166]

The Rise of the Concept of Tenure in American Universities

From the late nineteenth to early twentieth century, the higher education system in the USA was expanding as a handful of new privately funded universities were being established through large donations made by wealthy donors.[167] These contributions enabled, and were used to attract, faculty to continue their research at these universities and to further the industrial expansion of the West. Likewise, to provide incentives for attracting new faculty, universities used their funds to offer contractual agreements to individual faculty members so they could receive a leave of absence, known as a sabbatical, every seventh year of employment at the institution. With this incentive, universities and their donors encouraged faculty members to conduct research within their field of expertise and thereby have the university receive acclaim for the innovations they created.[168]

During the late nineteenth and early twentieth century, faculty made advancements in technology that benefited their universities through acquired patents and publications that were credited to the university;

however, no provisions were made to guarantee faculty employment after their research was completed. If their services were no longer required by the university, the faculty member had no claim to the research he/she conducted because, as viewed by the university administration, board of trustees and donors, the work had been done on university time and perhaps with the benefit of a paid sabbatical. This lack of job security led to increased tensions between faculty and administration as faculty began to feel as though they were disposable commodities with little or no employment security whose jobs would be terminated when their research was concluded.

As university faculty began to question administrative policies, they began to express their opinions on various issues which inevitably led to disagreements between them and the college's board of trustees and/or administration. These confrontations were attributed to several faculty members who challenged their termination through the court system. An example of a professor who challenged the status quo of the time regarding industrial monopolies, free trade, and the diminishment of the gold standard in the USA is the case of Richard Ely.[169]

In 1894, Ely, a University of Wisconsin economist, came under fire for his views on labor strikes and the right for laborers to boycott their workplace because of the perceived unfair and unsafe environment in which they were forced to work.[170] His views drew the attention of local journalists and several state legislators who called for his dismissal from the university. Although there was no set form of academic tenure in place at this time, the University of Wisconsin, as well as the Wisconsin Board of Regents, stood behind Ely and protected his academic freedom and safeguarded his employment at the university.

Such support for university faculty job security, however, was not common within higher education as is seen in the case of Edward Ross, a Stanford University professor, who was terminated from his appointment due to his controversial views on immigrant labor, train monopolies, and his attacks on the economic policies of Stanford's founder, Leland Stanford.[171] Ross's actions drew the attention of Mrs. Stanford who used her influence to force his termination from the university.[172] Following Ross's forced resignation on June 5, 1900, another Stanford professor, George Elliott Howard, spoke out against Ross's discharge from the university.[173] Howard's statements and actions also drew the ire of Mrs. Stanford and the university administration and he also was dismissed from his position at the university.[174] These two incidents at Stanford

University where administration and moneyed interests impacted faculty employment signaled the beginning of issues that would continue to surface across American academia pertaining to the rights of faculty to speak out and the impact such actions placed on their employment.

The Formation of the American Association of University Professors and a Definition of Tenure

From the beginnings of higher education in the USA dating back to the 1700s up to the twentieth century, the university's administration and financial supporters governed universities with a firm hand and tightly controlled the research agenda of their faculties.[175] However, industrial and business leaders during the Industrial Period of the United States (1820s to 1870s) looked to universities as places that were free from canonistic influences and where the pursuit of industrial and technical knowledge could be embraced, not dampened by differences in religious beliefs.[176] It was as industrial leaders began to recognize the value of higher education that Arthur Lovejoy, a philosophy professor at Johns Hopkins University, became aware of the lack of job security provided to faculty across the nation. As he began to develop a response to what he perceived as a lack of job security in higher education, he contacted eighteen colleagues at his university and persuaded them to co-sign a letter which he sent to peers of equal rank at nine other leading universities across the nation.[177] The purpose of this letter was to establish a society where academic professors could organize and develop approaches to protect their rights and the rights of their colleagues from university administration and college trustee boards and thwart occurrences similar to those that took place at Stanford.[178]

On January 1 and 2, 1915, the professors from these leading universities held their first organized meeting at the Chemists' Club in New York City. Out of this meeting was born the American Association of University Professors (AAUP) with John Dewey selected as the organization's first president.[179] A second result of this meeting was the development of a set of regulations that defined professional academic tenure and provided guidelines for its attainment.[180] This newly formed AAUP also identified university governing boards being heavily influenced by financial donors as an area of concern because these donors, who were primarily the industrial leaders of the time, propagated self-driven interests that limited the flexibility of university faculty members to conduct unrestricted research because they were bound to the special interests of the financial donor. The association viewed academic tenure as a way not only to provide a safeguard for faculty employment, but also an avenue for educators to conduct research outside the directives from the private sector. From this initial meeting in New York City, the AAUP became the professional organization to represent faculty rights in higher education.

As part of the work at this first meeting of the AAUP, a committee was formed to draft a statement describing the rights and freedoms shared by all faculty members in safeguarding their freedom of expression in the classroom. This committee, known as the Committee of Fifteen (also known as Committee A), produced what has become known as the AAUP's *1915 Declaration of Principles of Academic Freedom and Tenure*. In addition to the committee describing freedom of expression issues in their document, they also developed a rationale for tenure stating that, due to the lack of financial compensation for faculty, tenure should be viewed as a substitute for the wealth that was achievable outside of academia.[181] The Committee's recommendations went further when they suggested that faculty appointments be made by faculty and chairpersons following three specific elements: (1) clear employment contracts; (2) formal academic tenure; and (3) clearly stated grounds for dismissal.[182] Finally, their declaration provided a linkage between academic freedom and tenure noting that these issues reside somewhere between logic and practical concerns.[183] These two concepts (academic freedom and tenure) reflected the pressures of the time being placed on those in higher education for providing improved status and safeguards for faculty self-defense against unjustified termination.[184]

Since the creation of this Declaration of Principles of Academic Freedom and Tenure, the terms academic freedom and tenure clearly have been intertwined.[185] However, leading scholars of the time feared that the granting of tenure, which provided faculty job security, would force them to tolerate unproductive colleagues imposed on them by overzealous administrators, as well as a reduction in the number of qualified applicants for faculty vacancies at universities across the nation.[186] However, to alleviate the issues raised by these scholars, the AAUP emphasized that institutions of higher education follow the recommendations from the Committee of Fifteen and include a 10-year probationary period during which time a newly appointed faculty member could be terminated for lack of collegial performance.[187] In this probationary period, the newly appointed professor had to achieve academic tenure based on the institution's and/or state's standards or he/she could be terminated without cause.[188] In its attempt to further stress the importance the AAUP placed on the recommendations of the Committee of Fifteen, the association empowered the Committee to investigate allegations of fraudulent tenure practices by universities and other infractions against the policies established by the organization.

The first of these investigations conducted by Committee A occurred in April 1915. This inquiry was prompted by Lovejoy who, while traveling to New York from Johns Hopkins University, read that seventeen faculty members had resigned from the University of Utah in protest to the practices of the college administration and the manner in which the administration had unjustly terminated several faculty members from the university. Lovejoy, with the approval of AAUP president John Dewey, spent 4 days on the campus of the University of Utah investigating the allegations presented.[189] In his examination of the policies in existence at the University of Utah, Lovejoy uncovered that several faculty members had been terminated by the university administration for their expressing their disapproval of the Governor of Utah, William Spry, in a graduation speech that they had written.[190] In addition, Lovejoy also uncovered that all appointments at the University were for a 1-year term and that there were no set standards in any of the University's documents that described the policies and procedures for termination of faculty.[191] According to Lovejoy, grounds for dismissal were solely based on the whim of the University President and its board of trustees.[192] Although the recommendation of Lovejoy and the AAUP to reinstate the dismissed professors was ignored by the University president and board of trustees, this inquiry was a landmark in that it was the first time that the AAUP investigated what it considered to be the unwarranted termination of faculty members at a university.

A few years later, concerns continued to exist within higher education about academic freedom and academic tenure. In 1925, these concerns led an organization comprised of presidents and chancellors from American universities (the American Council on Education—ACE) to invite representatives from the AAUP and other educational organizations to a meeting for the purpose of discussing the principles of academic tenure and freedom.[193] During this conference, discussions were held on the principles of academic tenure and academic freedom and how these issues were to be applied within universities. The outcome of this meeting was a joint statement from the ACE and the AAUP which included the following: (1) an endorsement by college presidents that supported academic tenure as being essential to safeguarding the academic freedom of faculty members; and (2) the first attempt to develop codified rules for tenure-related disputes by the ACE and AAUP.[194]

Then, in 1940 the AAUP released a follow-up to their 1915 Declaration when they issued their Statement of Principles on Academic Freedom and Tenure. Within this Statement, the AAUP identified the inconsistency of policies on the termination process of faculty. The remedy they suggested to rectify this inconsistency was to state that no professor could be dismissed without adequate cause, except for extraordinary reasons related to financial emergencies. Furthermore, in this Statement the AAUP recommended reducing the probationary period to acquire tenure from 10 to 7 years. A key element of this Statement was that the AAUP identified that if a tenure-track faculty member did not receive tenure by the end of the identified probationary period, he/she could be terminated without cause if a peer review demonstrated a lack of professional progress in scholarship.[195] They also recommended that if tenure decisions were not made prior to the end of the probationary period, the faculty member would be granted tenure.[196]

Finally, this 1940 Statement of the AAUP supported the notion that faculty members should have the freedom to discuss topics within their classroom; however, they must exercise when discussing controversial issues with no relation to the subject they were teaching. Discretion also was advised for faculty who chose to write and/or speak on issues that might put them at odds with their university administration and to avoid conflict if at all possible. These pronouncements by the AAUP were considered important as they addressed the issue of academic freedom by stating that all faculty members have the freedom to discuss course-related topics within their classroom without fear of reprimand from their college's administration. However, with the start of World War II, little progress was made on the implementation of the principles addressed in the Statement and the role of the AAUP during the war was diminished as America's citizens postponed higher education to serve their country.

The Growth of Tenure as a Faculty Incentive Amid First Amendment Pressures

In the early twentieth century, higher education was not as well established as a means of career preparation as it is today. Students who attended college during this era were typically from the elite of the country.[197] The typical citizen of the late nineteenth and early twentieth century either did not have the money to attend college or did not see the advantage of pursuing higher education.[198] This pattern of advanced education being available only to a select few changed with the end of World War II as soldiers began returning home from the War without any opportunities for employment available to them.[199]

It was near the end of World War II that President Franklin D. Roosevelt and Congress were faced with economic issues related to returning to a non-war economy. These issues included: (1) the elimination of wartime production of goods, (2) determining how the country could adjust to meet the ever-growing demand of goods during peacetime, and (3) considering the role of the federal government in boosting the post-war economy.[200] Additionally, the federal government expressed concern about how the nation was going to meet the employment needs of servicemen returning home from the War.[201] In its attempt to address these issues, Congress passed the Servicemen's Readjustment Act (1944), also known as the G.I. Bill of Rights. The promise of this Act was to assist veterans in attending college without individual cost.[202] With the passage of this bill aiding returning service men and women, colleges and universities across the nation grew in size to accommodate the increased number of students. However, even though the GI Bill brought about an increased demand for higher education, university administrators failed to see a need for additional faculty despite the fact that there was an increased demand for the number of courses offered at their institutions.[203] Colleges and universities responded to this issue by offering their existing faculty various benefits including tenure. The lure of tenure was also used by administrators when they realized the need to attract new faculty to their institutions (Table 2.1, demonstrates how the number of students surpassed the number of faculty, located on page).[204]

With the War over and former servicemen attending institutions of higher education in increasing numbers, the AAUP's 1940 Statement of Principles on Academic Freedom and Tenure faced its first test in

Table 2.1 Expansion of Universities and Colleges between 1939 and 1969

Year	Number of institutions	Number of faculty	Number of students	Faculty/Student ratio
1939	1708	146,929	1,494,203	1:10.17
1949	1851	246,722	2,659,021	1:10.78
1959	2008	380,554	3,639,847	1:9.56
1969	2525	450,000	8,004,660	1:17.79

Source Data adapted from US Department of Education, "*Digest of Education Statistics: 1995,*" 175

the late 1940s and early 1950s in a time that has become known in US History as the McCarthy era. It was during this time that Senator Joseph McCarthy (R-WI) accused many academics of contributing to the Communist Party.[205] His premise was that the support academics were providing to the Communist Party allowed Soviet espionage efforts to develop within the USA.[206] McCarthy demanded that the accused identify the political party they supported and answer questions concerning their loyalty to the USA.[207] This overt political intrusion into the personal political life of academics threatened to jeopardize scholarly dialogue in higher education. However, because academic tenure was in place at many of the nation's institutions, a shield was provided for faculty which prohibited university administrators from dismissing those who refused to cooperate with McCarthy.[208]

In 1953, as a response to these actions by McCarthy, the AAUP leadership released a statement that placed restrictions on faculty members who actively participated in the Communist Party.[209] This statement, fueled by the drive of McCarthyism and the fear of Soviet intrusion into the nation's political infrastructure, made it clear to institutions of higher education that if a faculty member had an affiliation with the Communist Party, he/she could be terminated from his/her appointment.[210] However, this statement was in direct conflict with the First Amendment of the Constitution of the USA which assures a citizen's right to freedom of speech and association.[211]

Because of the AAUP's position on this issue, faculty support for the AAUP began to diminish. Evidence of this decline can be seen in a 1956 statement by the association which indicated that college administration was able to legitimately question faculty members about their political affiliations and determine their level of competency based on their affiliations.[212] However, not all faculty members were able to escape McCarthy's inquisition. Unfortunately, many, if not all, non-tenured instructors who refused to cooperate with McCarthy were terminated from their positions and did not receive any support from their professional association.[213]

In the years following the McCarthy era (late 1950s through the 1960s), the USA came under duress again as the rights of African-Americans were brought to the forefront of political debate.[214] This point in time, known as the Civil Rights Movement, witnessed events that were led by university faculty as they supported the desegregation of student bodies on college campuses across the nation. Although tenure provided faculty employment, they were not provided any safeguards for their actions outside of the classroom.[215] Many instructors who supported and who had taken an active role in the Civil Rights Movement were jailed for their involvement in protests on their campuses. Even though their right to freedom of speech and association was in question, tenure provided these individuals a modicum of protection to retain their jobs even after being incarcerated.[216]

An example of tenure as job security during this period can be seen in the protests of Russell Barrett in the early 1960s. Barrett was a tenured professor at the University of Mississippi during the Civil Rights Movement when the US Supreme Court ruled for the admission of its first black student, James Meredith. At that time (1962), university officials, as well as the state's governor, tried to block Meredith's admission to the university based solely on his ethnicity. Barrett, not supporting the actions of the university and state governor, launched several protests against the blocking of Meredith's admission.[217] Although the university did not condone his protests, Barrett encountered little administrative recrimination, a fact that has been credited to his tenure status at that time.[218]

With the protections tenure provided to faculty in the 1960s and early 1970s, many faculty felt they were able to voice their expressions concerning the issues of the time (i.e., Civil Rights Movement and Vietnam War) without retribution from university administrators.[219] In spite of the fact that tenure was in place at universities and colleges across the nation during the mid- to late 1960s, university officials still challenged the legality of faculty retaining employment based solely on the tenure system. Evidence of the challenges faculty faced regarding tenure and/ or their employment can be seen in the increased number of litigation

Table 2.2 Total number of US Supreme Court Cases 1930–1969

Decade	Number of Court Cases
1930–1939	54
1940–1949	94
1950–1959	69
1960–1969	146

Source Data adapted from US Supreme Court, "Dates of Early Supreme Court Decisions and Arguments."

cases during this period; a number that increased dramatically from previous decades.[220] As seen in Table 2.2, the increase in legal cases tried by the Supreme Court increased significantly as well during the 1960s, partially due to the fact that tenure was linked to the passage of the Civil Rights Act of 1964 (Title VII)[B].[221] This piece of legislation was designed to address employment discrimination issues, claims of breaching contracts of employment, racial segregation, and violations of due process and freedom of speech, thereby providing federal legislation to guarantee job security for faculty in higher education.[222]

As the 1960s ended and the decade of the 1970s began, the issue of a faculty member's job security was once again addressed by the US Supreme Court when it ruled on the legality of continuous employment granted to faculty through tenure. The landmark case for this issue was *Perry v. Sindermann* (1972) in which Sindermann, a faculty member for ten years within the University System of Texas, was working on 1-year renewable contracts.[223] In 1969, the System's Board of Regents decided not to renew his contract based on allegations of insubordination. Upon receiving his notice of non-renewal, Sindermann sued the Regents stating that their decision was based on his public criticism of the System's policies and procedures. His case wound its way through the courts until it reached the US Supreme Court which ruled that: (1) although there was a lack of a contractual or tenure right, the plaintiff's claims could not be dismissed; (2) a teacher employed for multiple years at an institution should be permitted to show that, while no explicit tenure system existed, a de facto tenure system was in place (as he had received continuous renewal for the nine previous years); (3) proof of such a system would not guarantee re-employment, but provide the plaintiff with the opportunity to receive a hearing; and (4) at such a hearing the grounds for his non-renewal of contract should be provided to him.[224] Therefore, because of the de facto state of tenure that had been awarded to him by the US Supreme Court, Sindermann was given the right to due process and essentially awarded the right to retain his position at the college. This tenure case, which dates back over 40 years, suggests that the re-examination of tenure during this time period was prompted not only by the politicization of elements within universities themselves, but also by external pressures from society such as the reduction of external funding, society's perception of education, and the Civil Rights Movement to name but three.[225]

Table 2.3 Percent of full-time instructional staff with tenure: 1980–2010

Academic year and type of institution	Tenured		
	Total	Male	Female
1980–1981			
Public institutions	68	72.8	54
4-year	62.7	71.1	47.5
PhD granting	64.5	71.3	42.8
Other 4-year	61.3	70.9	50.2
2-year	75.2	79.3	67.5
1990–1991			
Public institutions	62.9	67.8	45.3
4-year	61.7	68.6	43.9
PhD granting	65.2	71.6	43.6
Other 4-year	59.4	66.3	44
2-year	57.3	60.9	51.9
1999–2000			
Public institutions	55.9	62	45.6
4-year	53.2	60.3	39.3
PhD granting	50.4	58	34.5
Other 4-year	54.7	61.2	43.2
2-year	67.7	70.6	64.5
2009–2010			
Public institutions	50.6	56.3	42.9
4-year	47.9	54.6	38
PhD granting	45.7	52.9	34.1
Other 4-year	51.2	55.5	46.1
2-year	64.1	67.2	61.4

Source Data adapted from National Study of Postsecondary Faculty and can be found in US Department of Education Digest of Education Statistics (1997—Table 240) and Digest of Education Statistics (2010—Table 274)

From the 1950s to the 1990s, the number of tenure or tenure-track professors employed at universities far surpassed those of non-tenure-track instructors. A recent trend, however, as seen in Table 2.3 (located on the next page), is that universities are hiring faculty on single- or multi-year contracts which may or may not include guarantees of constitutional protection rather than providing faculty an opportunity to gain the security of employment associated with tenure.[226] There are several reasons associated with this change in employment practices on the part of universities. One of the reasons given for the weakening of the traditional concept of academic tenure is that faculties lack a unified voice across the nation as well as within their own institutions[227] and many faculty members now are concerned only about what they are receiving in security and wages; not what happens to their colleagues.[228] A second reason for the apparent demise of the tenure system is that it is viewed as placing a hardship on universities that are forced, because of tenure, to keep unproductive faculty who have little regard for the students they teach and who do not participate in university service-related areas.[229] Because of these feelings toward tenure, universities have begun to follow a trend of filling vacant faculty with non-tenure-track faculty.[230] If this trend continues, the question is raised as to what changes in the current approach to employment security will be needed if tenure is to survive.

Summary

Beginning in the seventeenth century, American higher education was dominated by religious institutions whose foremost purpose was to provide religious education to the moneyed elite males of the country in the hopes that these individuals would someday become clergy. These institutions were founded and controlled by donors who exercised their influence in the selection of faculty and administration of the university. However, students who had no desire for a religious education found that the only avenue available to them in higher education was to pursue their studies in Europe, or more specifically in Germany.

As the USA began its westward expansion, and with advances being made in technology, agriculture, and science during the mid- to late nineteenth century, the federal government began to take an active role in providing opportunities for citizens to gain land and to move away from traditional canonic education and toward advanced studies in agriculture and the technology of the time. This involvement of the federal government was seen by the passage of several acts—the two most significant of these acts being the Morrill Act of 1862 and the Hatch Act of 1887. These two acts not only provided funding for the creation of the nation's first state universities across the country, but also provided a means for research in the areas of agriculture and technology.

With the passage of these two acts, the federal government offered states supplemental funding to establish non-secular institutions of higher education. Those scholars who had gone to Europe to gain advanced degrees in the classical, non-religious tradition now were returning to the USA and finding positions in state-supported secular institutions. However, with these scholars came the concept of *Lehrfreiheit*, a German approach to teaching that these scholars had experienced during their studies while attending a German university.

Through the late nineteenth and early twentieth centuries, tension grew between university administrators and their faculty as the teaching staffs began to assert not only their rights to teach as they saw fit, but also to exercise their First Amendment rights on various social and political issues. The result of this heightened involvement led to several court cases regarding faculty employment security. Following several questionable terminations that were prompted by faculty members exercising their constitutional rights a group of faculty founded an organization designed to protect the rights of faculty. This organization, the American Association of University Professors (AAUP), defined the concepts of secure, continuous employment without fear of wrongful termination and academic freedom for university faculty across the nation.

Although the organization was silent for much of the 1940s due to the USA involvement in World War II, the merits of its continuous employment security proposition were tested shortly after the war concluded as the fear of Communism in all forms of American life was rampant. This issue was not alone in its challenge to faculty employment security. Each succeeding decade has had its own cause or causes for which some faculty have taken a stand and for which the employment security of those faculty have been tested. This involvement by university faculty in social and political causes has led to an increasing number of faculty terminations being challenged in the courts. These challenges will be examined in greater depth in the following chapter.

Finally, after World War II, university administrators found the promise of tenure as a successful incentive to retain existing faculty as well as to recruit new faculty. However, in recent years as higher education administrators observe faculty more concerned with their own personal issues and less concerned about issues they deem as unrelated to their own personal good, there appears to be a growing trend among higher education institutions to hire faculty in non-tenure-track positions. This approach to employment only serves to amplify the issues related to job security and strengthen the need for a careful examination of the court cases and the guarantees of the First and Fourteenth Amendments to the US Constitution.

Notes

1. Hastings Rashdall, "The Universities of Europe in the Middle Ages: Volume 1, Salerno, Bologna, Paris," (Cambridge: Cambridge University Press, 2010) (Rashdall 2010a).
2. Nuria Sanz and Sjur Bergan, ed, "The Heritage of European Universities," Volume 548, (Council of Europe, 2006) (Sanz and Bergan 2006).
   In 1155 Emperor Fredrick Barbarossa wrote the Authentica Habita which provided a set of rules, guidelines, and privileges for the medieval university. The Authentica Habita was the first attempt of providing written guidelines for universities.
3. Robert Rait, "Life in the Medieval University," Cambridge: Cambridge University Press (1918) (Rait 1918).
4. Metzger, supra, 3.
5. Rashdall, supra, 56.
6. Metzger, supra, 3.
7. Rait, supra, 58.
8. Charles Haskins, "The Rise of Universities," Ithaca: New York: Cornell University Press (1957) (Haskins 1957).
   The licentia docendi was also used as a way to determine if a student met certain qualifications enabling them to enter the guild as a student. This was a way for the guild to regulate who would receive their lectures.
9. Metzger, supra, 3.
10. Id.
11. Bergan, supra, 57.
12. Rashdall, supra, 56.
13. Haskins, supra, 63.
14. Metzger, supra, 3.
15. Walter Rüegg, "A History of the University in Europe: Volume 4, Universities Since 1945," (Cambridge: Cambridge University Press, 2010) (Rüegg 2010).
16. Rashdall, supra, 56.

17. Nuria Sanz and Sjur Bergan, ed, "The Heritage of European Universities, Volume 548," (Council of Europe, 2006) (Sanz and Bergan 2006).
18. Id.
19. Davide Cantoni and Noam Yuchtman (2010), "Medieval Universities, Legal Institutions, and the Commercial Revolution," http://www.people.fas.harvard.edu/~cantoni/universitiesdraft_20100608.pdf (Cantoni and Yuchtman 2010).
20. Sophia Menache, "Clement V: Volume 36 of Cambridge Studies in Medieval Life and Thought," (Cambridge: Cambridge University Press, 2003) (Menache 2003).
21. Frank Flinn, "Encyclopedia of Catholicism," (New York: New York, Infobase Publishing, 2010) (Flinn 2010).
22. Giuliana Cavallini, "Catherine Of Siena," (New York: New York, Continuum International Publishing Group, 2005) (Cavallini 2005).
23. Joëlle Rollo-Koster and Thomas Izbicki, "A Companion to the Great Western Schism (1378–1417)," (Boston: MA, Brill Publishing, 2009) (Rollo-Koster and Izbicki 2009).
24. Walter Ullmann, "A Short History of the Papacy in the Middle Ages," (London: England, Routledge Publishing, 2003) (Ullmann 2003).
25. Clinton Locke, "The Age of the Great Western Schism," (New York, The Christian Literature Co., 1896) (Locke 1896).
26. Id.
27. Rashdall, supra, 56.
28. Cantoni and Yuchtman, supra, 74.
29. Hastings Rashdall, "The Universities of Europe in the Middle Ages: Volume 2, Italy, Spain, France, Germany, and Scotland," (Cambridge: Cambridge University Press, 2010) (Rashdall 2010b).
30. "The Foundation of the University of Heidelberg," trans. E. F. Henderson (London and New York, 1892).
31. Metzger, supra, 3.
    Metzger also mentioned that along with the Protestant Reformation came a new form of university that did not require the funding of the Catholic Church. Furthermore, in the universitas magistrorum the professoriate was introduced as being secular in nature.
32. Sanz and Bergan, supra, 72.
33. Metzger, supra, 3.
34. Joel Mokyr, "The European Enlightenment, the Industrial Revolution, and Modern Economic growth," (Max Weber Lecture, European University, March 27, 2007), http://faculty.wcas.northwestern.edu/~jmokyr/Florence-Weber.PDF (Mokyr 2007).
35. Metzger, supra, 3.
36. Haskins, supra, 63.

37. Wilhelm Humboldt (1810), "On the Internal and External Organization of Institutions of Higher Education in Berlin," http://germanhistorydocs.ghi-dc.org/sub_document.cfm?document_id=3642 (Humboldt 1810).
38. Wilhelm Humboldt (1854), "The Sphere and Duties of Government," trans. by Joseph Coulthard, London: GB, John Chapman, http://files.libertyfund.org/files/589/Humboldt_0053_EBk_v6.0.pdf (Humboldt 1854).
39. Id.
40. Abraham Flexner, "Universities: American, English, German," New Brunswick and London, Transaction Publishers (1994) (Flexner 1994).
41. Rüegg, supra, 70.
42. Id.
43. Humboldt, supra, 92.
44. Walter Rüegg, "A History of the University in Europe. Vol. 3: Universities in the Nineteenth and Early Twentieth Centuries," (Cambridge: Cambridge University Press, 2004) (Rüegg 2004).
45. Toni Pierenkemper & Richard Tilly, "The German Economy During the nineteenth century," (London and New York: Berghahn Books, 2004) (Pierenkemper and Tilly 2004).
46. College of William and Mary, "Journal of the President and Masters of William and Mary College, May 4, 1768," William and Mary Quarterly (vol. 5, 1897).
   In 1693, King William III of England awarded a charter to provincial dignitaries in England's Virginia colony. This charter enabled the board to establish the College of William and Mary. The first example of a simplistic form of tenure was demonstrated in 1768 when the Board of Visitor's terminated half of the masters at the college and, in response, the president of the college and the masters proclaimed that they were a corporate entity and didn't answer to the board.
47. College of William and Mary, "The History of the College of William and Mary from its Foundation, 1693, to 1870," (Baltimore: John Murphy and Co., 1870) https://digitalarchive.wm.edu/bitstream/handle/10288/13574/historyofcollege1870coll.pdf?sequence=1.
   The universities at the time were secular in nature and prepared students for the clergy. An example of this can be seen with eighteenth-century faculty at the College of William and Mary. Faculty members at the college were required to take an oath of allegiance to both the crown and the Church of England.
48. Andrew Fleming West, "The Changing Conception of "The Faculty" in American Universities," San Francisco (1906).
49. Rudolph, supra, 51.

Although the General Court of the Massachusetts Bay colony passed legislation in 1636 that called for the creation of a college, it wasn't until 1638 that Harvard College was officially formed.
50. Edwin Duryea & Donald Williams, "The Academic Corporation: A History of College and University Governing Boards," (London: GB, Taylor & Francis, 2000) (Duryea and Williams 2000).
Harvard College received its name after its benefactor, John Harvard, died in 1638. In 1642 the General Court of the Massachusetts Bay Colony established the Board of Overseers, which was comprised of six magistrates and six ministers from surrounding churches. Likewise, the General Court of the Massachusetts Bay Colony questioned the legality of the Board of Overseers being able to establish a corporation out of the college.
51. General Court of the Massachusetts Bay Colony (1650), "Harvard Charter of 1650," http://hul.harvard.edu/huarc/charter.html.
The five fellows of the college were the five current masters of the college. At the time of the awarding of the 1650 charter, there were only five instructors employed at the college. The charter also permitted for the retainment of the Board of Overseers; however, the role of the Board of Overseers was to function as a second governing board for the college and not as the sole governing agent.
52. Metzger, supra, 3.
53. Id.
54. College of William and Mary, supra, 102.
55. King William III and Queen Mary II of England (1693), "The Charter of the College of William and Mary, in Virginia," http://scrc.swem.wm.edu/wiki/images/a/a9/AndrosCopyCharter.jpg.
The charter further defined that the president and the masters of the college would be a corporate entity from the moment of the college's inception.
56. Metzger, supra, 3.
57. College of William and Mary, supra, 101.
58. Id.
59. Metzger, supra, 3.
60. J. W. Bridge, "The Rev. John Bracken v. The Visitors of William And Mary College: A Post-Revolutionary Problem in Visitatorial Jurisdiction," 20 Wm. & Mary L. Rev. 415 (1979), http://scholarship.law.wm.edu/wmlr/vol20/iss3/2.
61. Id.
62. Id.
63. Bracken v. Visitors of Wm. & Mary College, 7 Va. (3 Call) 573, 579 (1790).
64. Id.

65. Bridge, supra, 115.
66. Bracken v. Visitors of Wm. & Mary College, 7 Va. (3 Call) 573, 579 (1790).
67. Bracken v. Visitors of Wm. & Mary College, 7 Va. (3 Call) 573, 579 (1790).
68. Lionel Stanley Lewis, "When Power Corrupts: Academic Governing Boards in the Shadow of the Adelphi Case," (Piscataway: New Jersey, Transaction Publishers 2000).
69. John Thelin, "A History of American Higher Education," Baltimore and London: Johns Hopkins University Press (2004) (Thelin 2004).
70. Rudolph, supra, 51.
71. Francis Wayland, "Thoughts on the Present Collegiate System in the United States," (Boston: US, Gould, Kendall & Lincoln 1842) (Wayland 1842).
72. Rudolph, supra, 51.
73. Metzger, supra, 3.
74. Lewis, supra, 123.
75. Metzger, supra, 3.
76. Josiah Quincy, "The History of Harvard University: Volume 1," (Cambridge: J. Owen, 1840) (Quincy 1840).
77. Metzger, supra, 3.
78. Id.
79. Josiah Quincy, "The History of Harvard University: Volume 2," (Boston: Crosby, Nichols, Lee & Co., 1860) (Quincy 1860).
80. Samuel Eliot Morison, "Three Centuries of Harvard, 1636–1936," (Boston: Harvard University Press 2001) (Morison 2001).
81. Quincy, supra, 134.
82. Amacher and Meiners, supra, at 7.

    During the eighteenth century, professional educators had a basic form of tenure which provided them job security as long as they supported the religious beliefs of the university/college. This agreement was in the form of a gentlemen's agreement. An example of this job security can be seen in Harvard Universities' appointment of professors with indefinite terms. However, at the beginning of the nineteenth century, this type of agreement was weakened when universities placed in their charters that faculty members held their positions at the leisure of the governing boards.
83. Loope, supra, 11.
84. Lawrence White, "Academic Tenure: Its Historical and Legal Meanings in the United States and Its Relationship to the Compensation of Medical School Faculty Members," 44 St. Louis L.J. 51 (Winter 2000), http://www.lexisnexis.com.proxy.lib.ilstu.edu/us/lnacademic/results/docview/docview.do?docLinkInd=true&risb=21_T9769416595&for

mat=GNBFI&sort=BOOLEAN&startDocNo=1&resultsUrlKey=29_ T9769416598&cisb=22_T9769416597&treeMax=true&treeWidth=0 &csi=139118&docNo=5.
During the seventeenth and eighteenth centuries, governance was the responsibility of the governing boards. These boards would appoint instructors, commonly referred to as masters, to instruct the students at the university. These appointments provided no job security and were commonly for a year at a time.
85. Amacher and Meiners, supra, at 7.
Prior to the AAUP's 1915 Declaration of Principles of Academic Freedom and Tenure, tenure was not a formal policy and faculty appointments were typically on a year-to-year basis.
86. White, supra, 139.
With the turn of the nineteenth century came the establishment of faculty appointments by "durante vita" (the life of the incumbent). Although this type of appointment did provide a form of tenure, faculty members could still be dismissed by an institution's governing board for the slightest reason.
87. Metzger, supra, 3.
The "out" of "up or out" was in reference to the limit of time that was allowed for a master to spend in temporary service, whereas the "up" was made possible by the creation of academic ranks at a university or college.
88. Rudolph, supra, 51.
The hierarchy of academic ranks came to be in 1891 at the University of Chicago as the university president, William Harper, established a system where a scholar could advance within the institution. Along with each advancement came a term appointment which ranged from 1-year terms to permanent employment.
89. Metzger, supra, 3.
90. Christopher Lucas, "American Higher Education: A History," New York: Palgrave Macmillan (2006) (Lucas 2006)
91. Metzger, supra, 3.
92. Morrill Act of 1862 7 U.S.C., § 301
The Morrill Act was originally established so that universities could be created in each state to educate students in agriculture, home economics, mechanical arts, and other professions that were deemed important for that time. The Morrill Act provided public lands to states so that each state could establish a land-grant college with the purpose of providing the most current scientific and technologically advanced concepts of the time to incoming, and existing, students in each state.
93. White, supra, 139.
The best known "economic" case is that of Edward Ross. Ross was a professor at Stanford University who had been dismissed from his

position due to his views on train monopolies and organized unions. His dismissal was influenced by a trustee of the university, Jane Lathrop Stanford.
94. Id.
95. Abraham Flexner, "Universities: American, English, German," New York: Oxford University Press (1930) (Flexner 1930).
96. Walter Metzger, "Academic Freedom in the Age of the University," New York: Columbia University Press (1961) (Metzger 1961).
97. According to Rudolph in "The American College & University: A History," the university student has the freedom in selecting what courses to take, the freedom to learn, the ability to move from one university to another, and to live his life as he sees fit. This freedom was less prominent in the American university when compared to the freedoms associated with Lehrfreiheit.
98. According to Rudolph in "The American College & University: A History," a professor that possess Lehrfreiheit has complete freedom of inquiry and teaching, as well as the freedom to present his research findings.
99. Prussia Constitution of January 31, 1850, title II, art. 20.
100. Metzger, supra, 151.
101. Id.
102. Prussia Constitution of January 31, supra, 154.
103. Rudolph, supra, 51.
104. Metzger, supra, 3.
105. Moore, supra, 12.
German universities developed during the Middle Ages as self-managing guilds which provided their guidance, or instruction, through long-standing traditions of mentor led instruction. To become a member of one of the established German guilds, an individual had to meet certain qualifications that were controlled by guild masters. The US version was much different in that American universities were controlled by external governing boards.
106. John Thelin, supra, 124.
Philanthropy in the early to mid-nineteenth century was closely linked to religion. College funding was supported by individuals in two ways: (1) devout donors to the English Church, who focused on missionary work, provided money to universities so that programs could be designed to bring Christianity to the American Indians and (2) university officials gained access to wills and bequests by defining that an individual's charitable contribution could be defined to include the education of colonial students so that these individuals could become missionary teachers to the Indians.
107. Rudolph, supra, 51.

Endowments allowed universities to plan for expansion, develop new departments, create advanced curriculum for new sciences and technology, and develop professional schools. The downside to benefactions was that it allowed benefactors to be placed on governing boards and effect the direction that the university would pursue in all areas of operation.

108. E. D. Sanders, "Definiteness of Appointment and Tenure," Science, 39 (June 19, 1914), http://www.jstor.org/stable/1639169?seq=6 (Sanders 1941).
109. Metzger, supra, 3.
110. Henry Dunster. "Papers of Henry Dunster and the Dunster and Glover families, 1638–1874: Memorandum of Henry Dunster, 1653 December," Boston: Harvard University Archives, http://oasis.lib.harvard.edu/oasis/deliver/deepLink?_collection=oasis&uniqueId=hua23004.

Rev. Jeremiah Chaplin, "Life of Henry Dunster: First President of Harvard College," (Boston: James R. OsGood and Company, 1872).

The termination of an educator based on their religious beliefs can be seen in Harvard College's first president, Henry Dunster. During the seventeenth century, the Massachusetts Bay Colony was comprised of Puritans. The Puritan religion required that children be baptized after birth. Dunster disagreed with this belief and refused to allow his own child to be baptized in 1651. During the same year, he also interfered with the baptism of another infant. Church officials from Boston and the surrounding area called for Dunster to resign as president from Harvard College. Dunster resigned from Harvard in 1654.

111. Amacher and Meiners, supra, at 7.

The nineteenth century brought new alternatives to existing religiously based universities. Students were now able to attend an institution that either had a religious focus or one that didn't have a canonical approach to education.

112. William Harper, "The President's Report: Administration," (Chicago: University of Chicago Decennial Publications (1), 1903) http://ia600305.us.archive.org/9/items/presidentsreport00univ/presidentsreport00univ.pdf (Harper 1903).
113. Nicholas Butler, "Scholarship and Service: The Policies and Ideals of a National University in a Modern Democracy," (New York: Charles Scribner's Sons, 1921), http://archive.org/stream/scholarshipands00butlgoog#page/n8/mode/2up (Butler 1921)
114. Metzger, supra, 151.
115. Board of Regents of the Kansas State Agricultural College v. B. F. Mudge, 21 Kansas Reports 223 (1878).

116. West Publishing Company, "The Pacific Reporter, Volume 56," (St. Paul: West Publishing Co., 1899).
117. Devol v. Board of Regents for the University of Arizona, 6 Ariz. 259, 56 Pac. 737 (1899).
118. Id.
119. Peterson, supra, 13.
120. Department of Agriculture Organic Act of 1862, ch. 72, 12 Stat. 387.
121. Id.
122. Homestead Act of 1862.
123. Id.
124. Dennis Johnson, "The Laws that Shaped America: Fifteen Acts of Congress and Their Lasting Impact," (New York: Routledge, 2009) (Johnson 2009).
125. Morrill Act of 1862 7 U.S.C., § 301.
126. U.S. Library of Congress. "Primary Documents in American History: Morrill Act of 1862," http://www.loc.gov/rr/program/bib/ourdocs/Morrill.html.
127. US Continental Congress, "Articles of Confederation," (1777, ratified 1781), http://memory.loc.gov/cgi-bin/ampage.
128. David Carleton, "Landmark Congressional Laws on Education," Chicago: Greenwood Publishing Group, (2002) (Carleton 2002).
129. US Continental Congress, "Land Ordinance of 1785," http://www.in.gov/history/2478.htm.
130. Id.
131. Carleton, supra, 183.
132. US Continental Congress, "Northwest Ordinance of 1787," http://memory.loc.gov/cgi-bin/ampage.
133. Id.
134. Harold Hyman, "American Singularity: The 1787 Northwest Ordinance, The 1862 Homestead And Morrill Acts, and the 1944 G.I. Bill," (Athens: University of Georgia Press, 2008) (Hyman 2008).
135. Carleton, supra, 183.
136. Jason Porterfield, "The Homestead Act of 1862: A Primary Source History of the Settlement of the American Heartland in the Late nineteenth century," (New York: The Rosen Publishing Group, 2005) (Porterfield 2005).
137. The National Archives, "The Homestead Act of 1862," http://www.archives.gov/education/lessons/homestead-act/.
138. Johnson, supra, 179.
139. Christy Steele, "Pioneer Life in the American West," (York: Gareth Stevens Publishing, 2005) (Steele 2005).

140. Howard Ottoson, "Land Use Policy in the United States," (Washington, D.C.: Beard Books, 2001) (Ottoson 2001).
141. Gillian Houghton, "The Transcontinental Railroad: A Primary Source History of America's First Coast-To-Coast Railroad," (New York: The Rosen Publishing Group, 2002) (Houghton 2002).
142. Steele, supra, 194.
143. Homestead Act of 1862
144. Hyman, supra, 189.
145. Mary Turner Carriel, "The Life of Jonathan Baldwin Turner," (Champaign: University of Illinois Press, 1911), https://archive.org/details/cu31924030583300 (Carriel 1911).
146. Id.
147. Coy F. Cross II, "Justin Smith Morrill: Father of the Land-Grant Colleges," (East Lansing: MSU Press, 1999). (Cross II 1999)
148. J.B. Turner, "Industrial Universities for the People," (Jacksonville: Morgan Journal Book and Job Office, 1853) (Turner 1853).
149. Edmund James, "The Origin of the Land Grant Act of 1862," (Champaign: University of Illinois Press, 1910) (James 1910).
150. Carleton, supra, 183.
151. Johnson, supra, 179.
152. Carleton, supra, 183.
153. According to Carleton in "Landmark Congressional Laws on Education," Morrill's proposal passed the House of Representatives with a vote of 105–100 and the Senate with a vote of 25–22.
154. James Buchanan to the House of Representatives of the USA (February 24, 1859) in James Richardson, "James Buchanan: A Compilation of the Messages and Papers of the Presidents," (Whitefish: Kessinger Publishing, 2004).
155. Coy F. Cross II, "Justin Smith Morrill: Father of the Land-Grant Colleges," (East Lansing: MSU Press, 1999).
156. Carleton, supra, 183.
157. Morrill Act of 1862 7 U.S.C., § 301.
158. Johnson, supra, 179.
159. Carleton, supra, 183.
160. Hatch Act 1887
    The purpose of the experiment stations was to establish a facility where research could be conducted so that solutions to food and agricultural problems could be found.
161. Id.
162. Arthur Cohen, "The Shaping of American Higher Education" San Francisco: Jossey-Bass (1998) (Arthur Cohen 1998).

Industrialization was a significant factor in the University Transformation Era. Farming was directly affected by this era as new farming equipment was used to enhance yields and impact exporting of goods. Likewise, the use of railroads during the industrialization period opened westward expansion, allowing for colonization of the westward lands in the USA.
163. Id.
Prior to the Civil War, there were only three universities established to educate African American students. These institutions were: (1) Cheyney University of Pennsylvania (1837), (2) Lincoln University (1854), and (3) Wilberforce University (1856). However, following the first 5 years after the Civil War 22 institutions (e.g. Clark College (combined with Atlanta College to form Clark Atlanta University)—1865, Howard University—1867, and Morgan State University (originally Centenary Biblical Institute)—1867 of higher learning were established to provide a higher education to children of recently freed slaves.
164. Rudolph, supra, 51.
165. Morrill Act of 1890.
166. U.S. Department of Agriculture. "1890 Land-Grant Institutions Grants Programs."
167. Loope, supra, 11.
Although significant donations from benefactors enabled newly formed universities to step outside of the secular emphasis utilized in higher education at that time, the influence of these benefactors on governing boards and university officials initiated the necessity for safeguards to be implemented which would provide a shield to protect a faculty member's ability to conduct research and provide instruction without fear of reprimand from university administration.
168. Cohen, supra, 217.
Sabbatical leaves were introduced at Harvard University in 1880 as a way to attract researchers to the university. The practice of utilizing sabbatical leave and federal funding for research was predominant during the first two decades of the twentieth century.
169. University of Wisconsin, "Richard Theodore Ely Papers, 1812–1963," http://digicoll.library.wisc.edu/cgi/f/findaid/findaid-idx?c=wiarchives; cc=wiarchives;q1=richard%20t.%20ely;rgn=main;view=text;didno=uw-whs-wis000mk#uw-whs-wis000mk.p1.
Stanley Rolnick, "Exceptional Decision: The Trial of Professor Richard T. Ely by the Board of Regents of the University of Wisconsin, 1894," http://libinfo.uark.edu/aas/titles.asp?letter=E.
Professor Ely had shown great interest in social reforms and reflected his thoughts on socialism in his writings during the early 1890s. In 1894

Professor Ely drew the attention of the Wisconsin State Superintendent of Public Instruction, Oliver E. Wells. Wells, who did not support Ely's views on social reform, launched an attack against the professor by referring to Professor Ely's theories as having utopian style beliefs and that Ely's doctrine was malicious in nature. Furthermore, Wells accused Ely of demanding the unionization of the employees at a local printing house for which he had printing work done. These accusations eventually led to a hearing before the Wisconsin Board of Regents on August 23, 1894, during which the Wisconsin Board of Regents discredited all claims against Ely.

170. Peterson, supra, 13.
171. Edward Alsworth Ross, "Seventy Years of It: An Autobiography," New York: ARNO Press (1977) (Edward Alsworth Ross 1977).
During the presidential campaign of 1896, Professor Ross took the position of supporting the Democratic movement for an inflationary monetary policy, known as the Free Silver movement. In the summer of 1896, Professor Ross gave two public speeches focused on the benefits of the replacing the Gold Standard with the less volatile Free Silver Standard. Although no action was taken against Ross, Stanford University President, David Star Jordan, offered him a 1-year leave of absence as long as he submitted a letter of resignation to him; however, Ross refused to resign. Ross then came under attack in 1899 for his opposition to the use of Asian laborers to build railroads. Jane Lathrop Stanford, the university's benefactor, called for Ross's dismissal based on his progressive views on free silver and the use of migrant Asian workers.
172. American Sociological Association, "Edward Alsworth Ross," http://www.asanet.org/about/presidents/Edward_Ross.cfm.
173. Id.
174. Ross, supra, 226.
After the dismissal/forced resignation of both Professor Ross and Professor Howard, several other Stanford faculty members resigned in protest to the university's actions.
175. Nelson, supra, 17.
Due to legislative appropriations and the pressure associated with external funding from private benefactors, university administrators used various means, such as termination of employment, to control unruly faculty members.
176. Lucas, supra, 145.
In the late nineteenth and early twentieth century, the nation moved from a religiously driven society to one that was secularized. The Carnegie Foundation, and its creator Andrew Carnegie, led the charge for universities to prepare their students to be the future leaders in

business and industry focusing on its financial support on universities that did not have a denominational affiliation.
177. Metzger, supra, 3.
178. Arthur Lovejoy, "Call: November 1914," Academe (May–June 1989).
179. American Association of University Professors, "Officers of the Association: 1915," http://www.jstor.org/stable/40216731.
180. American Association of University Professors, "General Report of the Committee on Academic Freedom and Academic Tenure: Presented at the Annual Meeting of the Association: December 31, 1915," http://www.jstor.org/stable/40216731.
181. Id.
182. American Association of College Professors, "1915 Declaration of Principles on Academic Freedom and Academic Tenure," http://www.aaup.org/AAUP/pubsres/policydocs/contents/1915.htm.
183. Id.
The AAUP identified that if academic freedom was to be safeguarded in American universities had to have a clear understanding of the principles that bear upon such a freedom. Likewise, AAUP noted that if such a freedom was to be awarded to university faculty, then there had to be an adoption by the university that would limit any infringement of that freedom. Academic tenure was designed to be a system that would be a means to an end, in as much as it would provide the freedom to conduct unrestricted research and enable a faculty member to have the freedom to teach without fear of reprisal from university officials.
184. Nelson, supra, 17.
The AAUP's 1915 Declaration of Principles of Academic Freedom and Tenure refers to how securing tenure brings with it a professional status to the person that has received it. Although the 1915 Declaration of Principles on Academic Freedom and Academic Tenure did not provide procedural guidelines for how to address dismissals of faculty, it did provide the basic outline for tenure and academic freedom and the rights that these principles provide to a faculty member.
185. American Association of College Professors, supra, 237.
186. Metzger, supra, 3.
187. Id.
188. Roger Geiger, "Perspectives on the History of Higher Education," Piscataway, NJ: Transaction Publishers (2008) (Roger Geiger 2008).
From the AAUP's 1915 Declaration of Principles on Academic Freedom and Academic Tenure, the recommended probation period for newly hired faculty members was 10 years. From its inception in 1916, the American Federation of Teachers (the AFT provides union support to both K-12 and higher education teachers) promoted for a

3-year probation period for all newly hired teachers. Many universities throughout the country failed to implement this AAUP recommendation due to the fact that there was no agreement for a set probationary period between the two leading teacher unions at the time, the AAUP and the American Federation of Teachers (AFT).
189. Daniel Pollitt and Jordan Kurland, "Entering the Academic Freedom Arena Running: The AAUP's First Year," (Academe, vol. 84, no. 4: July–August 1998) http://www.aaup.org/NR/rdonlyres/6B49A63E-F3BE-4801-829B-BB362DF5EE5B/0/TheFirstYear.pdf (Pollitt and Jordan (1998).
190. Walter Metzger, "The First Investigation," (AAUP Bulletin: Autumn 1961) http://aaup.org/NR/rdonlyres/FB879711-F81B-4C07-990E-D119EE2D3200/0/TheFirstInvestigation.pdf.
191. Pollitt and Kurland, supra, 244.
192. Id.
In 1915, Lovejoy was heading to New York City to see a play during his Easter vacation. While in Newark he happened to read in the editorial section of one of the New York newspapers about the resignation of seventeen faculty members at the University of Utah. After reading the editorial, Lovejoy learned that the seventeen members had resigned as a response to university officials terminating several faculty members without cause. After spending 4 days at the University of Utah, Lovejoy stated that the working conditions at the university were dismal.
193. American Association of University Professors, "American Council on Education," http://www.jstor.org/pss/40217376.
The purpose of the ACE's Conference on Academic Freedom and Tenure, held on January 2, 1925, was to discuss the problem that had been evident in the ACE and AAUP's response to claims of infringement on academic freedom, tenure violations, and violations in the promotion of faculty to higher ranks. While at this conference, Professor Leuschner, who was one of the delegates that represented the AAUP at the ACE's Conference, explained the difficulties that the AAUP had encountered concerning the infringement on academic freedom and the issuing of tenure to faculty. He further defined on how many of the issues discussed at the ACE conference had been overcome at the University of California. Leuschner stated that the university's board of trustees, university president, and the faculty had been cooperating to overcome any issues focusing on academic tenure, academic freedom, and the promotion of the faculty.
194. White, supra, 139.
195. American Association of College Professors, supra, 25.
196. Id.

197. Cohen, supra, 217.
Families needed their children to help work the family farm. A majority of the jobs for youth during this time required no additional training and could be learned via imitation or apprenticeship.
198. Cohen, supra, 217.
199. U.S. Department of Veteran Affairs, "VA History in Brief," http://www.va.gov/opa/publications/archives/docs/history_in_brief.pdf.
Before World War II, college and homeownership for the majority of Americans was unattainable. Upon the passing of the Servicemen's Readjustment Act in 1944, millions of Americans who had served their country during the time of war were able to attend college instead of attempting to find employment during an economic downturn experienced after the war.
200. Franklin D. Roosevelt, "Statement on Signing the G.I. Bill," http://docs.fdrlibrary.marist.edu/odgist.html.
On June 22, 1944, Franklin D. Roosevelt stated on the signing of the GI Bill that "…the members of the armed forces have been compelled to make greater economic sacrifice and every other kind of sacrifice than the rest of us, and they are entitled to definite action to help take care of their special problems."
201. U.S. Department of Veteran Affairs, "VA History in Brief," http://www.va.gov/opa/publications/archives/docs/history_in_brief.pdf.
202. Servicemen's Readjustment Act of 1944, P.L. 78–346, 58 Stat. 284m.
The Servicemen's Readjustment Act of 1944 provided three key benefits to individuals who served in the US Armed Forces. Servicemen and women were provided the opportunity to: (1) receive up to 4 years of education or training. This package would include up to $500 a year for college tuition and would cover college fees, the cost of books and supplies, and provide a monthly stipend for living expenses; (2) veterans were guaranteed a federal loan for the purchase of a home, farm or business with no down payment (veterans were able to apply for a loan up to $2000, with 50% guaranteed by the federal government); and (3) veterans were guaranteed unemployment compensation (veterans who had served in the military for a minimum of 90 days were able to receive a weekly payment of $20 for a total of 52 weeks)
203. US Department of Education, "Digest of Education Statistics: 1995."
204. James Richardson, "Tenure in the New Millennium," National Forum 79, no. 1 (1999) http://findarticles.com/p/articles/mi_qa3651/is_/ai_n8845167.
205. Cohen, supra, 217.
The quest for finding disloyal civil servants who supported Communist beliefs began in 1947 when President Truman ordered that all

federal employees be investigated to determine if they had any affiliation with an organization that was believed to be disloyal to the country. Although not a case against an academic, Dennis v. USA (1951) was the first federal case brought before the US Supreme Court to accuse an individual for their supposed loyalty to the Communist Party. The law that enabled Congress to initiate investigations of American citizens to determine their political loyalties was the Alien Registration Act, 18 U.S.C. § 2385 (1940). This Act (also known as the Smith Act of 1940) stated that it was illegal to "knowingly or willfully advocate, abet, advise, or teach the duty, necessity, desirability, or propriety of overthrowing the Government of the USA or of any State by force or violence, or for anyone to organize any association which teaches, advises, or encourages such an overthrow, or for anyone to become a member of or to affiliate with any such association."

206. U.S. Congress. Senate. Committee on Government Operations. Executive Sessions of the Senate Permanent Subcommittee on Investigations of the Committee on Government Operations. 83rd Cong., 1st sess., 1953–1954.

207. Senator Joseph McCarthy, telegram to President Harry S. Truman (February 11, 1950), http://www.archives.gov/education/lessons/mccarthy-telegram.

In the telegram from Senator Joseph McCarthy to President Truman, the Senator indicates that the spread of Communism has overrun the US Government, in particular the US State Department.

208. Loope, supra, 11. http://www.eric.ed.gov/ERICWebPortal/contentdelivery/servlet/ERICServlet?accno=ED382149.

In the late 1940s and through the mid-1950s, Senator Joseph McCarthy (R-WI) accused many academics for contributing to espionage for the Soviet Union against the USA. Even though many of the accused were innocent of the charges, a number were still targeted by McCarthy supporters and university administrators. Tenure, and more so due process and freedom of speech, provided a safeguard for these individuals so that they could not be dismissed from employment without cause.

209. Adam Clymer, "A.A.U.P. States Academic Freedom Standards Review of Past Year's More Significant Cases," (The Harvard Crimson, June 14, 1956), http://www.thecrimson.com/article/1956/6/14/aaup-states-academic-freedom-standards-review.

The AAUP released a statement that supported a faculty members' right to teach and stated that they could only be released from their duties if they were unfit to teach based on their incompetence, lack of integrity, misuse of academic prestige, misconduct, or conscious participation to overthrow the government.

210. Association of American Universities, "The Rights and Responsibilities of Universities and Their Faculties," http://www.aau.edu/policy/academic_rights.aspx?id=7212.

In this statement the AAU states that "When the speech, writing, or other actions of a member of a faculty exceeds lawful limits, he is subject to the same penalties as other persons. In addition, he may lose his university status."

211. U.S. Constitution, amend. 1.

The First Amendment of the Constitution of the USA protects the right for freedom of expression and religion. Freedom of expression includes freedom of speech, press, assembly and the implied rights of association and belief.

212. Philo Hutcheson, "Academic Freedom and Tenure - Roots of Academic Freedom, Restrictions on Academic Freedom, Tenure," http://education.stateuniversity.com/pages/1724/Academic-Freedom-Tenure.html.

213. Loope, supra, 11.

214. "King Leads the March on Washington," History.com, (August 28, 1963) http://www.history.com/topics/martin-luther-king-jr/videos#martin-luther-king-jr-leads-the-march-on-washington.

"Malcolm X on Black Nationalist Movement," History.com (March 12, 1964), http://www.history.com/topics/malcolm-x/videos#malcolm-x.

215. Metzger, supra, 3.

Academic tenure is a continuity of service, as defined by the Committee on Academic Tenure in Higher Education in 1973, and has no legal norm within the court system. The rules governing tenure are defined in the faculty handbook or faculty contract. The courts view these institutional documents as a form of state sub-legislation. If a faculty member violates one of the university policies, he/she can be terminated. However, if a faculty member is discharged from service contrary of university policy, and assuming that due process was awarded, the faculty member can be reinstated due to the policies of the university which are viewed by the courts as a form of state law.

216. Loope, supra, 11.

217. Meredith v. Fair, 83 S.Ct. 10 (1962).

The US Supreme confirmed the lower court's decision in the requirement of the University of Mississippi admitting James Meredith to the College of Law. Meredith was the first African American admitted to the University of Mississippi.

218. Russell H. Barrett, "Integration at Ole Miss," Chicago, IL: Quadrangle Books (1965) (Barrett 1965).

219. Texton v. Hancock, 359 So.2d 895 (1978).
In the Court's decision, it stated that a faculty member who is tenured has no more legal right to protection provided by the First and Fourteenth Amendment then a non-tenured faculty member would have to those same rights. Likewise, a professor and a citizen of the US, tenured or not, cannot be penalized for exercising their constitutional freedoms.
220. U.S. Supreme Court, "Dates of Early Supreme Court Decisions and Arguments," http://www.supremecourt.gov/opinions/opinions.aspx.
221. Id.
The number of cases seen before the US Supreme Court increased significantly during the decade of 1960–1969.
222. Civil Rights Act of 1964, Subchapter VI of Chapter 21 of 42 U.S.C. § 2000e.
223. Perry v. Sindermann, 408 U.S. 593 (1972).
224. Id.
225. Id.
226. Nelson, supra, 17.
227. American Association of University Professors, "Tenure and Teaching-Intensive Appointments (2010)," http://www.aaup.org/AAUP/comm/rep/teachertenure.htm.
In the AAUP's report, which was submitted to the Committee on Contingency and the Profession, it is stated that a majority of faculty positions are identified as teaching-intensive; however, these positions have been created outside of the tenure system. An outcome of this, according to the AAUP, is the replacement of the professoriate with instructors who have debilitated relationships between themselves, their peers, and campus life and thus separate instructional groups within education, those that are tenured and those that aren't.
228. Richardson, supra, 259.
With the percentage of part-time faculty and contract-based full time faculty on the rise, tenured faculty fight to retain their prestigious position awarded to them through the title of tenured professor. Part-time and contract-based professors focus their attention on salary and benefits. This focus on employment status and financial compensation creates a separation between the categories of employment allowing faculty groups to be played off against one another.
229. Robin Wilson, "Contracts Replace the Tenure Track for a Growing Number of Professors," (Chronicle of Higher Education, June 12, 1998), http://chronicle.com/article/Contracts-Replace-the-Tenur/98954/ (Wilson 1998).

230. American Association of University Professors, "The Status of Non-Tenure-Track Faculty (1993)," http://www.aaup.org/AAUP/comm/rep/nontenuretrack.htm.

References

Barrett, Russell H. 1965. *Integration at Ole Miss.* Chicago, IL: Quadrangle Books.
Butler, Nicholas. 1921. *Scholarship and Service: The Policies and Ideals of a National University in a Modern Democracy.* New York: Charles Scribner's Sons. http://archive.org/stream/scholarshipands00butlgoog#page/n8/mode/2up.
Cantoni, Davide, and Noam Yuchtman. 2010. *Medieval Universities, Legal Institutions, and the Commercial Revolution.* http://www.people.fas.harvard.edu/~cantoni/universitiesdraft_20100608.pdf.
Carleton, David. 2002. *Landmark Congressional Laws on Education.* Chicago: Greenwood Publishing Group.
Carriel, Mary Turner. 1911. *The Life of Jonathan Baldwin Turner.* Champaign: University of Illinois Press. https://archive.org/details/cu31924030583300.
Cavallini, Giuliana. 2005. *Catherine of Siena.* New York: Continuum International Publishing Group.
Christy, Steele. 2005. *Pioneer Life in the American West.* York: Gareth Stevens Publishing.
Cohen, Arthur. 1998. *The Shaping of American Higher Education.* San Francisco: Jossey-Bass.
Cross II, Coy F. 1999. *Justin Smith Morrill: Father of the Land-Grant Colleges.* East Lansing: MSU Press.
Duryea, Edwin, and Donald Williams. 2000. *The Academic Corporation: A History of College and University Governing Boards.* London: Taylor & Francis.
Flexner, Abraham. 1930. *Universities: American, English, German.* New York: Oxford University Press.
Flexner, Abraham. 1994. *Universities: American, English, German.* New Brunswick: Transaction Publishers.
Flinn, Frank. 2010. *Encyclopedia of Catholicism.* New York: Infobase Publishing.
Geiger, Roger. 2008. *Perspectives on the History of Higher Education.* Piscataway, NJ: Transaction Publishers.
Harper, William. 1903. *The President's Report: Administration.* Chicago: University of Chicago Decennial Publications. http://ia600305.us.archive.org/9/items/presidentsreport00univ/presidentsreport00univ.pdf.
Haskins, Charles. 1957. *The Rise of Universities.* Ithaca, NY: Cornell University Press.

Houghton, Gillian. 2002. *The Transcontinental Railroad: A Primary Source History of America's First Coast-To-Coast Railroad*. New York: The Rosen Publishing Group.

Humboldt, Wilhelm. 1810. *On the Internal and External Organization of Institutions of Higher Education in Berlin*. http://germanhistorydocs.ghi-dc.org/sub_document.cfm?document_id=3642.

Humboldt, Wilhelm. 1854. *The Sphere and Duties of Government*. trans. Joseph Coulthard. London: John Chapman. http://files.libertyfund.org/files/589/Humboldt_0053_EBk_v6.0.pdf.

Hyman, Harold. 2008. *American Singularity: The 1787 Northwest Ordinance, the 1862 Homestead and Morrill Acts, and the 1944 G.I. Bill*. Athens: University of Georgia Press.

James, Edmund. 1910. *The Origin of the Land Grant Act of 1862*. Champaign: University of Illinois Press.

Johnson, Dennis. 2009. *The Laws that Shaped America: Fifteen Acts of Congress and Their Lasting Impact*. New York: Routledge.

Locke, Clinton. 1896. *The Age of the Great Western Schism*. New York: The Christian Literature Co.

Lucas, Christopher. 2006. *American Higher Education: A History*. New York: Palgrave Macmillan.

Menache, Sophia. 2003. *Clement V: Volume 36 of Cambridge Studies in Medieval Life and Thought*. Cambridge: Cambridge University Press.

Metzger, Walter. 1961. *Academic Freedom in the Age of the University*. New York: Columbia University Press.

Mokyr, Joel. 2007. *The European Enlightenment, the Industrial Revolution, and Modern Economic Growth*. Max Weber Lecture, European University, 27 March 2007. http://faculty.wcas.northwestern.edu/~jmokyr/Florence-Weber.PDF.

Morison, Samuel Eliot. 2001. *Three Centuries of Harvard, 1636–1936*. Boston: Harvard University Press.

Ottoson, Howard. 2001. *Land Use Policy in the United States*. Washington, DC: Beard Books.

Pierenkemper, Toni, and Richard Tilly. 2004. *The German Economy During the Nineteenth Century*. London: Berghahn Books.

Pollitt, Daniel and Jordan Kurland. (1998). Entering the Academic Freedom Arena Running: The AAUP's First Year. *Academe* 84 (4): 45–52. http://www.aaup.org/NR/rdonlyres/6B49A63E-F3BE-4801-829B-BB362D-F5EE5B/0/TheFirstYear.pdf.

Porterfield, Jason. 2005. *The Homestead Act of 1862: A Primary Source History of the Settlement of the American Heartland in the Late Nineteenth Century*. New York: The Rosen Publishing Group.

Quincy, Josiah. 1840. *The History of Harvard University*, vol. 1. Cambridge: J. Owen.
Quincy, Josiah. 1860. *The History of Harvard University*, vol. 2. Boston: Crosby, Nichols, Lee & Co.
Rait, Robert. 1918. *Life in the Medieval University*. Cambridge: Cambridge University Press.
Rashdall, Hastings. 2010a. *The Universities of Europe in the Middle Ages: Volume 1, Salerno, Bologna, Paris*. Cambridge: Cambridge University Press.
Rashdall, Hastings. 2010b. *The Universities of Europe in the Middle Ages: Volume 2, Italy, Spain, France, Germany, and Scotland*. Cambridge: Cambridge University Press.
Rollo-Koster, Joëlle, and Thomas Izbicki. 2009. *A Companion to the Great Western Schism (1378–1417)*. Boston, MA: Brill Publishing.
Ross, Edward Alsworth. 1977. *Seventy Years of It: An Autobiography*. New York: ARNO Press.
Rüegg, Walter. 2010. *A History of the University in Europe: Volume 4, Universities Since 1945*. Cambridge: Cambridge University Press.
Rüegg, Walter. 2004. *A History of the University in Europe. Vol. 3: Universities in the Nineteenth and Early Twentieth Centuries*. Cambridge: Cambridge University Press.
Sanders, E.D. 1914. Definiteness of Appointment and Tenure. *Science*, 39: 890–896. http://www.jstor.org/stable/1639169?seq=6.
Sanz, Nuria, and Sjur Bergan (eds.). 2006. *The Heritage of European Universities*, vol. 548. Strasbourg: Council of Europe.
Thelin, John. 2004. *A History of American Higher Education*. Baltimore: Johns Hopkins University Press.
Turner, J.B. 1853. *Industrial Universities for the People*. Jacksonville: Morgan Journal Book and Job Office.
Ullmann, Walter. 2003. *A Short History of the Papacy in the Middle Ages*. England: Routledge Publishing.
Wayland, Francis. 1842. *Thoughts on the Present Collegiate System in the United States*. Boston: Gould, Kendall & Lincoln.
Wilson, Robin. 1998. Contracts Replace the Tenure Track for a Growing Number of Professors. *Chronicle of Higher Education* 44 (40): A12.

CHAPTER 3

Tenure-Related Issues in the Lower Courts: Decisions and Ramifications

As seen in Chap. 2, faculty concerns related to the freedom of faculty to teach their classes as they saw fit without retribution from university administration, and the issue of faculty job security date back to the eleventh century. As the American higher education system developed through the Colonial Period, it was not until the twentieth century that these issues came to prominence with the case of Edward Ross at Stanford. It was this case that spurred the American Association of University Professors (AAUP) to take a stand and demand protections that their freedoms of speech and their rights to due process, although guaranteed in the Constitution, would be assured prior to termination. The position of this organization was that, although these rights and protection were guaranteed by the First and Fourteenth Amendments to the US Constitution, additional protection was warranted because many boards of trustees and higher education administrators were terminating faculty without regard to these amendments. Such actions brought rise to the initial concept of tenure as put forth by the AAUP in 1915. This chapter begins with an examination of the criticisms leveled against tenure which is followed by a review of significant lower court decisions related to faculty protection based on the First and Fourteenth Amendment.

CRITICISMS OF TENURE

Many critics of tenure contend that it guarantees job security, promotes mediocrity among professors, and makes it difficult for university administrators to terminate instructors who are no longer effective in the classroom while they are working with students and peers or both.[1] Impressions such as these, by no means, place all higher education faculty members in the category of being unproductive. While it's unfair to broadly level these charges against college and university faculty as a whole, such accusations may be correct for some faculty members who reach a point in their professional career where their energy for educating students and conducting research has diminished to an unproductive level.

Within the current system of tenure, non-tenured professors conduct research, serve on numerous university committees, and have scores of student advisees with tenure and promotion/advancement as the ultimate rewards for their efforts.[2] However, once tenure and promotion are attained, the individual's desire for teaching is often replaced with the desire to conduct research on narrow topics of personal interest or becoming a recluse and not taking part in any university activities.[3] Such departures from the profession may have the faculty member seeking to remove himself/herself from teaching, perhaps more so for younger faculty members than a seasoned faculty member.[4] According to Riley, the reason faculty members remove themselves from teaching and focus more on research is based on how senior faculty members require a high number of publications for younger faculty members to achieve tenure.[5] As tenured faculty withdraw into their own area of specialization, universities and colleges are hampered with employees who seem to do the minimum to benefit the institution and/or their students.[6]

Tenure is a system designed to provide a means of security for a professor's academic freedom and remove politics from a faculty member's daily interaction with his/her colleagues and administration.[7] However, tenure within higher education does not really remove politics from an academician; rather, it shifts politics to the first 7 years of a professor's career, when he/she, typically, goes through the application process for tenure and often promotion.[8] This fear of not receiving tenure has led many non-tenured faculty members to present course materials in a manner other than that which they would do otherwise if they had tenure, for their concern is that if they do not teach the way their senior peers expect, they will not be recommended for tenure by the tenure committee. As Shearer points out, the fear that non-tenured faculty members have toward not being granted tenure establishes a professional environment where liability is not equally possessed between non-tenured and tenured faculty.[9] Furthermore, Shearer states that tenure is viewed by many faculty and administrators as a lifetime guarantee of employment with little or no process built into it for disciplinary action in the event an instructor performs less than satisfactory in the classroom, in the conducting of research, or in his/her participation in university/community service.[10] Politicians critical of academic tenure cite this lack of consistency (no recourse for poor performance once tenure is granted) as a key reason to chastise higher education for keeping tenure as well as stating that tenure is an archaic system within education that handicaps university administrators when they attempt to terminate incompetent or non-productive professors. In this argument, tenure does little to promote academic freedom.[11]

A second criticism of tenure is that it influences the quality of instruction as seen in the economic downturn which began early in the twenty-first century. Scholars have identified that institutions with over 60% of their faculty tenured are headed toward financial instability, and that those institutions with a high percentage of tenured faculty are courting disaster because of the perceived lack of flexibility on the part of the university administration to adjust to regional and national trends in the employment market.[12] This trend regarding tenure was first noted in 1980, almost 30 years before the recession of 2008. Within this timeframe, colleges/universities attempted to shift scarce resources based on the community and national environment. However, since the 2008 recession, the national unemployment rate has hovered around 8% and those who are employed typically become concerned with the stability of their own job.[13] Society's perception of tenure in academia is that it provides a safeguard to an education-related job for life and that faculty members are insulated from scrutiny and pressure for enhanced performance.[14] This public perception has led to a national disdain for tenure which has been validated by Gross and Simmons in a recent article. Using a survey technique, these researchers found that business and community leaders view the use of academic tenure as a way to protect professors from accountability and productivity, an element required of employees in other professions.[15]

However, tenure as it now stands seems largely dysfunctional because of the limits it places on institutional flexibility and the university's ability to respond to community and business educational needs.[16] This issue of university flexibility as it relates to tenure is the reality of diminishing enrollments in specific academic programs. Therefore, a conflict develops between the need of the institution for flexibility to meet societal demands and the faculty concerns for job security.[17] It is this lack of flexibility in the reallocation of human resources that places a university in gridlock when it attempts to adapt to societal demands.

TENURE AND THE FIRST AMENDMENT

Although employment security for faculty within American colleges and universities existed prior to the twentieth century in the form of faculty contracts (generally 1-year renewable contracts), the actual use of the word "tenure" and its granting to faculty after a period of 7 years of satisfactory service (initially 10 years), was brought to the forefront when Edward Ross, a professor at Stanford University, was terminated for his controversial views on immigrant labor and railroad monopolies.[18] Up until this time (1900), faculty members across the nation felt that the university was a place where they could pursue knowledge and explore new ideas without fear that university administration would terminate them for their beliefs that might be considered outside the norm of common practice within society.[19] However, the role university administration played in the personal well-being of academics changed during the early twentieth century from one where the administration was viewed as a barrier between the professor and the board of trustees to one where the administration acted as an outside agent that supported external influences infringing on the interests of the faculty.[20]

This perceived change in the view of the administration by faculty meant that faculty were no longer solely concerned with the influences of their peers and colleagues as they sought promotion and advancement in their respective fields, but forces outside of academia, from state and federal legislators and monied individuals well-connected to the university, added stress to faculty security. Jastrow addressed this issue of faculty security best when he stated that: "(t)he professor was diverted by manifold cares beyond the class-room or laboratory or study; and found that his availability for the purpose of the organization directly affected his influence, his value, preferment, his status."[21] It was the Ross dismissal (discussed in length in Chap. 2) that served as a catalyst in spurring faculty interest to seek more than the job security promised by the

1-year renewable contract being used by higher education administration as faculty sought additional protection for their academic freedom and freedom of speech as protected in the First Amendment of the US Constitution.[22]

First Amendment and Faculty Rights

According to the American Association of University Professors' (AAUP) *1940 Statement of Principles on Academic Freedom and Tenure*, academic freedom cannot exist without the presence of tenure as, without tenure, faculty dismissals were at the whim of the administration or the board of trustees.[23] A question that is frequently raised concerning the need for tenure is, because the First and Fourteenth Amendments to the Constitution provides protections to all citizens, including academics[24] regardless of their tenure status,[25] is tenure needed? It can be argued that the need for a system within academia to protect a faculty member's freedom to deliver course materials in the classroom is unwarranted because the freedom of speech (his/her academic freedom) is protected by the First Amendment.[26] Additionally, it can be argued that tenure lays no claim to the guarantee of lifetime employment with a university; instead, it only provides that no person retained as a full-time faculty member beyond a probationary period may be dismissed without adequate cause and that the person being dismissed be provided the right of due process, a right guaranteed every citizen by the Fourteenth Amendment.[27] The end of this argument against the need for tenure then is that all necessary safeguards are already in place and therefore tenure is not necessary for the safeguarding of academic freedom.[28]

Within academia, however, there are numerous examples that illustrate how a university's administration has honored a professor's academic freedom without tenure being part of the equation. One such example, though without legal involvement, but involving the issue of tenure nonetheless in which a faculty member's Constitutional rights were recognized, occurred in 2000 when Edward Said, a professor at Columbia University, hurled a rock toward an Israeli guardhouse while visiting Israel. Said, a fully tenured faculty member at Columbia University, had expressed his views throughout his professional career on the conflicts between Israel and Palestine. After viewing a picture of Said throwing a rock at an Israeli guardhouse, Columbia University students, as well as the surrounding community, demanded that he be terminated;

however, the university provost, Dr. Jonathan Cole, determined that there were no grounds for seeking disciplinary action against Said for his display of anger toward the guardhouse.[29]

In his response to the university as a whole regarding the Said incident, Cole referred to the institution's faculty handbook and its wording of the protections provided to faculty and students on the topic of academic freedom. As referenced in the University's faculty handbook:

> *Academic freedom* implies that all officers of instruction are entitled to freedom in the classroom in discussing their subjects; that they are entitled to freedom in research and in the publication of its results; and that they may not be penalized by the University for expressions of opinion or associations in their private or civic capacity; but they should bear in mind the special obligations arising from their position in the academic community.[30]

The faculty handbook went further and defined the term officers of instruction:

> ...*as* any person whose appointment in the Columbia Corporation is primarily for teaching, whether full-time or part-time, with or without tenure, whatever his or her title or type of appointment held, and whether or not assigned to membership in any Faculty....[31]

According to Cole, in this case, academic tenure did not provide any legal protection to the professor and that the same protection awarded to Said would have been awarded to any non-tenured faculty member or student of the university.[32]

A second example of academic freedom being protected without the issue of tenure being involved, but which involved legal proceedings, is found in the Kentucky case of *Hardy v. Jefferson Community College* (2001).[33] In 1995, Hardy was employed by Jefferson Community College as an adjunct instructor in the Communication Department where he taught two courses: Basic Public Speaking and Introduction to Interpersonal Communication. Historically, at the end of each semester, the college offered Hardy a new term of employment for the upcoming semester and continued this form of employment from his initial contract until the end of the summer semester, 1998. During his time at the college, Hardy's student evaluations, as well as reviews conducted by his supervisor, indicated that he excelled at delivering instruction and was viewed by his students and colleagues as being an outstanding professor.[34]

In May, 1998, Hardy was informed by his supervisor, Dean Besser, that he would be teaching three sections of various communication courses the upcoming fall semester. Although he had been informed of his assigned fall teaching load for the upcoming semester, he was never asked to sign any form of intent to teach for the courses to which he was assigned, the method for employment to which he was accustomed.[35] When Spring Semester 1998 ended, Hardy was assigned to teach a summer section of Introduction to Interpersonal Communication in which the student enrollment for this course included nine African-Americans, an Asian American, and one foreign exchange student from Switzerland.[36]

As the summer semester progressed, Hardy used a variety of pedagogical approaches to present his course information. In one class session, on the topic of language and social constructivism, he chose to delve into a discussion and analysis of common words in the American language that were historically used to marginalize various minorities within the American culture.[37] During the ensuing discussion, Hardy elicited student interaction and responses on how daily conversation could be used to marginalize minority groups. This interaction with student participation led to the use of terms such as "nigger," "faggot," "lady," and "bitch" to describe how daily language could be used as a way to demoralize minority groups.[38] At the end of the class, Hardy was approached by an African-American student who objected to the in-class activity and the use of terms such as "nigger" and "bitch." The student further claimed that using such terms was in direct violation of the professor's own policy on the use of offensive language in the classroom. This policy, as noted in the course syllabus stated: "In order to make all class members comfortable enough to participate, there will be no abusive (i.e. sexist, racist, otherwise derogatory) language in discussion."[39]

Realizing that the in-class activity had offended the student, Hardy apologized. However, the student, as well as several other African-American students, did not accept the professor's apology and decided to complain about the professor's use of degrading language during the in-class activity and how the activity permitted the use of offensive words within the classroom. After meeting with their local minister, Reverend Louis Coleman, the students and the minister approached the college president (Dr. Green) and complained about the use of racially driven terms during the in-class activity. The students and their pastor demanded that appropriate action be taken against Hardy for permitting the use of the offensive terms in class. In their meeting with the college president, Coleman threatened the college president indicating that if appropriate actions were not taken against the instructor, the African-American enrollment at the college would decrease significantly.[40]

Following a discussion about the incident between Green and Besser, Besser met with Hardy to question him about the use of the offensive terms used in the class. In their meeting, Besser asked Hardy why he allowed the term "nigger" to be used within his class when his syllabus explicitly provided a statement that no such language would be tolerated in the course.[41] Hardy attempted to explain that the terms used during the in-class activity were used as a way to analyze how highly offensive terms can be and how they can negatively affect an individual. Furthermore, he indicated that the discussion was never abusive in nature nor did it focus on a particular race or ethnicity.[42]

Although Hardy attempted to explain what the intended use of the activity was within the class, Besser continued to challenge the use of the in-class activity. Realizing the seriousness of the event, Hardy asked the dean if there was anything he could do to rectify the situation.[43] Instead of answering the question, Besser simply informed him that a community leader representing the interests of the African-American student population had met with the college president and threatened to affect the college's enrollment if action was not taken against the instructor.[44]

At the end of the summer semester, 1998, Hardy received a letter from the assistant dean of students for the college, Dr. Denise Gray, indicating that the student, who had discussed the incident at the outset, was satisfied with the resolution provided for the situation.[45] Shortly thereafter, but prior to the start of the fall semester, Hardy received a voice mail from Besser stating that there were no courses available for him to teach in the 1998 fall semester, contradicting what he had been told the previous May.[46] After receiving the dean's message, Hardy requested to meet with Besser and Gray to discuss the situation.[47] During this meeting, Hardy was informed that the situation had been resolved to the complaining student's satisfaction; however, when he asked them to elaborate on what the resolution had been, Gray and Besser were silent.[48]

After receiving limited feedback from either dean, Hardy filed suit against the college stating that his rights, as protected under the

First and Fourteenth Amendment of the Constitution of the USA, had been violated. In his complaint, Hardy identified that the college had retaliated against him for exercising his rights of freedom of speech and academic freedom. In response to his claims, the college filed a complaint requesting for the case to be dismissed based on various grounds in relation to 12(b)(6) of the Federal Rules of Civil Procedure.[49] The defendant further claimed that Hardy's claims were not permissible since the college was part of the state's public educational system and protected by the Eleventh Amendment.[50] In the defendants' claim of protection under the Eleventh Amendment, they indicated that if any judgment were to be filed against either the college or deans in question, who were acting in their official capacity as a college official, such an award would be against the state.[51] Furthermore, Green and Besser claimed that they were protected by qualified immunity since Hardy had no constitutionally protected right for using the "N" and "B" words.[52]

After hearing the case, the US District Court for the Western District of Kentucky addressed the various claims made by both the defendant and the plaintiff. In its opinion, the court stated that, because the college was identified as an arm of the state, and because the college and its deans were functioning in their official capacity, and because any judgment found against them would be paid out of the state's treasury, the defendant's plea for immunity provided by the Eleventh Amendment was granted.[53] However, on the defendant's plea for qualified immunity against the plaintiff's claim of violation of his First Amendment rights, the District Court found that Hardy's speech was considered a matter of public concern and that his right to speak on such topics is a protected right.[54] Furthermore, regarding Hardy's claim of retaliatory action by the college, the District Court identified that if Hardy could prove that the college had retaliated against him for exercising his constitutionally protected rights, he then would have met any state law protecting against retaliatory actions.[55] However, in the District Court's ruling it stated that because Hardy had failed to demonstrate sufficient evidence to support his First and Fourteenth Amendment claims, the court granted the defendant's request for dismissal of these claims.[56]

Green and Besser challenged the District Court's ruling not awarding them qualified immunity. In the appeal to the US Court of Appeals for the Sixth Circuit, Green and Besser identified that Hardy's in-class speech should not have been identified as a "public concern" and thus not protected by the First Amendment. Furthermore, both deans identified that Hardy's dismissal was due to his questionable teaching methods which led to "nothing more than an internal employment dispute."[57] According to Hardy, the claim of his dismissal being nothing more than an employment dispute was unwarranted because he was questioned by Besser about the use of the "N" word in his class.[58] Hardy further claimed that during their meeting, Besser informed him that if he "were not a white male, this would not be an issue."[59]

When the case was heard by the US Court of Appeals for the Sixth Circuit, the Court addressed the various claims made by the plaintiff and the defendant noting that the claims encompassed two areas: (a) First Amendment retaliation; and (b) qualified immunity. Concerning the retaliation claim submitted by Hardy, the Court identified that the US Supreme Court had previously identified that a public employee retains his First Amendment rights when his speech addresses matters that are classified as a public concern and that the public employee should not fear retaliation from his employer.[60] In the Court's ruling on this issue, it referred back to two US Supreme Court cases (*Pickering v. Board of Education*[61] and *Perry v. Sindermann*[62]) where the topic of a public employee's comments was deemed as a matter of public concern and that an employee's employment status as untenured did not have any effect on the employee's constitutional rights.

During the Court's process for determining whether or not an employee's speech is deemed as a public concern, the Court indicated that the US Supreme Court ruled in *Connick v. Myers* (1983) that if the speech in question relates "to any matter of political, social, or other concern to the community that then that speech touch(ed) upon matters of public concern."[63] Questioning on the applicability of *Pickering*, the defense referred to *Bonnell v Lorenzo* (2001)[64] and stated that Hardy's allowing of racially charged words within the classroom were not a matter of public concern and were not protected by the First Amendment[65]. However, the Court ruled that since Hardy's speech was related to the subject matter, specifically since his lecture focused on how certain words had a social and political impact on society, unlike *in Bonnell*, Hardy's speech was identified as a matter of public concern and thus speech protected by the First Amendment.[66] Furthermore, after subjecting Hardy's claims of retaliation against protected speech, the Court identified that Hardy's speech met all parts of the "Pickering balancing test"[67] and that his allowing vulgar terms to be used in his class had no negative impact on the college or students.[68]

On the issue of qualified immunity, the defendants had indicated that they were qualified to receive immunity because any reasonable college official would have disagreed on Hardy's allowance of vulgar speech in the classroom as being protected by the First Amendment.[69] In its response to the defense's stance on qualified immunity, the Court stated that the question was whether or not it was reasonable to assume that Green and Besser truly believed that by not renewing Hardy's contract, based on his allowance of certain forms of in-class speech, that their act was lawful.[70] The defendants claimed that, in this case, since there was no precedent set by the courts for a university's ability to release a faculty member due to a faculty member's use of vulgar speech in the classroom, they should be awarded qualified immunity.

However, in the Court's ruling it pointed out that there had been several cases where the courts had identified academic freedom as being a public concern which had the ability to impact the social and political values of the nation.[71] Likewise, the Court stated that in *Dambrot v. Central Michigan University* (1995) where an athletic coach used the "N" word in a speech, the Court ruled that the coach intended that the word was motivational with its purpose being to influence public opinion, and therefore, the coach's speech was then deemed as a matter of public concern and protected by the First Amendment.[72] In the Court of Appeals verdict, it ruled that Green and Besser had retaliated against Hardy for his permitting of vulgar terms in an in-class activity, and as such was lawfully unreasonable.[73] The case was remanded back to the lower court.

Several key concepts of academic freedom and academic tenure are apparent in the *Hardy* case. First, in the Court's ruling it stated that any speech that is deemed as a matter of public concern is awarded the protection offered by the First Amendment of the US Constitution. Second, even though a college employee may not be awarded the protection of tenure, the lack of tenure does not negatively affect the rights provided to each citizen of the USA. Third, concerning the use of vulgar language within a university professor's course, the Court referred to the differences between Hardy's case to that of *Bonnell*. In its judgment, the Court stated that when the use of language is related to the subject matter, the speech is then classified as a matter of public concern and is protected by the First Amendment. As can be seen in this case, a professor's constitutional right for the protection of freedom of speech was guaranteed by the protections awarded him by the First Amendment of the Constitution, without regard for his tenure status.

State and federal courts have commonly preserved the right of a professor's academic freedom within the classroom. However, a third case of academic freedom being protected without the issue of tenure being raised is in the case of *Churchill v. The University of Colorado at Boulder* (2011). In this case, while the university investigated allegations of protected speech, other issues of misconduct were uncovered that led to the dismissal of the faculty member.

Churchill was a tenured professor in the Department of Ethnic Studies at the University of Colorado at Boulder from 1990 to 2007. During spring semester, 2005, after having agreed to speak at Hamilton College in New York, a controversy developed around the professor and an essay he had written in 2001. When the Hamilton College student body became aware of Churchill's agreement to speak at their school, the school's student newspaper ran an article focused on an essay Churchill had written entitled "On the Justice of Roosting Chickens." In this essay Churchill claimed that the September 11, 2001 attacks on the USA were an unavoidable response to the unjust policies of the USA.[74] Furthermore, he went on to say that "mindful of the hideous human costs attending the propensity of Good Americans, like Good Germans, to dodge responsibility by anchoring professions of innocence in claims of near-total ignorance concerning the crimes of their corporate state...."[75]

As publicity grew around the essay, the University of Colorado's Board of Regents decided to call a special meeting to discuss the essay and the surrounding publicity.[76] At this specially called meeting of the Board, the Interim Chancellor, Dr. Phillip DiStefano, announced that an in-depth investigation would be conducted on the claims made against Churchill's completed works. According to the interim chancellor, the purpose of the investigation was to answer two questions: (1) in accordance with Board of Regents guidelines, were any of Churchill's works justification for his dismissal and (2) if his work did violate Board policy, was his work protected by the First Amendment.[77]

An ad hoc committee was formed by DiStefano to review Churchill's work and to determine if any of his work could be classified as inappropriate in its context. This committee consisted of the Interim

Chancellor, the Dean of the School of Law, and the Dean of the College of Arts and Sciences. Upon the conclusion of their review, the committee identified that five of Churchill's works were protected by the First Amendment; however, during their investigation the committee uncovered nine instances of research misconduct.[78] With this new information, DiStefano requested that the Standing Committee on Research Misconduct (SCRM) look into the claims brought forward against Churchill[79] and an investigative sub-committee[80] was created by the SCRM to review the claims. In its attempt to prevent any conflict of interest during the sub-committee's selection process, the SCRM elicited Churchill's input for possible individuals to place on the committee.[81]

After hearing evidence presented by the university administration and Churchill, the investigative sub-committee concluded its investigation and presented its report. In its report, the sub-committee identified that Churchill had committed research misconduct in "five areas: (1) falsification, (2) fabrication, (3) plagiarism, (4) failure to comply with established standards regarding author names on publications, and (5) serious deviation from accepted practices in reporting research results."[82] However, the sub-committee was split on the seriousness of the offense with three of the five committee members calling for his dismissal while the other two calling for his suspension for 2 weeks along with a loss of pay during the suspension. Following his review of the sub-committee's recommendation, Churchill was provided an opportunity to respond before the SCRM to the allegations made against him. After hearing his rebuttal to the charges, the nine-member panel of the SCRM agreed that he had conducted research misconduct. Of the nine members of the Committee, six of the members called for his dismissal with three recommending suspension without pay (this minority opinion of the SCRM was also divided with two of the three calling for a 5-year suspension and one wanting a 2-year suspension).[83]

In his response to the SCRM's recommendation, DiStefano wrote to the Board of Regents indicating that the university's recommendation in this case was that Churchill should be dismissed from his position citing that his research misconduct demonstrated behaviors that were below the acceptable level of professional integrity at the university.[84] Upon hearing of the chancellor's recommendation for his dismissal, Churchill requested a hearing before the Faculty Senate Committee on Privilege and Tenure alleging that the university had selectively enforced college policies and that university administration's actions were in retaliation for his use of free speech.[85] In addition, Churchill claimed that he had not been provided an opportunity to hear the charges against him nor address the allegations.

After permitting the university administration and Churchill to present evidence before the Privilege and Tenure Committee of the Faculty Senate, the Committee submitted their report to the interim chancellor. In their report, they stated that the university had provided sufficient evidence in proving that Churchill had clearly conducted research misconduct and had demonstrated professional integrity that fell below the minimally accepted level at the university. According to the Privilege and Tenure Committee, Churchill had committed: "(1) three instances of evidentiary fabrication by ghostwriting and self-citation, (2) two instances of evidentiary fabrication, (3) two instances of plagiarism and (4) one instance of falsification."[86] Furthermore, the Committee stated that Churchill had been unsuccessful in providing sufficient evidence to support his claims of the university not providing him due process. In its recommendations, two of the committee members called for Churchill's dismissal and three members agreed that he should be suspended without pay for 1 year and have his academic rank lowered to Associate Professor.[87]

Following his review of the various committee recommendations, the university president, Dr. Brown, determined that the examples of research misconduct were severe and had a negative impact on the university. The recommendation of Brown to the Board was that Churchill be dismissed for research misconduct.[88] In accordance with the Board of Regents Policy, Section 5-I, IV,[89] the Regents notified Churchill of the recommendation for his dismissal and following a hearing before the Regents, Churchill was dismissed by a vote of eight to one.[90]

Upon receiving the decision by the Board of Regents, Churchill chose to have his case moved to the judicial venue of the City and County of Denver District Court where he claimed that the university had violated his First Amendment rights when they had terminated him for his use of free speech.[91] Furthermore, he claimed that the investigation was an adverse employment action and that his Civil Rights had been violated. Prior to the start of the trial, both parties agreed to stipulations that would allow for the case to proceed more quickly. These agreed upon stipulations were: (1) the University waived its right to immunity provided under the Eleventh Amendment[92] and (2) Churchill agreed to allow the University and Board of Regents to utilize any defense that would have been permissible by any university official or Regent's member acting in their official capacity.[93]

After the plaintiff and the defendant presented their evidence before the court, the university requested that Churchill's claim of the university conducting an unlawful investigation be adjudicated as a direct verdict because, according to the university, the investigation was not an adverse employment action.[94] The Court sided with the university on their request for a direct verdict and Churchill's claim that the university violated his First Amendment rights was moved to a jury trial. Siding with Churchill, the jury stated that "the Board of Regents of the University of Colorado use[d] [Churchill's] protected speech activity as a substantial or motivating factor in the decision to discharge [him] from employment."[95] Furthermore, the jury indicated that the University and the Board of Regents failed to provide evidence that supported their claim that Churchill had been terminated for reasons outside of the areas protected by the First Amendment. Although the jury sided with Churchill, they awarded him $0 in past noneconomic damages and $1 in past economic loss.[96]

Claiming quasi-judicial immunity, the university filed a post-trial motion alleging that the university and the Board of Regents were immune from Churchill's claim of violating his First Amendment rights. The Court granted this request stating that the Board of Regents had functioned as a judicial entity and had acted in a quasi-judicial manner when it decided to dismiss Churchill, thus allowing the Regents to receive quasi-judicial immunity.[97] Likewise, recognizing that he had received no financial compensation from the jury, Churchill filed a post-trial motion requesting that he be reinstated at the university at his former rank and salary.[98] On this issue, the Court stated that the professor was not capable of receiving reinstatement because such an allowance would "disregard the jury's implicit finding that Churchill had suffered no actual damages that an award of reinstatement would prospectively remedy."[99] Furthermore, the Court ruled that if they were to grant Churchill's request, the university's authority to set standards of scholarship would then be in question. Likewise, with the animosity from Churchill toward the university, the Court ruled that granting reinstatement of the professor would only lead to discontent at the workplace.[100]

Shortly after receiving the verdict of the District Court, Churchill filed an appeal with the Court of Appeals of Colorado for Division Five alleging that the lower court had erred in its decision when they: (1) granted the university the right to receive a direct verdict believing that the evidence he presented would lead a jury to siding with him, (2) allowed the university to claim quasi-judicial immunity when they were not qualified to receive such immunity, and (3) denied the professor's motion for reinstatement to the university at his former rank and salary.[101] In his appeal, Churchill indicated that the university and the Board of Regents were not qualified to receive immunity because they did not meet four qualifying reasons for the granting of immunity. These qualifying reasons are: (1) the Board of Regents were not comprised of a body of judicial officers, (2) the Board of Regents displayed bias in their decision which kept them from understanding his discipline, (3) there was no feasible way to review the decision of the Regents, and (4) the university and the Board of Regents did not qualify for quasi-judicial immunity.[102]

In its review of the qualifying reasons as put forth by Churchill, the Court of Appeals of Colorado stated that the question of quasi-judicial immunity is a question of law that should be determined by the Court. To support this decision, the Court referred to *Miller v. Davis* (2008) in which the US Court of Appeals for the Ninth Circuit stated that "Whether a public official is entitled to absolute immunity is a question of law...."[103] Furthermore, the court also referred to *Brewer v. Blackwell* (1982) where the US Court of Appeals for the Fifth Circuit stated "whether an official is protected by judicial immunity is a question of law...."[104] In its decision the Court ruled that the issue of quasi-judicial immunity had been defined within the federal courts and that "...the nature of the decision reached by the University and its Regents, and the process by which that decision was reached, shared enough characteristics with the judicial process to warrant absolute immunity from liability." The Court perceived "no error in the trial court's analysis which looked to the nature and process of the University and the Regents' activities in concluding that there was enough functional similarity between their actions and the judicial process to justify the application of quasi-judicial immunity."[105]

Regarding Churchill's claim that the Board of Regents functioned under bias in their decision to terminate him, the Court of Appeals of Colorado identified that the defendant misunderstood the purpose of quasi-judicial immunity and that if the Board of Regents functioned under the cloak of fear of lawsuit, any decision for the termination of an employee that they would make would be biased by that fear. The Court stated that "Decisions to discipline professors who do not meet standards of integrity or scholarship will no doubt be unpopular and disputed. But such self-policing does not indicate bias and it ought not subject faculty and the Regents to liability for enforcement. Otherwise academic freedom would not be preserved."[106] Furthermore, the Court of Appeals of Colorado referred to *Feldman v. Ho* (1999) where the US Court of Appeals for the Seventh Circuit indicated that a university's academic independence is protected by the Constitution, just like a faculty member's own speech. In that decision Justices Frankfurter and Harlan referred to the four freedoms of a university as the ability "to determine for itself on academic grounds who may teach, what may be taught, how it shall be taught, and who may be admitted to study."[107] The Seventh Circuit concluded that "the Constitution does not commit to decision by a jury every speech-related dispute, for if it did, that would be the end of a university's ability to choose its faculty—as it is speech that lies at the core of scholarship, and every academic decision is in the end a decision about speech."[108] In addition, the Colorado Court of Appeals further defined that it was within the ability of the lower court to rule on the request for reinstatement of Churchill. Because the Court of Appeals found that there had been no evidence of abuse in the lower court's decision, the Court of Appeals of Colorado saw no reason to overturn the lower court's ruling.[109]

Addressing the final claim of the defendant, that the university's decision in terminating him was in retaliation for his use of protected speech, the Court indicated that an investigation into an employee's conduct is not in itself an adverse employment action. For an employment action to be adverse, the action must alter the individual's terms of employment, which did not occur in the case of Churchill.[110] To support this claim, the Court referred to *Altonen v. City of Minneapolis* (2007) where the US Court of Appeals for the Eighth Circuit stated that the burden of proof for an alleged adverse employment action has to negatively affect materially the terms of employment and falls on the shoulders of the plaintiff.[111]

In their decision, the Court took into account that, as the university conducted their investigation on the allegations of research misconduct, Churchill still received his salary and benefits allotted to all faculty members employed by the university. Where Churchill claimed that his First Amendment rights were infringed upon as his use of free speech led to the investigation that caused his dismissal from the university, however, according to the Court of Appeals of Colorado, for a claim to be made where retaliation by an employer is executed due to an individual's use of protected speech, the Pickering test must be applied.[112] The Pickering test, which was developed and utilized by the US Supreme Court in *Pickering v. Board of Education* (1968), determines...

1. whether the speech was made pursuant to an employee's official duties
2. whether the speech was on a matter of public concern
3. whether the government's interests, as employer, in promoting the efficiency of the public service are sufficient to outweigh the plaintiff's free speech interests
4. whether the protected speech was a motivating factor in the adverse employment action
5. whether the defendant would have reached the same employment decision in the absence of the protected conduct.[113]

When applying the Pickering test, the plaintiff must be able to prove how his/her use of protected speech led to the adverse employment action on the part of the employer. Contrary to the claims made by the defendant, when held to the standards of the Pickering test, it was evident that the actions of the university were in response to research misconduct and not the use of protected speech by Churchill. Likewise, during the university's investigation it was stated that five of Churchill's controversial works were protected by the First Amendment; therefore, the claim of infringement of his First Amendment rights was unsupported by the evidence presented to the Court.[114] Upon receiving the ruling from the Court of Appeals of Colorado, Churchill appealed the decision to the Supreme Court of Colorado; however, citing the evidence presented in the Court of Appeals, the Supreme Court of Colorado affirmed the decision of the lower court.[115]

In the case of *Churchill*, the plaintiff (Ward Churchill) claimed that the University of Colorado at Boulder had violated his First Amendment rights when they had terminated him for his use of protected speech; however, as demonstrated in the testimony presented by the defendant, during its investigation of Churchill's publications, the university identified that Churchill's publications were protected under academic freedom (the First Amendment) and that no actions were taken against him for the views he had displayed within his writings with no relationship to his tenure status. The issues that had led to the termination of Churchill were clearly outside the realm of academic freedom and focused on Churchill's misconduct in conducting research as noted in several of his published works.

A fourth example of a recent lower court decision that related to a faculty member's academic freedom and its connection to the First Amendment of the US Constitution is that of *Adams v. Trustees of the University of North Carolina-Wilmington* (2011). In this case, Adams was hired as an assistant professor of criminology by the University of North Carolina, Wilmington Campus to teach in the Department of Sociology and Criminal Justice. During his probationary period, which lasted a total of 5 years, Adams received high teaching evaluations from his supervisor and students, received two faculty awards, had articles published, and was an active participant in university-related service activities.[116] Upon the completion of his probationary period, without question from his peers and university administration, Adams received tenure and the new academic rank of associate professor.

Several years after his promotion, Adams changed his religious beliefs and became a Christian, a change that redefined his moral and ideological views.[117] As his religious beliefs grew stronger, he became increasingly vocal about his views on the moral and political state of the university and nation. In 2004, he published a book entitled *Welcome to the Ivory Tower of Babel: Confessions of a Conservative College Professor* which contained past articles that he had published on Townhall.com as well as new works he had written. Although his views on the moral well-being of the nation had changed, his ability to be an effective teacher was confirmed as he continued to receive positive reviews from his supervisor and students.[118]

Over the years Adams became even more vocal in his views and tension began to develop between him and several of his colleagues at the university. As these tensions progressed, complaints from the Board of Trustees and the surrounding community began to find their way to the university administration concerning his public expressions of his beliefs and values.[119] However, even though the university administration did not support Adams' views or the way he presented them to the public, they recognized his right to freedom of speech and academic freedom and agreed that he was able to express his thoughts without the fear of retaliation from the administration. At one point following the release of his book, Adams was approached by the interim chair of his department, Dr. Levy, who asked him to "alter the tone of his speech to be less 'caustic' and more 'cerebral' 'like William F. Buckley' in order to 'make things a whole lot more pleasant around the office.'"[120]

Several months after publishing his book, Adams submitted his application for promotion to full professor. According to the Faculty Handbook at the University of North Carolina-Wilmington, faculty promotion is reviewed in four areas: (1) teaching ability; (2) research conducted or artistic achievement; (3) service to the university and community; and (4) scholarship and professional development completed.[121] In addition to these four areas, the review process for promotion places an emphasis on the significance of teaching excellence and research conducted or artistic achievement attained, items which carry the most weight in the decision process for the awarding of promotion and tenure.[122] Within the Faculty Handbook specific guidelines were quite specific regarding the requirements to be met for an applicant to be promoted to full professor. According to the handbook, for a faculty member to be awarded academic rank as a full professor, the candidate must "have exhibited during her/his career distinguished accomplishment in teaching, a tangible record of research or artistic achievement, and a significant record of service."[123] In Adams' application packet, he included all of the required documents plus a list of published and pending publication articles and books (including the *Welcome to the Ivory Tower of Babel: Confessions of a Conservative College Professor* book).[124]

After completing his application for promotion, Adams submitted his packet to the chair of the department, Dr. Cook. Following promotion guidelines identified within the Faculty Handbook, Cook forwarded Adams' packet to the senior most department faculty members requesting their feedback on Adams' request for promotion. Upon receiving the recommendation from the senior faculty members, Cook compiled their responses and placed them in a document that summarized the overall themes of the comments submitted by the senior faculty.[125] Cook then called a meeting with the senior faculty members to discuss their comments and recommendations. During this meeting, the scholarly works Adams had submitted were reviewed and discussed for their scholarly content. According to those who participated in the meeting, the difficulty in reviewing the works was because "they were not peer-reviewed or traditional academic writing related to his academic discipline."[126] The outcome of the meeting was that seven of the nine senior faculty members in the department voted to deny Adams' request for promotion. Supporting the recommendation of the faculty, Cook recommended that Adams' request be denied.

Upon receiving notification of denial for his promotion, Adams requested a written response from the department chair identifying the reasons for the decision to not promote him. In her response to Adams, Cook explained that the decision "...was based exclusively on the promotion application and supplementary materials [that he had] submitted and [with Cook's] consultation with the senior faculty in accordance with existing UNCW policies and procedures. [Cook] indicated an overwhelming consensus of the senior faculty did not support the promotion and found the lack of support from the senior faculty provided compelling evidence that Adams' record [did] not merit promotion to professor at [that] time."[127]

Adams followed the receipt of Cook's explanation by filing a claim with the US District Court for the Eastern District of North Carolina that the University of North Carolina—Wilmington had violated his First Amendment rights and retaliated against him stating that the university's decision to deny him promotion was based on his protected speech. Furthermore, Adams claimed that he had been denied the constitutionally protected right to due process. Finally, Adams alleged that according to Title VII of the Civil Rights Act of 1964, he had been discriminated against for his religious views and that those views played a role in the university's decision to not promote him.[128]

The defendants, who had been named in their individual and official capacities, requested summary judgment and that the claims against them be dismissed in accordance to Federal Rule of Civil Procedure 12(b)(6).[129] After granting the motion submitted by the defense, the District Court indicated that Adams' claims for violation of Title VII of religious discrimination and monetary claims against the defendants acting in their official and individual capacities were denied based on Federal Rule of Civil Procedure 12(b)(6).[130] Furthermore, the District Court referred to *Garcetti v. Ceballos* (2006) where the US Supreme Court ruled that when a public employee is speaking in his official capacity, he is not speaking as a citizen[131] (*Garcetti* is further reviewed in Chap. 4). In the Court's decision, they indicated that the focus of this case was not placed on the speech itself, but the role of the speaker when it was said.[132]

Upon receiving the opinion of the District Court, Adams appealed to the US Court of Appeals for the Fourth Circuit. In filing his appeal,

Adams submitted claims based on three actions committed by the university: (1) the university had discriminated against him because of his religion, a violation of Title VII of the Civil Rights Act of 1964; (2) the university had violated his First Amendment rights when they based their decision for his request of promotion on his protected speech; and (3) that the university had violated his right to equal protection awarded him under the Fourteenth Amendment.[133] Adams further claimed that the lower court's decision to grant the defendant's request for summary judgment was erroneous because the court had misconstrued the law when reviewing the defendant's claims.[134]

In deciding this case, the US Court of Appeals for the Fourth Circuit referenced the US Supreme Court when it stated that the courts had been reluctant to interfere with educational matters and a faculty member's academic freedom.[135] The Court identified that in its support with the District Court; Adams had failed to provide evidence supporting his claim of religious discrimination and, in fact, had failed to prove how the defendant treated him differently from his colleagues who held different religious beliefs than himself. Furthermore, the Court defined that for Adams' claim of religious discrimination to be supported, the plaintiff needed to show how his religious views were a motivating factor in the university's decision to deny his request for promotion, an issue which he was unable to document.[136] The Court also stated that for Adams to be successful in his claim of religious discrimination, he had to prove that he had been the victim of religious discrimination and that he had to provide the burden of evidence for discrimination against the burden-shifting analysis as cited in *McDonnell Douglas v. Green* (1973).[137] For Adams to meet this criterion as mentioned by the Court, he would have to "show that: (1) he belongs to a protected class; (2) he suffered an adverse employment action; (3) at the time of the adverse action, he was performing his job at a level that met his employer's legitimate expectations and was qualified for the promotion; and (4) he was rejected under circumstances giving rise to an inference of unlawful discrimination."[138] According to the Court, the District Court did not err in its decision by indicating that Adams had not proven he was denied promotion based on religious discrimination.

In reference to Adams' claims that the District Court erred in granting summary judgment for the defendant on his First Amendment claims, the US Court of Appeals referenced to *Suarez Corporation Industries v. McGraw* (2000) where the US Court of Appeals stated that the "right to be free from retaliation by a public official for the exercise of that right" is a right protected by the Constitution of the USA.[139] However, basing their opinion on *Pickering* and *Garcetti*, the Court further explained that "while government employees do not lose their constitutional rights at work, the Supreme Court has repeatedly held that the government may impose certain restraints on its employees' speech and take action against them that would be unconstitutional if applied to the general public."[140] The Court referenced to their ruling in *McVey v. Stacy* (1998) where they had identified that the complexity between a public employee acting as a citizen when the employee has commented on matters of public concern and the ability of government acting as an employer by providing a public service, the Court had to determine…:

1. "whether the public employee was speaking as a citizen upon a matter of public concern or as an employee about a matter of personal interest;
2. whether the employee's interest in speaking upon the matter of public concern outweighed the government's interest in providing effective and efficient services to the public; or
3. whether the employee's speech was a substantial factor in the employee's [adverse employment] decision."[141]

Referencing the McVey test (items one through three listed above), the US Court of Appeals stated that the District Court had erred when it had only applied the first step of the test and identified that Adams had spoken in his official capacity and not that of a citizen. Furthermore, the Court explained that the lower court had misinterpreted *Garcetti* in several areas. According to the Court, the District Court faltered when it: (1) held that protected speech was converted to unprotected speech based on its use after the fact; and (2) applied Garcetti without acknowledging the language used within the Supreme Court's decision indicating that the Court's analysis on freedom of speech did not apply to education.[142] Likewise, the District Court faltered when it concluded that Adams' speech, which had been protected by the First Amendment, had turned into unprotected speech after the speech had been made.[143]

In its decision, the US Court of Appeals for the Fourth Circuit reversed the lower court's ruling on summary judgment on Adams' First Amendment claims and affirmed the lower court's granting of summary judgment for the defendant on Adams' Title VII claim.[144] The Court remanded the case back to the US District Court for the Eastern District of North Carolina for further proceedings.

In the case described above, the concept of academic freedom was challenged within Adams. In the Court's ruling, it stated that "...the underlying right Adams asserts the Defendants violated—that of a public employee to speak as a citizen on matters of public concern—is clearly established and something a reasonable person in the Defendants' position should have known was protected."[145] It is the purpose of academic freedom to protect faculty members' freedom of speech without the fear of reprimand from his/her employer. In its decision, the Court of Appeals for the Fourth Circuit stated that "...we conclude Adams' speech was clearly that of a citizen speaking on a matter of public concern. Adams' columns addressed topics such as academic freedom, civil rights, campus culture, sex, feminism, abortion, homosexuality, religion, and morality. Such topics plainly touched on issues of public, rather than private, concern."[146] As can be seen in this case, a professor's constitutional right to freedom of speech was upheld through the First Amendment of the US Constitution.

Tenure and the Fourteenth Amendment

Although tenure is seen by many as providing a faculty member with lifelong employment security, the AAUP in its 1940 Statement of Principles on Academic Freedom and Tenure addresses financial exigency as a just cause that could lead to the termination of a faculty member.[147] However, the process of dismissing a tenured faculty member is laden with paperwork and legalities, causing many university administrators to hesitate in proceeding with faculty layoffs or retrenchment.[148] Although institutions in higher education commonly resist pursuing faculty layoffs because of a financial crisis, there have been instances where faculty members have been dismissed due to a university's financial exigency. In some instances, faculty members have challenged their dismissal based on a university's financial shortfalls through the courts; however, the courts have generally sided with the universities in their decisions. The following three lower court cases serve as examples of where institutions of higher education used financial exigency in a termination of faculty members. In each case, the faculty member had been awarded the right to due process.

The first of the three cases to be discussed is that of Annette Bignall. Bignall was employed as an adjunct instructor at North Idaho College from 1961 to 1969 and, at the start of the 1969 academic year, accepted a full-time faculty position at the college.[149] She continued at North Idaho College until 1973 when she was informed by the college president, Dr. Barry Schuler, that her contract would not be renewed for the upcoming academic year.

The issues that led Schuler to permit Bignalls contract to expire were related to several conversations he had with the Board of Trustees over the reduction of the college's student enrollment.[150] In one of those meetings, the discussion arose on how projected increases in student enrollment had led the college to hire additional faculty, but since there had been a significant decrease in enrollment the college now was overstaffed. The outcome of this meeting was that Schuler was directed by the Board to release two full-time faculty members in an effort to help with the college's depleting cash flow caused by the decrease in student enrollment.

To determine which faculty members would be terminated, the president met with all the department heads at the college to discuss faculty evaluations and identify the needs of the college. In these discussions, the department heads noted that Bignalls teaching style was not as academically sound as that of her colleagues and that there had been several student complaints concerning her favoritism toward specific students in the classroom. On January 10, 1973, Schuler notified Bignall of her non-renewal via a letter of non-renewal. However, within the letter he sent to her, he did not include the reason for her dismissal.[151]

Upon receiving Shuler's letter, Bignall enlisted her spouse, an attorney, to respond to the letter requesting an explanation for her non-renewal.[152] In correspondence between the Bignalls and the college president, it was identified that the decision to terminate Bignall was based on a decision made by the college's Board of Trustees requiring the dismissal of two full-time faculty members.[153] Upon receiving this information, the Bignalls requested a hearing before the Board of Trustees; however, the Board's attorney informed the Bignalls (by letter) that because the Board of Trustees viewed her as a probationary employee, she was not entitled to a Board hearing.[154] Furthermore, the Board's attorney indicated that if the Bignalls could provide the Board with evidence indicating that she was tenured, the Board would then reconsider their position on her dismissal.[155]

When the couple received the Board's response to their request for a hearing, they viewed it as a denial and proceeded to file suit in the US District Court for the District of Idaho. In their suit, they claimed that Mrs. Bignall had been denied her constitutionally protected right to due process because her husband had recently represented several minority students enrolled at the college. Mr. Bignall alleged that his actions of representing these students were protected by the First Amendment and that his wife's dismissal from the college was in retaliation for this issue.[156]

In their submission to the Court, the Bignalls called for a preliminary injunction halting the dismissal of Mrs. Bignall from her faculty position.[157] Although the Court denied this request, the Court ordered the college's Board of Trustees to provide a hearing to the plaintiff prior to the start of the 1973–1974 academic year. Following the direction of the District Court, the Board conducted hearings during August and September 1973, the outcome of which led to the Bignalls' withdrawing from the hearings when the Board refused to allow their counsel access to confidential personnel files of other professors who had been considered for non-reemployment.[158]

Following this action on the part of the Bignalls, they returned to the District Court alleging that, although the college's Board had conducted hearings on the matter of Bignalls dismissal, their counsel had not been granted access to records that were pertinent to their case.[159] During the Court's findings, it was concluded that even though Bignall was classified as being a de facto tenured faculty member, she had forfeited any right to administrative due process when she had prematurely terminated the August hearing held on her behalf. Furthermore, the Court stated that the college's actions for her non-renewal were based on a valid, non-discriminatory reason (financial exigency) which was not influenced by the actions of her husband.[160]

In their appeal to the US Court of Appeals for the Ninth Circuit, the Bignalls alleged that Mrs. Bignalls right to due process had been violated. According to their claim: (1) she did not receive proper notification, or a hearing, prior to the president's decision on not renewing her contract; and (2) although the Board of Trustees identified that her non-renewal of contract was based on a significant drop in student enrollment, the true reason for her termination, according to the Bignalls, was based on the prejudice of the Board of Trustees.[161] Finally, in their claim the Bignalls defined how the Board of Trustees had violated the college's tenure policy when they were unable to demonstrate how the college was suffering from a financial exigency with the termination of the plaintiff.

Within the Court's verdict in this case, it referenced the decision handed down by the US Supreme Court in *Perry*.[162] In this case, the Supreme Court stated that a de facto tenured faculty member has the right to receive ample notice of his/her non-renewal, as well as being awarded the opportunity to request a hearing where the individual can be informed of the reasons for dismissal and then challenge that decision if so desired.[163] However, the Court explained that even though a de facto tenured faculty member had the right to a hearing, it expressed that it was only the right to a hearing that would be awarded and that having such a hearing did not warrant the need for a change in the decision that had been made regarding the individual's employment.

The plaintiff's attorney referred to *Perry* and how, in similar fashion to that particular Supreme Court case, Bignall had a right to receive ample notice of her dismissal and then receive a hearing prior to Schuler's identifying her as one of the two faculty members to be dismissed. However, the Court answered this issue when it referred to a case heard before the Court of Appeals for the Third Circuit. In *Chung v. Park* (1975), the Court ruled that "a pre-termination hearing is not a hearing held prior to any decision to terminate, as [the plaintiff] suggests, but rather a hearing held prior to a termination of benefits.... In the present case, any hearing held prior to the end of the academic year would be a pre-termination hearing."[164] Similar to *Chung*, the Bignalls tried to unjustifiably define that a hearing had to be awarded to the plaintiff prior to the decision being made to not renew Mrs. Bignalls contract.[165]

Concerning the issue of a pre-dismissal hearing, the US Court of Appeals for the Ninth Circuit identified that the college had provided Bignall the required hearing as directed by the District Court. The Court pointed out, however, that it was the Bignalls who had opted to discontinue the hearing process which had led them back to the District Court to file a suit against the college for the alleged violation of the plaintiff's Fourteenth Amendment rights. Furthermore, the Court stated that....

When the Bignalls unilaterally halted the hearing, they aborted the decision-making process. The hearing could have resolved the controversy, and given the District Court, whose review would not normally be de novo, a full record to evaluate. The College violated the Bignalls' procedural rights only if it offered an inadequate hearing. If the suggested procedure would have been adequate, the Bignalls cannot state a claim under the Civil Rights Act for a denial of their procedural rights when they themselves elected to forego a complete hearing."[166]

At this point, the plaintiffs contended that the hearing they received was flawed in nature because the Board, which was focused on the financial standing of the institution, was biased because it was the entity that had instructed the president of the college to terminate two faculty members.[167] However, the Court identified that the claims made by the plaintiff were supported by no facts that would have the Court believe that there was any prejudice on the part of the Board in their decision-making process. In its response to this accusation, the Court referred to several cases where the courts had identified that even though it is not unreasonable for there to be a risk of a "hearing panel" being biased, especially if the panel is the originator of the decision in question, the courts have commonly allowed for governing boards to hold hearings in response to employee terminations (i.e., *Brubaker v. Board of Education*,[168] *Swab v. Cedar Rapids Community School District*[169] and *Simard v. Board of Education*[170]). However, the Court of Appeals for the Ninth Circuit did acknowledge that if Bignall was identified as being de facto tenured, the college was then unreasonable in notifying her of her non-renewal in the fashion they had.[171] According to the Court, the purpose of providing ample notice of termination to an individual is so the individual has the opportunity to address the justification for his/her dismissal.[172]

The Court agreed with the Bignalls when it stated that the letter received by Mrs. Bignall from Dr. Schuler did little more than inform the plaintiff of her contract being non-renewed.[173] Additionally, the Court cited that there had been no correspondence indicating that the college's decision for the termination of the two faculty members was driven by the college's financial exigency. The Court also questioned the motive of the college for not disclosing the financial shortfalls of the institution prior to the Board's August hearing.[174] In its decision, the Court even went as far as to state: "At this point the Bignalls lacked time to prepare a rebuttal. Even under the usually malleable due process standard, the notice of the basis for Mrs. Bignalls non-retention was inadequate."[175]

The Court did, however, agree with the District Court in its ruling on the topic of due process. Because the District Court had directed the college to provide a hearing where the plaintiff would be provided with the reasons for her non-reemployment, the Court of Appeals for the Ninth Circuit confirmed that the plaintiff had then been provided reasonable due process.[176] Furthermore, the Court questioned the Bignalls because, even though pre-trial information had clearly shown that the college was suffering from a financial exigency, the Bignalls made no effort to dispute the claims of the college needing to reduce faculty numbers.

When the Ninth Circuit addressed the District Court's confirmation of Bignalls status of de facto tenure, it referred to the US Supreme Court's ruling on de facto tenure in *Perry*. In that case the Supreme Court stated that de facto tenure was awarded to an individual when "the promisor's words and conduct in the light of the surrounding circumstances" deemed the action appropriate.[177] Mrs. Bignalls claim of de facto tenure was based on a single general statement made to her by the college president when she was hired indicating that she would have tenure after 3 years.[178] In itself, such a general statement provides insufficient terms for the awarding of tenure to a faculty member nor is it reasonable to assume that the president of the college has the authority to make an offer without the support of the college faculty or Board of Trustees.

Finally, the Bignalls referred to the faculty handbook from 1963, 1965, and 1968 in which it was stated that a faculty member would automatically have his/her contract renewed after having taught three consecutive years, unless discharged thereafter for cause.[179] It was established during litigation that, although there had been no mention of financial exigency within the faculty handbook, while acting as an ad hoc committee on academic freedom and tenure, Mrs. Bignall had signed a report stating that no other statement on academic tenure and academic freedom were needed beyond that of the AAUP's *1940 Statement on Academic Freedom and Tenure*.[180] Her signature on this report was crucial to her case as within the AAUP's Statement it is mentioned that a tenured faculty member could be released from employment if an institution was suffering from financial exigency.[181]

In the case described above, the concept of tenure, or more specifically de facto tenure, was raised. In the Court's ruling, it stated that "the Bignalls were provided with adequate due process protection and that the college non-retained Mrs. Bignall for valid, constitutionally permissible reasons."[182] The purpose of tenure is to guarantee faculty members the right of due process and in its decision, the Court of Appeals for the Ninth Circuit stated that a "...tenured faculty member has a right to notice," and "a hearing, at [her] request, where [she] could be informed of the grounds for [her] non-retention and challenge their sufficiency."[183] Furthermore, although in the eyes of the Court of Appeals for the Ninth Circuit, Mrs. Bignall did not possess any form of tenure; however, she still received the same right to her constitutionally protected right to due process. As can be seen in this case, a professor's constitutional right to due process is not awarded through tenure but rather through the Fourteenth Amendment of the US Constitution.

A second example of a case where a faculty claimed that she did not receive due process and was terminated because of a university's financial stability is that of *The Board of Community College Trustees for Baltimore County—Essex Community College v. Jane Adams* (1997).[184] Although this was a state case, the ruling of the Court of Special Appeals for the state of Maryland supported the ability of a university to release a tenured faculty member because of the institution's declaration of a financial exigency. This case was documented by the AAUP in their report entitled *Academic Freedom and Tenure: Essex Community College (Maryland)*.[185]

In 1991, Essex Community College was notified by the state and county government that there would be drastic cutbacks to the college's operating budget. Because of this reduction in state and county funding (a shortfall of $7.6 million for the 1992 academic year), the college began to review its current employee complement and the variety of academic programs it offered. To prepare for this shortfall of funding, the board of trustees and the college administration held several meetings to determine which areas and individuals would be affected. From these meetings the following decisions were reached: (1) over the next several years the college would have to downsize several academic programs and college activities; (2) the college's mission and values had to be redefined and protected from the financial exigency that the college was facing; and (3) the department chairs would be required to utilize a defined process for accomplishing the reduction in the number of academic programs.[186] Through these meetings, the administration developed a process to be implemented by division chairs to ascertain which programs to eliminate from their offerings. It was under this process, named the Four Flags for Andy,[187] that each program was evaluated through the use of three elements: (1) size of student enrollment; (2) size of each course section; and (3) other considerations deemed relevant by the college administration.[188]

After the process for determining program viability was put in place, the dean of instruction at the college, Dr. Andrew Snope, sent a memorandum to all college employees identifying the issues the college was facing and the process to be used in addressing the college's financial problems. In his memorandum, the dean indicated that the college may either make recommendations for the reduction of a program or for the continuation of a program without change. In addition, his memo indicated that unless the college declared itself as being in a financial exigency, the recommendations would not include a reduction of the faculty/staff complement.[189]

The Four Flags for Andy program was then forwarded to a committee comprised of the Dean of Instruction, a representative of the faculty senate, a representative of the academic council, and a representative of the counseling area.[190] In September 1992, the committee was charged by the Board of Trustees and college president to review every program at the college and grade each program on its budgetary worth, program enrollments, community needs, and cost of operation (known as the Four Flags of Andy). After administering the Four Flags for Andy approach to each program, the committee made its recommendations on addressing the financial challenges facing the college.[191]

In its recommendation to the president, the committee identified seven academic programs (one being the Office Technology program) to be terminated. Such an action of program termination was noted as inevitably leading to the dismissal of ten tenured full-time faculty. The president of the college reported the committee's recommendations to the Board of Trustees, who, along with the college president, approved the recommendations for the elimination of the seven programs.[192]

In March 1993, the faculty members in the seven programs identified for termination met with their respective department chairs and the Dean of Instruction to discuss the recommendations made by the committee. It was at this meeting that the Dean of Instruction informed the faculty members that the programs in which they taught would be curtailed at the end of the academic year and that they would be terminated as of July 1, 1994. Following this notification of termination, the faculty members submitted documentation to the college president indicating why their positions and academic programs should be allowed to continue at the college; however, no change was made in the administration's decision.[193]

In response to their termination, a Faculty Appeals Committee was formed to investigate the claims made by the college administration regarding the college's alleged financial exigency; however, after an investigation by this committee it was determined that the faculty members who were to be terminated had been terminated for reasons outside the definition presented in the faculty contract for the termination of a tenured faculty member. Furthermore, the Appeals Committee noted that during their investigation they were unable to find any formal declaration by the college of a financial exigency, the reason given for the program curtailments and faculty layoffs.[194]

In response to the claims of the Faculty Appeals Committee, the college's attorney responded via a letter that: "Thus, because the elimination of the program in question as one means of addressing [the college's] financial difficulties, and because the elimination of the programs eliminated the subject matter of the contract, then neither party could be required to perform their obligation under the contract."[195] Following the outlined procedures defined in the faculty handbook, the faculty filed a grievance against the college president alleging that they had been wrongfully terminated; likewise, because they were all tenured faculty, they noted that they should not have been released from service since their termination was not derived from a contract-defined reason for termination.[196] After a wait of several months, the faculty members' grievance was heard before the Board of Trustees. Upon hearing the information provided by both sides of the argument, the Board denied the request of the faculty for their reinstatement.[197]

As a direct result to the elimination of the college's academic programs (more specifically the Office Technology program) and the subsequent termination of the program's faculty members, Jane Adams and Gwen Nicholson, both tenured professors in the Office Technology program, submitted a request to the Circuit Court of Baltimore County for a mandamus relief in an effort to halt the college's Board of Trustees actions against the terminated faculty members.[198] The plaintiffs claimed that the reason for their termination was due to the college's decision to eliminate the academic program in which they both taught. Furthermore, since the elimination of the program led to their termination, and because their termination had not been caused by any of the defined reasons for termination listed within the faculty contract (i.e., immorality, dishonesty, misconduct in office, incompetency, insubordination, or willful neglect of duty[199]), the plaintiffs stated that the college had violated the terms of the faculty contract.[200]

Upon review of the faculty contract, the District Court found no indications in the faculty contract that provided guidelines for the curtailment of academic programs which would lead to the termination of faculty teaching within that program. Likewise, the Court found that the contract did not provide guidance for faculty reassignments, retraining, or relocations in the event a program was curtailed due to a financial exigency.[201] According to claims submitted by the plaintiffs, the terminated faculty members should have had the right to continue their employment at the college; however, the faculty members indicated that because the Board of Trustees refused to conduct a hearing on the matter of the curtailment of their academic program, the college violated their right to due process.[202] Finally, the plaintiffs noted that since their dismissal from the college, other faculty members with less tenure had been brought back to teach. In addition, on behalf of Adams and Nicholson, an outside faculty agency reviewed the events at the college and concluded that both professors had been improperly terminated because both individuals were qualified to teach courses in other disciplines and should have been reassigned to do so within the college.[203]

In response to the claims made by the plaintiffs, the defendant alleged that the use of the writ for a mandamus relief was inappropriate due to the fact that the Board's decision, which was based on state law, was non-appealable.[204] Furthermore, the defendant's attorney stated that "to the extent that the…complaint seeks to have this court control or direct the statutorily mandated authority over the expenditure of public monies allocated to the Board, mandamus relief is likewise unavailable as decisions concerning expenditures of public funds are by their very nature, discretionary actions as to which mandamus relief will not lie."[205] The defendants further claimed that the plaintiffs should not have been able to request writ for mandamus relief because their termination, as well as the elimination of the seven academic programs, was the result of severe financial difficulties that the college was experiencing at the time of their dismissal.[206]

In the Court's ruling, it stated that "…it is the Court's opinion that I should strike all of the testimony regarding that particular defense and should grant the writ of mandamus."[207] According to the Court, the cause for termination of a tenured faculty member was clearly defined within the faculty contract. However, because the non-renewal of the professors was for reasons not defined within the faculty contract, their release from the college was erroneous in nature.

The college appealed the District Court's ruling to the Court of Special Appeals for the State of Maryland. In the appeal, the Court ruled that because of the state's reduction in the state budget, which directly led to a financial shortfall for Essex Community College in state funding, a clear understanding can be made of the legitimacy of the financial crisis faced by Essex Community College. In addition, the Court noted that the national academic community recognized that tenured faculty members could be terminated for reasons related to a financial crisis.[208] When the Court commented on the appellant's reliance on the AAUP's 1940 Statement of Principles on Academic Freedom and Tenure, it noted that the Statement recognized that termination of a tenured faculty member could occur in the event of a financial exigency. Finally, on the matter of the claim for infringement of the appellants' due process right, the court referred this claim back to the lower court.[209]

As seen in the previous case that focused on faculty tenure and judicially enforceable termination of a tenured faculty member, in *The Board of Community College Trustees for Baltimore County—Essex Community College* the Court of Special Appeals for Maryland was required to determine the conditions that a tenured faculty member could be discharged from service at a college. In the Court's ruling it stated that "We note...that if tenured teachers could force schools to maintain programs, courses, and positions, the teachers would, themselves, be the policymakers—rather than the administrative bodies of the colleges. This is especially pertinent when a college is a publicly supported institution, such as the appellant. The institution cannot compel the legislative and executive branches of government to fund programs."[210] Furthermore, the Court of Special Appeals for Maryland stated that, within this case, on the matter of financial exigency, "...the courts are also ill situated, under the circumstances here present, to compel funding of institutions that are mandated into existence by legislative policy and where that branch of government has the power to abolish the entity it has created if it has the will."[211] Finally, the Court defined that it was inappropriate for the plaintiffs to request a writ for mandamus relief that directed the college to reappoint tenured faculty members to positions that no longer were available at the institution, especially since their termination was in response to reasons unrelated to personal or professional aspects of their employment.[212] Although the faculty members in this case had been dismissed from their positions at the college, their right to due process had been met when the college provided them the opportunity to a hearing in which they were presented with the reasons for their discharge and then provided an opportunity to address the governing board of the college for the reasons that they had been terminated.

The third and final lower court case related to faculty due process to be examined is that of *Katz vs. Georgetown University* (2001).[213] In this case, Dr. Katz began his employment at Georgetown University's Medical Center as a clinical professor. At the time of his employment, the university's Medical Center consisted of five areas: (1) School of Medicine; (2) School of Nursing; (3) a hospital that contained the clinical portion for both schools; (4) the Community Practice Network; and (5) the Faculty Practice Group.[214] Because Katz was employed as a clinical instructor, most of his work was conducted within the university's hospital; however, his duties did include a minimal amount of medical research and some teaching responsibilities within the School of Medicine. After completing a 5-year probationary period, he was awarded tenure in 1985.

During the 1996 academic year, the university began facing financial challenges that were mostly characterized as a cause of financial shortcomings within their Medical Center. In February 2000, in an attempt to relieve some of the financial burdens of the institution, the university's Board of Director's entered into an agreement with MedStar Health, Inc. to transfer the operations of the university's hospital and its clinical practices to MedStar while leaving control of the medical school to the university.[215] Because the university transferred control of its clinical practices to MedStar, there was no need for Georgetown University to retain its clinical faculty which led to the termination of 330 faculty members. Katz, one of the 330 faculty members released from their contract with the university, was, at that time, a tenured full-time faculty member within the Department of Surgery at Georgetown University with 20 years of service.

On March 29, 2000, Katz was notified that, because of the financial downturn of the institution, his employment at the university would be terminated on June 30, 2000. In the letter he received from the university, it was stated that any faculty member assigned to the hospital would be eligible for employment with MedStar Health, Inc. Katz was also informed that if interested, he could pursue a non-tenured track faculty position with the university. Because he was tenured, he was offered a severance buyout package of $750,000.[216] In June, 2000, he was offered 1 year of employment by MedStar Health, Inc. as a non-tenured faculty member working within the once university-owned hospital. To compensate him for the difference between his university salary ($500,000) and that offered by MedStar ($345,000), Georgetown offered to pay him $155,000 on a monthly installment plan for 1 year. Katz agreed to accept the monthly installment plan offer, but did not accept the employment offered by MedStar or the severance package offered by the university.[217]

On June 15, 2000, Katz filed a grievance against the university challenging his termination. In his grievance, he indicated that the university had improperly terminated him when they did not follow the faculty handbook by denying him a 1-year notification of his dismissal.[218] After presenting his evidence to a three-person grievance committee, the committee supported Katz's claim and indicated that the professor should have been provided a 1-year notification of his upcoming dismissal.[219] The committee forwarded its decision to the University's Grievance Code Committee who, in turn, supported the decision of the panel.

Upon receiving the Committee's decision, the university's administration appealed to the University's President, Father Leo O'Donovan, who issued a final judgment that dismissed Katz's grievance claims.[220] According to the University President, the institution's grievance process had not been designed as a way for the institution's faculty to second guess the decisions made by its Board of Directors.[221] Furthermore, the president indicated that although Katz had been a tenured professor at the university, having tenure did not provide protection to any faculty member in the event that he/she would be dismissed from the university due to a financial exigency.[222]

Then, in the following March, Katz filed suit in the US District Court for the District of Columbia against the university seeking a motion for a preliminary injunction. In his suit, Katz sought to be reinstated as a tenured faculty member and have the university provide him with a 1-year notification of termination.[223] Furthermore, Katz sought to receive back pay for the period of time that the institution had dismissed him from their employment.[224] Katz indicated that he challenged the legality of his termination and stated that the university did not have the right to end his contract as well as stating that the university was required to provide him a 1-year notice prior to his termination. The District Court's ruling sided with the university, whereupon Katz appealed the decision to the US Court of Appeals for the District of Columbia Circuit.

Upon hearing the case, the Appeals Court ruled that there was no merit in Katz's request for a preliminary injunction because there was no merit in his demand of an entitlement to a 1-year notice of his termination. The Court used a four-step process to merit the validity of the defendant's claim for a preliminary injunction. This process included: (1) would there be a strong likelihood for the plaintiff to win based on the merits of the case; (2) if the plaintiff were to lose the case would he suffer from unrecoverable injury; (3) would the awarding of an injunction cause irreparable damage to any of the other interested parties; and (4) would public interest benefit if the preliminary injunction was awarded to the plaintiff?[225]

In the Court's review of the plaintiff's request for preliminary judgment, it referred to *Ross-Simons of Warwick, Inc. v. Baccarat* (1996) where the US Court of Appeals for the First Circuit stated that when there was a claim for a preliminary injunction that the "...likelihood of success is the main bearing wall of the four factor framework."[226] Furthermore, the Court of Appeals ruled that in Katz's claims he had been unable to show how there was "...irreparable injury that would entitle him to injunctive relief."[227] Likewise, the Court explained that "...although we apply a four-factor test in weighing a request for a preliminary injunction, such relief never will be granted unless a claimant can demonstrate a fair ground for litigation."[228]

The argument Katz put forward claimed that the University's Faculty Handbook (1999) was the binding contract between the faculty and the university and that, within the handbook, several facts were stated that supported the requirement of the university to provide him with a 1-year notification before termination. This handbook wording is as follows:

1. ...those officers of instruction who by reason of their qualifications have been appointed to one of the four full-time tenure-eligible academic ranks (which in ascending order are Instructor, Assistant Professor, Associate Professor, and Professor) constitute the Ordinary Faculty of the University.
2. For one regularly appointed to the Ordinary Faculty the normal term of employment is 1 year, renewable annually. The appointment may be extended to 7 years.
3. Notice of non-reappointment will be given in writing to members of the Ordinary Faculty...

4. Not later than July 31st in the year prior to termination after two or more years of service.[229]

However, in reviewing the Faculty Handbook, the Court of Appeals noted that these claims had no legal bearing because of the following reasons:

1. According to the faculty handbook...
   (i) "Tenure may be defined as a mutually acknowledged expectation of continuing employment that is terminable by the University only for just cause (as for professional incompetence or moral turpitude of the faculty member, for grave economic stringency on the part of the University, or for reasons of major changes in institutional aims)."[230]
2. According to the Court, "The argument [presented by Dr. Katz] is pointless because it is absolutely clear that the notice of non-reappointment provision in the Faculty Handbook has nothing whatsoever to do with the termination of tenured faculty members for just cause."[231]
3. According to the Court, "Dr. Katz can point to no provision in the Faculty Handbook that requires the University to give 1-year's notice to a tenured faculty person who is subject to termination for just cause."[232]

The Court of Appeals further stated that no reasonable person would assume that the university was required to provide Katz 1-year notice prior to his termination. Furthermore, within the faculty handbook "... grave economic stringency on the part of the university" was identified as just cause for the termination of a faculty member.[233] Finally, the Court stated that because there were no university policies identifying a requirement of the school to give the professor back pay, Katz's request was deemed unwarranted.[234]

The issues of academic tenure and due process are essential elements in the Court's decision. As seen in its ruling, the Court stated that, as described in the university's faculty handbook, tenure provides a faculty member with continued employment until there is just cause for termination. In this case, the Court agreed that a financial exigency was demonstrated by the institution which led to the dismissal of the faculty member.[235] Second, even though the faculty member's contract was not renewed with the university, he was provided the right to due process. In its review of the evidence, the Court took into account the recommendations of the Grievance Panel, Grievance Code Committee, and the President of the University; however, it was the faculty handbook that clearly defined the guidelines for due process and the dismissal of a faculty member. As can be seen in this case, a professor's constitutional right for due process was guaranteed by the protections awarded him under the Fourteenth Amendment of the US Constitution.

SUMMARY

As discussed in Chap. 2, tenure was originally introduced into academe to protect a faculty member's right to research and lecture on topics without the fear of reprimand from university officials.[236] However, over the years tenure has gradually come to be seen by politicians and the public as a system that reduces the flexibility of a university to adapt to community needs and realign resources as university officials see fit.[237] In addition, tenure has been viewed as tending to distort faculty member's efforts of job performance by placing strong incentives at the beginning of his/her career, but once tenure is received, there typically are no additional tangible incentives available to motivate faculty to better serve the university.[238] Inevitably, according to tenure critics, this form of job security leads to universities being forced to continue with employees who provide no observable benefit to the institution and reduce the institution's ability to adjust to community and national needs.

As seen in the cases discussed in this chapter, it is a widely accepted standard that a university can release a faculty member due to a financial exigency regardless of the language in the faculty contract or handbook providing that the faculty member has been granted due process.[239] In the cases cited, it is clear that financial exigency has been upheld by the courts as a reason for faculty termination, although faculty still have the right to seek legal injunctions against their institutions if they feel they were denied due process, were a victim of a breach of contract or wrongful termination. Cases where universities have proven financial exigency as the reason for the termination of faculty, such as those cited in this chapter, have been upheld by the courts.[240] However, where a faculty member's freedom of speech was the issue for termination, the courts have tended to rule on the side of the professor.

Notes

1. J. Peter Byrne, "Academic Freedom without Tenure?," American Association for Higher Education (1997) (Byrne 1997).
2. Levitt, supra, 49.
   Tenure provides a system where newly appointed faculty members face strong incentives at the beginning of their careers, but once they are awarded tenure, there are only meek incentives available to them at best.
3. Andrew Hacker and Claudia Dreifus, "*Higher Education?*" New York, NY: St. Martin's Press (2011) (Hacker and Dreifus 2011).
   According to the authors, tenure cannot be proven to have an impact on productive research and teaching; however, it can have a negative effect on both research and instruction by creating a sense of entitlement and enable professors to redirect their focus from the classroom to other areas of interest.
4. Naomi Riley, "The Faculty Lounges: And Other Reasons Why You Won't Get the College Education You Paid for," (Plymouth, UK: The Rowman & Littlefield publishing Group, inc., 2011) (Riley 2011).
5. Id.
6. Levitt, supra, 49.
7. Elisa Shearer, "The Penultimate Word: The Need to Re-evaluate the Tenure System," *The Houghton Star* (March 7, 2011), http://www.houghtonstar.com/commentary/the-penultimate-word-the-need-to-re-evaluate-the-tenure-system-1.2074235 (Shearer 2011).
   According to the author, supporters of tenure indicate that tenure takes the politics out of a professor's position. However, the author indicates that tenure simply places politics and stress during the first 7 years of their career.
8. Jeffrey Williams, "The Other Politics of Tenure," *College Literature*, 26:3 (Fall 1999) (Williams 1999).
9. Shearer, supra, 292.
   Tenure provides a system where non-tenured faculty members are restricted by their fear of not attaining tenure and are not focused on their accountability within the classroom. However, tenured faculty members fear no repercussions from administration for almost anything they may do.
10. Id.
11. Brian Maffly, "Bill to end Higher-Ed Tenure dies in Committee," *The Salt Lake Tribune* (February 23, 2011), http://www.sltrib.com/sltrib/home/51298790-76/tenure-faculty-herrod-professors.html.csp 9) (Maffly 2011).
12. Moore, supra, 12.

13. US Department of Labor, "Labor Force Statistics from the Current Population Survey (November 4, 2011)," http://www.bls.gov/cps/ (US Department of Labor 2011).
14. Erwin Chemerinsky, "Is Tenure Necessary to Protect Academic Freedom?," *American Behavioral Scientist*, 41, no. 5 (1998) (Chemerinsky 1998).
15. Neil Gross and Solon Simmons, "Americans' Views of Political Bias in the Academy and Academic Freedom," *Research* (May 22, 2006), http://www.aaup.org/NR/rdonlyres/DCF3EBD7-509E-47AB-9AB3-FBCFFF5CA9C3/0/2006Gross.pdf (Gross and Simmons 2006). Gross and Simmons, with the help of Princeton Survey Research Associates International in conducting the survey, found that out of a thousand randomly questioned Americans, 80.7% believed that tenure protects incompetent faculty. Furthermore, 57.9% surveyed believe that awarding tenure to faculty removes incentives for hard work.
C. Peter Magrath, "Eliminating Tenure without Destroying Academic Freedom," *Chronicle of Higher Education* (February 28, 1997), http://chronicle.com/article/Eliminating-Tenure-Without/77875/.
The view of society towards higher education is that the institution of higher education is no longer accountable to the community and that it has lost its focus on undergraduate students.
16. David Breneman, "Alternatives to Tenure for the Next Generation of Academics," *American Association for Higher Education* (1997) (Breneman 1997).
17. Moore, supra, 12.
18. Richardson, supra, 259.
According to the AAUP, the first nationally recognized tenure case in higher education was with the termination of Edward Ross from Stanford University. Co-founder of the AAUP, Arthur Lovejoy, used this incident to spur the creation of the AAUP in 1915.
19. Joseph Jastrow, "The Administrative Peril in Education," (*The Popular Science Monthly*, vol 81: January–June, 1912) (Jastrow 1912).
20. Id.
21. Id.
22. Byrne, supra, 286.
American Association of College Professors, supra, 4.
23. American Association of College Professors, supra, 25.
According to the AAUP's 1940 Statement of Principles on Academic Freedom and Tenure, academic freedom and economic security are vital to the quality of education provided to students; therefore, tenure and academic freedom are inseparable and vital to the instruction provided by faculty members and to the success of an institution.

24. Byrne, supra, 286.
Byrne asks the question of whether tenure is truly necessary to protect faculty members', as well as students', academic freedom in the classroom. As he points out in his article, faculty members, as well as students, have the same right to academic freedom as their tenured counterparts.
25. In Perry v. Sindermann (408 U.S. 593 (1972)), the US Supreme Court ruled that even though a professor may not have tenure, non-renewal of that person's contract would violate their Fourteenth Amendment rights if such action taken by the university was based on the defendant's First Amendment rights. Furthermore, if that person was able to show that they had the expectancy of reemployment they then would be guaranteed the right of due process, which is awarded to all people of the US under the Fourteenth Amendment.
26. Byrne, supra, 286.
The author also identifies that for academic freedom to be prevalent at a university without tenure, a grievance process must be outlined. This process is guaranteed to all citizens by the Fourteenth Amendment of the Constitution of the USA. Byrne also stated that the Supreme Court has ruled on numerous cases where the First Amendment protects academic freedom.
27. In the AAUP v. Bloomfield College (129 NJ Super. 249, 322 A.2d 846 (1974)), it was demonstrated that tenure only provides an individual with the legally guaranteed right to due process. Tenure does not provide a guarantee to lifetime employment. However, since due process is guaranteed to every American citizen through the Fourteenth Amendment of the Constitution of the USA, then faculty members have the same constitutionally protected right.
28. Byrne, supra, 286.
29. Jonathan Cole, "The University Responds: 'On the Matter of Edward Said'," *Columbia Spectator* (October 20, 2000), http://www.columbiaspectator.com/2000/10/20/university-responds-matter-edward-said (Cole 2000).
The Provost for Columbia University, Dr. Cole, stated that there is no right more fundamental to self-expression of university faculty members than that of the freedom to express one's thoughts and beliefs without the fear of reprimand. Furthermore, Dr. Cole identified that the same action taken by the university, one of support for Dr. Said's academic freedom, would have been taken even if a student at the university had protested in the same fashion as Dr. Said had.

30. Columbia University, "*The Faculty Handbook*," Columbia University (2008), http://www.columbia.edu/cu/vpaa/handbook/appendixb.html (Columbia University 2008).
31. Id.
32. Cole, supra, 314.
33. Hardy v. Jefferson Community College, 260 F.3d 671 (2001).
34. Hardy v. Jefferson Community College, 260 F.3d 671 (2001).
35. Hardy v. Jefferson Community College, 260 F.3d 671 (2001).
36. Hardy v. Jefferson Community College, 260 F.3d 671 (2001).
37. Hardy v. Jefferson Community College, 260 F.3d 671 (2001).
38. Hardy v. Jefferson Community College, 260 F.3d 671 (2001).
39. Hardy v. Jefferson Community College, 260 F.3d 671 (2001).
40. Hardy v. Jefferson Community College, 260 F.3d 671 (2001).
41. Hardy v. Jefferson Community College, 260 F.3d 671 (2001).
42. Hardy v. Jefferson Community College, 260 F.3d 671 (2001).
43. Hardy v. Jefferson Community College, 260 F.3d 671 (2001).
44. Hardy v. Jefferson Community College, 260 F.3d 671 (2001).
45. Hardy v. Jefferson Community College, 260 F.3d 671 (2001).
46. Hardy v. Jefferson Community College, 260 F.3d 671 (2001).
47. Hardy v. Jefferson Community College, 260 F.3d 671 (2001).
48. Hardy v. Jefferson Community College, 260 F.3d 671 (2001).
49. Federal Rules of Civil Procedure govern the civil procedure used in the US district courts. Rule 12(b) identifies pre-trial motions that can be filed and which commonly lead to lawsuits that have been identified as having insufficient legal basis and are commonly dismissed.
50. The Eleventh Amendment of the US Constitution deals with a state's sovereign immunity. Sovereign immunity identifies that a state, or a branch of a state, cannot do any legal wrong and is thus immune from any civil action or criminal prosecution.
51. Hardy v. Jefferson Community College, 260 F.3d 671 (2001).
52. Qualified immunity provides protection to government employees from liability for the violation of a person's protected constitutional rights.
53. Hardy v. Jefferson Community College, 260 F.3d 671 (2001).
54. Hardy v. Jefferson Community College, 260 F.3d 671 (2001).
55. Hardy v. Jefferson Community College, 260 F.3d 671 (2001).
56. Hardy v. Jefferson Community College, 260 F.3d 671 (2001).
57. Hardy v. Jefferson Community College, 260 F.3d 671 (2001).
58. Hardy v. Jefferson Community College, 260 F.3d 671 (2001).
59. Hardy v. Jefferson Community College, 260 F.3d 671 (2001).
60. Hardy v. Jefferson Community College, 260 F.3d 671 (2001).
61. In *Pickering v. Board of Education*, 391 U.S. 563 (1968), the US Supreme Court ruled that a teacher's comments (in this case which

focused on school fund raising) touched on a matter of public concern and could not be used for the individual's dismissal. Furthermore, the Court devised a three-prong test (later called the Pickering balancing test or just the Pickering test) for determining if speech was considered protected: "(1) did the individual demonstrate how their speech was a matter of public concern, (2) did the individual demonstrate how their speech was a motivating factor in the decision of the employer and (3) in its decision, was the court able to balance the interests of the individual as a citizen commenting on the topic and was the employer's interest a way of promoting a public service?"

62. In *Perry v. Sindermann*, 408 U.S. 593 (1972), the US Supreme Court ruled a professor's lack of tenure did not defeat his claim of his lack of re-employment was in retaliation for his use of constitutional protected speech.

63. *Connick v. Myers*, 461 U.S. 138 (1983).
Myers was an assistant district attorney in Louisiana. Her supervisor had indicated that she would be transferred to a different section of criminal court to try cases; the plaintiff strongly disagreed with the transfer. The plaintiff distributed a questionnaire concerning the transfer policies of the office. Myers was then informed by the district attorney that she was being terminated for her refusal to accept the transfer and that the questionnaire that she had distributed was a form of insubordination. Myers filed suit alleging that she had been wrongfully terminated for reasons that infringed upon freedom of speech.

64. In *Bonnell v Lorenzo*, 241 F3d 800 (6th Cir. 2001), *the* US Court of Appeals for the Sixth Circuit ruled that a college professor's use of vulgar words within the classroom was not considered a matter of public concern if the language used was not pertinent to the subject matter. Although the Court identified that the speech Bonnell used was unprotected by the First Amendment, they did state that a professor's rights to academic freedom and freedom of expression are paramount in the academic setting."

65. Hardy v. Jefferson Community College, 260 F.3d 671 (2001).

66. Hardy v. Jefferson Community College, 260 F.3d 671 (2001).

67. Pickering v. Board of Education, 391 U.S. 563 (1968).
The Pickering Test is used to evaluate the interests of an employer with the rights of an employee's freedom of speech.

68. Hardy v. Jefferson Community College, 260 F.3d 671 (2001).

69. Hardy v. Jefferson Community College, 260 F.3d 671 (2001).

70. Hardy v. Jefferson Community College, 260 F.3d 671 (2001).

71. Hardy v. Jefferson Community College, 260 F.3d 671 (2001).

In the Court's ruling, it identified Dambrot v. Cent. Mich. Univ., 55 F.3d 1177, 1189 (6th Cir. 1995) and Swank v. Smart, 898 F.2d 1247 (7th Cir. 1990) as being two prime examples where the courts had identified the purpose for the freedom of speech (academic freedom) as being the a way to safeguard the "advancement of knowledge, the transformation of taste, political change, cultural expression, and the other objectives, values, and consequences of the speech that is protected by the First Amendment."

72. Dambrot v. Central Michigan University, 55 F.3d 1177, 1189 (6th Cir. 1995).
During a speech that Dambrot delivered to the men's basketball team at Central Michigan University (plaintiff was the head basketball coach at the university), Dambrot used the word nigger. The university gained wind of the coach's use of the N word and conducted an interview with the African American players on the team, to which all of them had indicated that they had not been offended by what the coach had said. However, a former team player went to a university official and complained about the coach's use of the N word during team speeches. After being confronted by the university official, the plaintiff agreed to a suspension for his use of language that was against the university's discriminatory harassment policy. News of the incident was leaked to the school newspaper in which an article was printed portraying the coach's apology as being cynical in nature. Dambrot was then approached by the AD and informed that he was being terminated from his position. Dambrot filed suit against the university alleging that his termination had been fueled by his use of the N word and that his First Amendment rights (and academic freedom) had been violated.
73. Hardy v. Jefferson Community College, 260 F.3d 671 (2001).
74. Ward Churchill, "On the Justice of Roosting Chickens: Consequences of American Conquest and Carnage," (Oakland: AK Press, 2003) (Churchill 2003).
75. Id.
76. Churchill v. The University of Colorado at Boulder, Colo. App. (2010).
77. Churchill v. The University of Colorado at Boulder, Colo. App. (2010).
78. Churchill v. The University of Colorado at Boulder, Colo. App. (2010).
79. Churchill v. The University of Colorado at Boulder, Colo. App. (2010).
80. The sub-committee included members from the SCRM as well as five additional professors who were not on the committee.
81. Churchill v. The University of Colorado at Boulder, Colo. App. (2010).
82. Churchill v. The University of Colorado at Boulder, Colo. App. (2010).
83. Churchill v. The University of Colorado at Boulder, Colo. App. (2010).
84. Churchill v. The University of Colorado at Boulder, Colo. App. (2010).

85. Churchill v. The University of Colorado at Boulder, Colo. App. (2010).
86. Churchill v. The University of Colorado at Boulder, Colo. App. (2010).
87. Churchill v. The University of Colorado at Boulder, Colo. App. (2010).
88. Churchill v. The University of Colorado at Boulder, Colo. App. (2010).
89. University of Colorado at Boulder, "Regent Policies," https://www.cu.edu/regents/Policies/.
90. Churchill v. The University of Colorado at Boulder, Colo. App. (2010).
91. Churchill v. The University of Colorado at Boulder, Colo. App. (2010).
92. US Constitution, amend. 11.
93. Churchill v. The University of Colorado at Boulder, Colo. App. (2010). The significance in allowing the university and Board of Regents to utilize any form of defense that would have been available to an individual acting in their official capacity was that the institution could claim quasi-judicial immunity.
94. Churchill v. The University of Colorado at Boulder, Colo. App. (2010).
95. Churchill v. The University of Colorado at Boulder, Colo. App. (2010).
96. Churchill v. The University of Colorado at Boulder, Colo. App. (2010).
97. Churchill v. The University of Colorado at Boulder, Colo. App. (2010).
98. Churchill v. The University of Colorado at Boulder, Colo. App. (2010).
99. Churchill v. The University of Colorado at Boulder, Colo. App. (2010).
100. Churchill v. The University of Colorado at Boulder, Colo. App. (2010).
101. Churchill v. The University of Colorado at Boulder, Colo. App. (2010).
102. Churchill v. The University of Colorado at Boulder, Colo. App. (2010).
103. Miller v. Davis, 521 F.3d 1142, 1145 (9th Cir. 2008).
Davis, a prisoner in the California state prison system, filed suit requesting that he be removed from the vexatious litigant list. He alleged that he had not been provided a hearing where he could hear the violations that he had supposedly committed and thus, did not receive due process.
104. Brewer v. Blackwell, 692 F.2d 387, 390 (5th Cir. 1982).
The plaintiffs were employed by a tree pruning company. They were directed to dump a load of tree limbs into a ravine. However, they were arrested after it was discovered that there was garbage in the load. They were charged with a felony for contaminating the water supply. In response, the plaintiffs filed a suit against the arresting officer, the chief of police, and the town. Judicial immunity was awarded to the police offer.
105. Churchill v. The University of Colorado at Boulder, Colo. App. (2010).
106. Churchill v. The University of Colorado at Boulder, Colo. App. (2010).
107. Feldman v. Ho, 171 F.3d 494, 497 (7th Cir. 1999).
108. Feldman v. Ho, 171 F.3d 494, 497 (7th Cir. 1999).
109. Churchill v. The University of Colorado at Boulder, Colo. App. (2010).

110. Churchill v. The University of Colorado at Boulder, Colo. App. (2010).
111. Altonen v. City of Minneapolis, 487 F.3d 554, 560 (8th Cir. 2007).
    Altonen was a lieutenant for the Minneapolis police department. During her time with the police department, she had been promoted to inspector but informed that the position served at the leisure of the chief of police. In October 2003, the chief of police had resigned from his position to which Altonen submitted her name for chief of police. After not advancing through the interview process, Altonen publically placed her support with the current deputy chief who was also seeking the position of chief of police. Although Altonen supported the deputy chief, another candidate had been awarded the position as chief of police. Throughout the year, Altonen had been critical of the new police of chief and then on May 16, 2004, Altonen had been reassigned to a new division with a $12,000 cut in salary. Altonen filed suit against the chief of police and the city alleging that her demotion was in response to her support of the deputy chief for the position of chief of police which violated her First Amendment rights.
112. Churchill v. The University of Colorado at Boulder, Colo. App. (2010).
113. Pickering v. Board of Education, 391 U.S. 563 (1968).
114. Churchill v. The University of Colorado at Boulder, Colo. App. (2010).
115. Churchill v. The University of Colorado at Boulder, Colo. (2011).
116. Adams v. Trustees of the University of North Carolina-Wilmington, 640 F.3d 550 (4th Cir. 2011).
117. Adams v. Trustees of the University of North Carolina-Wilmington, 640 F.3d 550 (4th Cir. 2011).
118. Adams v. Trustees of the University of North Carolina-Wilmington, 640 F.3d 550 (4th Cir. 2011).
119. Adams v. Trustees of the University of North Carolina-Wilmington, 640 F.3d 550 (4th Cir. 2011).
120. Adams v. Trustees of the University of North Carolina-Wilmington, 640 F.3d 550 (4th Cir. 2011).
121. University of North Carolina-Wilmington, "Faculty Handbook," (University of North Carolina-Wilmington, 2012), http://uncw.edu/facsen/documents/2012_Faculty_Handbook.pdf (University of North Carolina-Wilmington 2012).
122. Adams v. Trustees of the University of North Carolina-Wilmington, 640 F.3d 550 (4th Cir. 2011).
123. University of North Carolina-Wilmington, supra, 406.
124. Adams v. Trustees of the University of North Carolina-Wilmington, 640 F.3d 550 (4th Cir. 2011).
125. Adams v. Trustees of the University of North Carolina-Wilmington, 640 F.3d 550 (4th Cir. 2011).

126. Adams v. Trustees of the University of North Carolina-Wilmington, 640 F.3d 550 (4th Cir. 2011).
127. Adams v. Trustees of the University of North Carolina-Wilmington, 640 F.3d 550 (4th Cir. 2011).
128. Adams v. Trustees of the University of North Carolina-Wilmington, 640 F.3d 550 (4th Cir. 2011).
129. Federal Rule of Civil Procedure 12(b)(6) calls for the dismissal of charges if it appears to the court that the plaintiff cannot provide support to their claims that would entitle them to relief (Conley v. Gibson, 1957).
130. Adams v. Trustees of the University of North Carolina-Wilmington, 640 F.3d 550 (4th Cir. 2011).
131. Garcetti v. Ceballos, 547 U.S. 410 (2006).
132. Adams v. Trustees of the University of North Carolina-Wilmington, 640 F.3d 550 (4th Cir. 2011).
133. Adams v. Trustees of the University of North Carolina-Wilmington, 640 F.3d 550 (4th Cir. 2011).
134. Adams v. Trustees of the University of North Carolina-Wilmington, 640 F.3d 550 (4th Cir. 2011).
135. Adams v. Trustees of the University of North Carolina-Wilmington, 640 F.3d 550 (4th Cir. 2011).
136. Adams v. Trustees of the University of North Carolina-Wilmington, 640 F.3d 550 (4th Cir. 2011).
137. McDonnell Douglas Corp. v. Green, 411 U.S. 792 (1973).
    In this case, the US Supreme Court developed a set of standards to be used for determining if a request for summary judgment under a Title VII claim has the necessary evidence to prove that an individual had been discriminated against.
138. Adams v. Trustees of the University of North Carolina-Wilmington, 640 F.3d 550 (4th Cir. 2011).
139. Suarez Corporation Industries v. McGraw, 202 F.3d 676, 685 (4th Cir. 2000).
140. Adams v. Trustees of the University of North Carolina-Wilmington, 640 F.3d 550 (4th Cir. 2011).
141. McVey v. Stacy, 157 F 3d 271 (4th Cir. 1998).
    The three-prong test is known as the McVey test.
142. Adams v. Trustees of the University of North Carolina-Wilmington, 640 F.3d 550 (4th Cir. 2011).
143. The defendant concurred with the US Court of Appeals that when Adams had initially made the speech in question it had been protected under the First Amendment as free speech.

144. Adams v. Trustees of the University of North Carolina-Wilmington, 640 F.3d 550 (4th Cir. 2011).
145. Adams v. Trustees of the University of North Carolina-Wilmington, 640 F.3d 550 (4th Cir. 2011).
146. Adams v. Trustees of the University of North Carolina-Wilmington, 640 F.3d 550 (4th Cir. 2011).
147. Gross and Simmons, supra, 300.
148. D. Frank Vinik, "Lessons from Costly Tenure Denial Claims," (*Risk Research Bulletin: Faculty and Staff Employment*, February 2007). http://www.uky.edu/Provost/APFA/Department_Chairs/Lessons_ costly.pdf (Vinik 2007).
149. Bignall v. North Idaho College, 538 F.2d 243, 248 (CA9 1976).
150. Bignall v. North Idaho College, 538 F.2d 243, 248 (CA9 1976).
151. Bignall v. North Idaho College, 538 F.2d 243, 248 (CA9 1976).
152. Bignall v. North Idaho College, 538 F.2d 243, 248 (CA9 1976).
153. Bignall v. North Idaho College, 538 F.2d 243, 248 (CA9 1976).
154. Bignall v. North Idaho College, 538 F.2d 243, 248 (CA9 1976).
155. Bignall v. North Idaho College, 538 F.2d 243, 248 (CA9 1976).
156. Bignall v. North Idaho College, 538 F.2d 243, 248 (CA9 1976).
157. Bignall v. North Idaho College, 538 F.2d 243, 248 (CA9 1976).
158. Bignall v. North Idaho College, 538 F.2d 243, 248 (CA9 1976).
159. Bignall v. North Idaho College, 538 F.2d 243, 248 (CA9 1976).
160. Bignall v. North Idaho College, 538 F.2d 243, 248 (CA9 1976).
161. Bignall v. North Idaho College, 538 F.2d 243, 248 (CA9 1976).
162. Perry v. Sindermann, 408 U.S. 593 (1972) is discussed in Chap. 2 of this book.
163. Bignall v. North Idaho College, 538 F.2d 243, 248 (CA9 1976).
164. Chung v. Park, 514 F.2d 382 (3d Cir. 1975).
    Professor Chung had been employed at Mansfield State College for 5 years. At the end of his 5th year, he was informed that his contract would not be renewed for the upcoming academic year. Even though a lower court had identified that the plaintiff had gained tenure after his third year of employment at the college, the plaintiff had been informed by the college president of the reasons for his dismissal prior to a hearing. Furthermore, the plaintiff had been given ample opportunity to prove how his termination was unreasonable but had been unable to provide evidence supporting his claims.
165. Bignall v. North Idaho College, 538 F.2d 243, 248 (CA9 1976).
166. Bignall v. North Idaho College, 538 F.2d 243, 248 (CA9 1976).
167. Bignall v. North Idaho College, 538 F.2d 243, 248 (CA9 1976).
168. Brubaker v. Board of Education, 502 F.2d 973 (7th Cir. 1974).

Brubaker, and several of her colleagues, had been terminated from their positions as eighth grade teachers for distributing obscene reading materials (pamphlets on the Woodstock Rock Festival) to their students. The superintendent of the school district approached the teachers and asked if they had made the brochures available to their students, which they affirmed. The issue was then raised before the school board and in a closed session the board had voted to terminate the teachers. A meeting was requested by legal representation for the teachers to which the request had been denied. Brubaker, as well as the other teachers, filed suit alleging that their First and Fourteenth Amendment rights had been violated. In the court's ruling, it indicated that academic freedom had not been violated since the material was outside the goals of the educational objectives.

169. Swab v. Cedar Rapids Community School District, 494 F.2d 353 (8th Cir. 1974).
Swab was a public teacher who had been terminated in Iowa. Iowa did not have a tenure law; however, according to the school board, the issue of due process is satisfied under Iowa Code § 279.13. Swab disagreed with the school board's assessment of the state code and filed suit alleging that she had not received the right of due process. The court ruled that since she had been given the opportunity to hear the allegations against her, and be represented, that her right to due process had been met.

170. Simard v. Board of Education, 473 F.2d 988 (2nd. Cir. 1973).
Simard was a non-tenured public school teacher who served on a year-to-year contract. He was notified by the school superintendant that his contract would not be renewed due to reasons of insubordination. Simard requested a hearing before the board of education to hear the allegations against him. A hearing was conducted where the board supported Simard's dismissal. The plaintiff filed a claim alleging that his First and Fourteenth Amendment rights had been violated. The court ruled that (1) there had been no evidence that his freedom of speech had been violated and (2) that since Simard had been granted a hearing before the board of education his right to due process had been met.

171. Bignall v. North Idaho College, 538 F.2d 243, 248 (CA9 1976).
172. Bignall v. North Idaho College, 538 F.2d 243, 248 (CA9 1976).
173. Bignall v. North Idaho College, 538 F.2d 243, 248 (CA9 1976).
174. Bignall v. North Idaho College, 538 F.2d 243, 248 (CA9 1976).
175. Bignall v. North Idaho College, 538 F.2d 243, 248 (CA9 1976).
176. Bignall v. North Idaho College, 538 F.2d 243, 248 (CA9 1976).
177. Perry v. Sindermann, 408 U.S. 593 (1972).
178. Bignall v. North Idaho College, 538 F.2d 243, 248 (CA9 1976).

179. Bignall v. North Idaho College, 538 F.2d 243, 248 (CA9 1976).
180. Bignall v. North Idaho College, 538 F.2d 243, 248 (CA9 1976).
181. American Association of College Professors, supra, 25.
182. Bignall v. North Idaho College, 538 F.2d 243, 248 (CA9 1976).
183. Bignall v. North Idaho College, 538 F.2d 243, 248 (CA9 1976).
184. The Board of Community College Trustees for Baltimore County—Essex Community College v. Jane Adams, 117 Md. App. 662 (1997).
185. American Association of College Professors, "Academic Freedom and Tenure: Essex Community College (Maryland)," *Academe* (May–June, 1995), http://www.aaup.org/NR/rdonlyres/3AE6F378-6EEF-4D4F-8A52-8A2DC4CA4300/0/Essex.pdf (American Association of College Professors 1995).
186. Id.
187. The Four Flags for Andy program was named after the first name of the college's Dean of Instruction, Dr. Andrew Snope. The reference to "flags" indicated which programs were to be eliminated from the college. Each flag represented a negative fact about the reviewed program; the more flags that a program received, the less justifiable it was to keep that program active at the college. As indicated in the title of the program, "four" represented any program that had received four negative marks or "flags" and was marked for elimination.
188. The Board of Community College Trustees for Baltimore County—Essex Community College v. Jane Adams, 117 Md. App. 662 (1997).
189. The Board of Community College Trustees for Baltimore County—Essex Community College v. Jane Adams, 117 Md. App. 662 (1997).
190. The Board of Community College Trustees for Baltimore County—Essex Community College v. Jane Adams, 117 Md. App. 662 (1997).
191. The Board of Community College Trustees for Baltimore County—Essex Community College v. Jane Adams, 117 Md. App. 662 (1997).
192. The Board of Community College Trustees for Baltimore County—Essex Community College v. Jane Adams, 117 Md. App. 662 (1997).
193. The Board of Community College Trustees for Baltimore County—Essex Community College v. Jane Adams, 117 Md. App. 662 (1997).
194. The Board of Community College Trustees for Baltimore County—Essex Community College v. Jane Adams, 117 Md. App. 662 (1997).
195. The Board of Community College Trustees for Baltimore County—Essex Community College v. Jane Adams, 117 Md. App. 662 (1997).
196. The Board of Community College Trustees for Baltimore County—Essex Community College v. Jane Adams, 117 Md. App. 662 (1997).
197. The Board of Community College Trustees for Baltimore County—Essex Community College v. Jane Adams, 117 Md. App. 662 (1997).

198. A mandamus relief is an order of a court directing an entity to stop an action that they are taking against the plaintiff.
199. The Board of Community College Trustees for Baltimore County—Essex Community College v. Jane Adams, 117 Md. App. 662 (1997).
200. The Board of Community College Trustees for Baltimore County—Essex Community College v. Jane Adams, 117 Md. App. 662 (1997).
201. The Board of Community College Trustees for Baltimore County—Essex Community College v. Jane Adams, 117 Md. App. 662 (1997).
202. The Board of Community College Trustees for Baltimore County—Essex Community College v. Jane Adams, 117 Md. App. 662 (1997).
203. The Board of Community College Trustees for Baltimore County—Essex Community College v. Jane Adams, 117 Md. App. 662 (1997).
204. Maryland Code, § 16-103 (1974, 1997).
In the Education Article of the Maryland code, the board of trustees for a community college has the authority to have general control over the community college. Furthermore, the board of trustees has the authority to set the salaries and tenure of the president and faculty of the college.
205. The Board of Community College Trustees for Baltimore County—Essex Community College v. Jane Adams, 117 Md. App. 662 (1997).
206. The Board of Community College Trustees for Baltimore County—Essex Community College v. Jane Adams, 117 Md. App. 662 (1997).
207. The Board of Community College Trustees for Baltimore County—Essex Community College v. Jane Adams, 117 Md. App. 662 (1997).
208. The Board of Community College Trustees for Baltimore County—Essex Community College v. Jane Adams, 117 Md. App. 662 (1997).
209. The Board of Community College Trustees for Baltimore County—Essex Community College v. Jane Adams, 117 Md. App. 662 (1997).
210. The Board of Community College Trustees for Baltimore County—Essex Community College v. Jane Adams, 117 Md. App. 662 (1997).
211. The Board of Community College Trustees for Baltimore County—Essex Community College v. Jane Adams, 117 Md. App. 662 (1997).
212. The Board of Community College Trustees for Baltimore County—Essex Community College v. Jane Adams, 117 Md. App. 662 (1997).
213. Katz v Georgetown University, 246 F.3d 685 (District of Columbia Circuit 2001).
214. Katz v Georgetown University, 246 F.3d 685 (District of Columbia Circuit 2001).
215. Katz v Georgetown University, 246 F.3d 685 (District of Columbia Circuit 2001).
216. Katz v Georgetown University, 246 F.3d 685 (District of Columbia Circuit 2001).

217. Katz v Georgetown University, 246 F.3d 685 (District of Columbia Circuit 2001).
218. Georgetown University, "Faculty Handbook (1999)," http://www11.georgetown.edu/president/facultysenate/Archives/FacHandbook/faculty-handbook-1999.pdf.
219. Katz v Georgetown University, 246 F.3d 685 (District of Columbia Circuit 2001).
220. Katz v Georgetown University, 246 F.3d 685 (District of Columbia Circuit 2001).
221. Katz v Georgetown University, 246 F.3d 685 (District of Columbia Circuit 2001).
222. Katz v Georgetown University, 246 F.3d 685 (District of Columbia Circuit 2001).
223. Katz v Georgetown University, 246 F.3d 685 (District of Columbia Circuit 2001).
224. Katz v Georgetown University, 246 F.3d 685 (District of Columbia Circuit 2001).
225. Katz v Georgetown University, 246 F.3d 685 (District of Columbia Circuit 2001).
226. Ross-Simons of Warwick, Inc. v. Baccarat, Inc., 102 F.3d 12, 16 (1st Cir. 1996).
227. Katz v Georgetown University, 246 F.3d 685 (District of Columbia Circuit 2001).
228. Katz v Georgetown University, 246 F.3d 685 (District of Columbia Circuit 2001).
229. Georgetown University, "Faculty Handbook (1999)," http://www11.georgetown.edu/president/facultysenate/Archives/FacHandbook/faculty-handbook-1999.pdf.
230. Id.
231. Katz v Georgetown University, 246 F.3d 685 (District of Columbia Circuit, 2001).
232. Katz v Georgetown University, 246 F.3d 685 (District of Columbia Circuit, 2001).
233. Katz v Georgetown University, 246 F.3d 685 (District of Columbia Circuit, 2001).
234. Katz v Georgetown University, 246 F.3d 685 (District of Columbia Circuit, 2001).
235. According to the AAUP's 1940 Statement of Principles on Academic Freedom and Tenure, financial exigency is a justifiable reason for the termination of a tenured, or non-tenured, faculty member.
236. American Association of College Professors, supra, 25.
237. Moore, supra, 12.

238. Levitt, supra, 49.
   A problem with the type of system that provides strong incentives in the beginning of someone's career but weak incentives after a probationary period is that universities then are compelled to retain employees who do nothing for the institution or their students.
239. American Association of College Professors, supra, 25.
240. Robb Jones, "The Rest of the Story: The Costs of Tenure Litigation are far Greater than the Dollars You Spend," (*Reason & Risk* 8:1, Spring 2000) http://www.uky.edu/Provost/APFA/Department_Chairs/Rest_of_story.pdf (Jones 2000).
   The author indicates that the cost of tenure litigation goes far beyond that of a financial strain to the institution and the affected faculty member. Claims dealing with the denial of tenure also have a human cost, one dealing with time spent by those involved in the litigation, energy diverted by university officials and faculty, and the focus of university employees being diverted from the institutions academic mission.

References

American Association of College Professors. 1995. Academic Freedom and Tenure: Essex Community College (Maryland). *Academe* 81 (May–June): 40–50. http://www.aaup.org/NR/rdonlyres/3AE6F378-6EEF-4D4F-8A52-8A2DC4CA4300/0/Essex.pdf.

Breneman, David. 1997. *Alternatives to Tenure for the Next Generation of Academics*. American Association for Higher Education.

Byrne, J. Peter. 1997. *Academic Freedom without Tenure?* American Association for Higher Education.

Chemerinsky, Erwin. 1998. Is Tenure Necessary to Protect Academic Freedom? *American Behavioral Scientist* 41 (5): 638–651.

Churchill, Ward. 2003. *On the Justice of Roosting Chickens: Consequences of American Conquest and Carnage*. Oakland: AK Press.

Cole, Jonathan. 2000. The University Responds: 'On the Matter of Edward Said'. *Columbia Spectator*, October 20. http://www.columbiaspectator.com/2000/10/20/university-responds-matter-edward-said.

Columbia University. 2008. *The Faculty Handbook*. Columbia University. http://www.columbia.edu/cu/vpaa/handbook/appendixb.html.

Gross, Neil, and Solon Simmons. 2006. Americans' Views of Political Bias in the Academy and Academic Freedom. *Research*, May 22. http://www.aaup.org/NR/rdonlyres/DCF3EBD7-509E-47AB-9AB3-FBCFFF5CA9C3/0/2006Gross.pdf. Accessed 22 May 2006.

Hacker, Andrew, and Claudia Dreifus. 2011. *Higher Education?* New York: St. Martin's Press.

Jastrow, Joseph. 1912. The Administrative Peril in Education. *The Popular Science Monthly* 81 (January–June): 495–515.
Jones, Robb. 2000. The Rest of the Story: The Costs of Tenure Litigation are Far Greater than the Dollars You Spend. *Reason & Risk* 8 (1). http://www.uky.edu/Provost/APFA/Department_Chairs/Rest_of_story.pdf.
Maffly, Brian. 2011. Bill to End Higher-Ed Tenure Dies in Committee. *The Salt Lake Tribune*, February 23. http://www.sltrib.com/sltrib/home/51298790-76/tenure-faculty-herrod-professors.html.csp9.
Riley, Naomi. 2011. *The Faculty Lounges: And Other Reasons Why You Won't Get the College Education You Paid for*. Plymouth: The Rowman & Littlefield Publishing Group.
Shearer, Elisa. 2011. The Penultimate Word: The Need to Re-evaluate the Tenure System. *The Houghton Star*, March 7. http://www.houghtonstar.com/commentary/the-penultimate-word-the-need-to-re-evaluate-the-tenure-system-1.2074235.
University of North Carolina-Wilmington. 2012. *Faculty Handbook*. University of North Carolina-Wilmington. http://uncw.edu/facsen/documents/2012_Faculty_Handbook.pdf.
US Department of Labor. 2011. Labor Force Statistics from the Current Population Survey. http://www.bls.gov/cps/. Accessed 4 Nov 2011.
Vinik, D. Frank. 2007. Lessons from Costly Tenure Denial Claims. *Risk Research Bulletin: Faculty and Staff Employment*, February 2007. http://www.uky.edu/Provost/APFA/Department_Chairs/Lessons_costly.pdf.
Williams, Jeffrey. 1999. The Other Politics of Tenure. *College Literature* 26 (3): 226–241.

CHAPTER 4

Landmark Cases in Higher Education on Academic Freedom and Tenure

In the preceding chapter, the issue of job security in higher education was examined through the use of several key lower court cases which focused on the topic of faculty protection as guaranteed by the First Amendment to the Constitution of the USA. Through an examination of the cases presented there, it was found that the lower courts ruled that faculty members had their freedom of speech protected regardless of their tenure status. In the cases cited where the courts ruled against the faculty member, their decisions affirmed the individual's freedom of speech and maintained that their decision was based on issues other than those associated with the individual's First Amendment rights.

Through the years, faculty members in higher education have sought various approaches to ensure their job security, with tenure seeming to be the most effective. However, when issues related to faculty employment have been brought before the courts, the issue of tenure has been superseded by rights granted every citizen in the First and Fourteenth Amendments to the US Constitution. In this chapter five landmark federal cases related to academic freedom and tenure will be examined including their ramifications and the precedents they established. In the discussion of these cases, the courts' reliance on the First Amendment (Freedom of Speech) and Fourteenth Amendment (Due Process) of the US Constitution will be noted for their impact on the courts' decisions. Each case will end with a brief précis and an overall summary will conclude the chapter.

Background

Throughout the years, the concept of tenure is one that has been foreshadowed by challenges on academic freedom and freedom of speech. Although completely separate in principle, the terms academic freedom and tenure typically have been viewed by faculty as one and the same within academia. This linkage came about in 1940 when the American Association of University Professors (AAUP) issued their *Statement of Principles on Academic Freedom and Tenure* which claimed that academic freedom and tenure were inseparable.[1] Since then, the organization has maintained that academic freedom and tenure are a guarantee for faculty members that provides them the freedom to teach, conduct, and report on research, and be active as citizens, in and out of the university walls, without fear or favor from university administration.[2]

The concept of academic freedom and the freedom it provides faculty members to develop new ideas within their classrooms cannot be disputed; however, whether or not tenure is still needed, or ever was needed, to protect those rights remains. It must be noted, however, that tenure becomes the right of an academic only after a defined probationary period, but once he/she attains tenure, it is continued until retirement unless some unforeseen circumstances arise. Those faculty members without tenure still enjoy the same rights to academic freedom as their colleagues who have been awarded tenure because of the rights granted to them by the First and Fourteenth Amendments of the US Constitution, regardless of their academic rank.[3]

In its *1940 Statement of Principles on Academic Freedom and Tenure*, the AAUP stated that academic freedom cannot be achieved in higher education without the job security provided by tenure.[4] Before this statement can be evaluated, however, one must first examine the conditions under which an institution would seek to deny incoming faculty the right of tenure or attempt to remove existing faculty from their institutions. Historically, institutions of higher education typically give one of two reasons for seeking to remove or deny tenure to existing faculty or incoming faculty. The first of these reasons for eliminating tenure among faculty is provided by Byrne who notes that removal of tenure facilitates the dismissal of faculty whose interaction with students, either in the classroom setting or in the advisory role, may be deemed unacceptable based on peer and/or administrative review.[5] While it is a common misconception that tenured faculty cannot be removed for poor performance, examples exist where tenured faculty have been terminated for performing substantially below the university's accepted standards.[6]

A second rationale that institutions may use for tenure's removal was noted by Chait. His argument is that institutions seek to remove tenure to maintain their flexibility to increase or decrease faculty numbers within specific academic programs based on student enrollment, community needs/trends, and institutional goals.[7] By having the ability to adjust the faculty compliment based on external factors permits institutions to follow shifts in student and community demands for particular courses and programs.[8] Chait argues that tenure prohibits institutions the flexibility needed and, therefore, programs that are no longer deemed vital or pertinent to the health of the university maintain their faculty complement, thus denying the institution the ability to shift scarce resources to potential new growth programs.[9]

Using the reasoning noted above for the abolishment of tenure in higher education has led to a variety of cases that have found their way to the higher courts. In each of the cases to be cited in this chapter, the faculty member has claimed he/she was denied academic freedom or freedom of speech in his/her defense and has appealed lower court decisions to either the Appeals Court or, if not successful at that level, to the US Supreme Court. The courts in their decisions have addressed the established legal precedent that protects a professor's constitutional rights while in the classroom without fear of reprimand from his/her administration and the protection available to the professor without tenure. The following judicial summaries are considered landmark cases in the area of academic freedom and freedom of speech within higher education. Their significance illustrates that the First and Fourteenth Amendments of the US Constitution provides the right of freedom of religion and expression and the right to due process, including professors in higher education. These rights protect the academic from government interference that may infringe on his/her rights, including dismissals that violate the individual's freedom of speech or right to Due Process.[10]

Federal Landmark Cases

During the 1950s, the USA had just come out of World War II, was facing an increasing threat from the Soviet Union known as the Cold War, was engaged in a "police action" called the Korean War, and feared that its political infrastructure was being overrun by Communist sympathizers. This era, known as the Red Scare, saw Senator Joseph McCarthy (R-WI) lead Congressional hearings against American citizens as he scrutinized their political affiliations and alleged that most, if not all, of the accused were affiliated with the Communist Party. Among those being investigated by Senator McCarthy were academics, many of whom he claimed were Communist sympathizers. He and his investigative committee placed the academics they questioned under oath and inferred that their loyalty was to the Communist Party and that the topics they taught their students were tainted with Communist philosophy. It is against this background that the first case in this chapter is considered.

Sweezy v. New Hampshire (1957)

During the heightened sensitivity about Communist activity in the country, and in particular higher education, the first reported court case related to academic freedom as a legal right was brought forward. *Sweezy* had its genesis when, in 1953, the State Legislature of New Hampshire adopted a joint resolution that provided for the legal investigation of individuals identified as having committed subversive activities against the state and federal government. In their resolution, the legislature stated that:

> ...the attorney general is hereby authorized and directed to make full and complete investigation with respect to violations of the subversive activities act of 1951 and to determine whether subversive persons as defined in said act are presently located within this state. The attorney general is authorized to act upon his own motion and upon such information as in his judgment may be reasonable or reliable....[11]

Under the Subversive Activities Act of 1951, New Hampshire's attorney general, Louis Wyman, was directed by the state legislature to conduct a formal investigation of any individual that was deemed as having committed any subversive act. Furthermore, the attorney general was given the authority to proceed with criminal prosecution whenever evidence was discovered that an individual had violated the Act.[12] As directed by state law, Wyman investigated various allegations to determine if there were any subversive persons working in the state government. His directive from the legislature was to make recommendations on new legislation to address the legislature's concern about state employees who were active members of hostile political parties that planned the possible overthrow of the US Government.[13] On January 5, 1954, Wyman subpoenaed Paul Sweezy, a guest lecturer at the University of New Hampshire, to inquire about his past conduct and political associations. During his testimony before the state legislature, Sweezy answered questions concerning his political association with the Communist Party. In addition, he provided clarification that, although he had helped co-found the *Monthly Review*, a magazine that was self-defined as an independent socialist magazine,[14] he had never been associated with an organization or participated in a program whose focus was the overthrow of the government of the USA.[15]

In Wyman's interrogation of Sweezy, the attorney general questioned Sweezy's military service in World War II and his later participation in the Scientific and Cultural Conference for World Peace of 1949. Throughout his interrogation, Sweezy cooperated and responded to the questions he was asked; however, when he was questioned about his affiliation with the Progressive Party and contents of a lecture that he had delivered to students in a humanities course at the University of New Hampshire, he stated that he would not answer any questions that were not pertinent to the subject about which he was being questioned or those that threatened his constitutional rights under the First Amendment.[16] At the conclusion of Sweezy's interrogation by the attorney general, Wyman decided not to pursue any further actions to elicit an answer on the questions that Sweezy refused to answer.

Several months after Wyman's initial investigation of Sweezy, the attorney general re-summoned him to appear before the state legislature on June 3, 1954, to provide further testimony about his alleged association with the Communist Party.[17] During this interrogation the attorney general focused on an article that Sweezy had co-authored. In this article, the authors expressed that they despised how the USA used violence to promote a form of social order that the authors believed would inevitably fall.[18] According to the transcripts of the hearing, the attorney general questioned Sweezy about the article and how it referred to a resistance that would form against such a social order. In particular, Wyman focused on what the authors stated would inevitably lead to violence from an oncoming socialism that would be less morally corrupt than the capitalistic approach of the USA.[19]

Sweezy responded to the claims made by the attorney general during the hearing by stating that "...he viewed himself as a classical Marxist and more specifically a socialist and that the article in question promoted his political and social views of the government."[20] Once again the attorney general questioned Sweezy's affiliation with the Progressive Party and that party's association with the Progressive Citizens of America, an organization that was considered to be a front for the American Communist Party. During Wyman's questioning, the topic of Sweezy's wife's affiliation with the Progressive Citizens of America Party also was raised. To these additional accusations, Sweezy responded as he did during his initial appearance before the state legislature earlier in 1954 by stating that he refused to answer questions he deemed as irrelevant to the subject matter about which he was being questioned or those that threatened his constitutional rights which were protected under the First Amendment.[21]

In the cross-examination of Sweezy, Wyman introduced questions about a lecture Sweezy delivered to a humanities class on March 22, 1954, as a guest lecturer at the University of New Hampshire. During the attorney general's questioning, Sweezy was asked:

1. What was the subject of your lecture?
2. Didn't you tell the class at the University of New Hampshire on Monday, March 22, 1954, that Socialism was inevitable in this country?
3. Did you advocate Marxism at that time?
4. Did you express the opinion, or did you make the statement at that time that Socialism was inevitable in America?
5. Did you in this last lecture on March 22 or in any of the former lectures espouse the theory of dialectical materialism?[22]

The response Sweezy offered to these questions was similar to his previous stand on matters he deemed irrelevant to the subject matter about which he was being questioned. He further stated that the questions referring to his March 22 class lecture were not pertinent to the matter under inquiry. In his concluding remarks at the questioning, Sweezy stated that such questioning infringed upon an area protected by the First Amendment.[23]

Following the June 3 cross-examination, the attorney general petitioned the Superior Court of Merrimack County, New Hampshire to require Sweezy to answer the questions that he had refused to answer during the legislative hearings. Upon hearing the argument presented before them, the Superior Court of Merrimack County ruled that the questions asked of Sweezy were pertinent to the attorney general's investigation. The Court summoned Sweezy as a witness and insisted that he answer the questions presented to him by Attorney General Wyman.[24] When Sweezy again refused to answer the questions put to him by the attorney general, the Court held him in contempt of court and sentenced him to the county jail. Believing that his constitutional rights were being infringed upon, Sweezy appealed the lower court's decision and submitted an appeal to the Supreme Court of New Hampshire alleging that his right of political affiliation had been violated when he was questioned about his association with the Progressive party. Furthermore, Sweezy alleged that the state's Subversive Activities Act had violated his Fourteenth Amendment rights by empowering the attorney general with the authority to interrogate an individual based on his/her political affiliations.[25]

The Supreme Court of New Hampshire's opinion focused on two different topics of questions asked by the plaintiff and how those questions were pertinent to the investigation being conducted by the attorney general. These topics were: (1) the questions asked of Sweezy that dealt with the lectures he had provided as a lecturer at the University of New Hampshire; and (2) the questions that focused on Sweezy's association with the Progressive Party and the Progressive Citizens of America.[26] After hearing the evidence presented before it, the Supreme Court of New Hampshire affirmed the lower court's decision.

Upon receiving the decision of the Supreme Court of New Hampshire, Sweezy petitioned the US Supreme Court alleging that his rights, protected by the First and Fourteenth Amendments of the US Constitution, were being nefariously breached. During its adjudication of his case, the US Supreme Court identified that, when exercising the power associated with the investigative process, such power cannot infringe on sensitive areas such as freedom of speech, freedom of political association, and freedom of the communication of ideas, especially within the academic community.[27] Furthermore, the Court stated that in a previous decision by the US Supreme Court, *Wieman v. Updegraff* (1952), the Court held that a loyalty oath prescribed by the State of Oklahoma for all of its state employees violated the requirements of due process as identified by the Fourteenth Amendment.[28] The Court linked its decision from *Wieman* to New Hampshire's use of its Subversive Activities Act of 1951 and stated that the New Hampshire Act also was deemed as unconstitutional.[29] In its decision, the US Supreme Court stated that "...the inviolability of privacy belonging to a citizen's political loyalties has so overwhelming an importance to the well-being of our kind of society that it cannot be constitutionally encroached upon on the basis of so meager a countervailing interest of the State as may be argumentatively found in the remote, shadowy threat to the security of New Hampshire allegedly presented in the origins and contributing elements of the Progressive Party and in petitioner's relations to these."[30] Finally, the Court concluded that in the "...political realm, as in the academic, thought and action are presumptively immune from inquisition by political authority,"[31] thus reversing the decision of the Supreme Court of New Hampshire.

In this case, the plaintiff (Paul Sweezy) was summoned before the state legislature to answer questions concerning his political affiliation with the Communist and Progressive political parties. During his testimony, Sweezy refused to answer any questions that he believed were protected by the First Amendment of the US Constitution. In its ruling, the US Supreme Court indicated that: (1) an academic's thoughts and actions are immune from political oversight; (2) a citizen's right to political affiliation is protected by the First Amendment; and (3) the safeguarding of a state interest cannot infringe on a citizen's constitutionally protected right of due process and political affiliation. The authority that had been awarded to the state attorney general, as demonstrated in *Sweezy*, by the state legislature encroached upon Sweezy's constitutionally protected rights which were upheld within the federal court system even though the defendant had not been awarded academic tenure.

Keyishian v. Board of Regents of the University of the State of New York (1967)

Almost a decade after the US Supreme Court ruled on *Sweezy*, another case was brought before the Court that challenged academic freedom's protection under the First Amendment of the US Constitution (*Keyishian v. Board of Regents of the University of the State of New York* [1967]).[32] The precedence in this case can be traced back to the McCarthy era (late 1940s–1954) when several states began implementing laws that required state employees to declare if they had ever been associated with the Communist Party. It was during this time that the State of New York passed The Feinberg Law,[33] a law used to enforce two earlier statutes which permitted the state to deem individuals unemployable for state positions if they were classified as having committed any treasonable act or using any seditious word which could be classified as a treasonable act.[34]

As required by The Feinberg Law, all state employees (both newly hired and those seeking reappointment), including those employed by the state university system, were required to sign a certificate (Feinberg Certificate) to confirm that they never had been associated with the Communist Party.[35] Furthermore, if state university employees had been associated with the Communist Party, they were required to communicate that fact to the President of the University System of the State of New York.[36] Once a professor signed the Feinberg Certificate, university administrators were instructed to complete an annual evaluation of each faculty member to determine if any evidence was uncovered linking the employee to a subversive organization, which was a direct violation of the Feinberg Law.[37] If such evidence was found, in accordance with the Feinberg Law, the university administration was directed to recommend the faculty member for dismissal.

In June 1965, the Feinberg Certificate was rescinded by the New York Legislature when it announced that no person employed by the state would be deemed ineligible for continued employment based solely on their refusal to sign the Feinberg Certificate.[38] Even though the requirement of a state employee signing the Feinberg Certificate was rescinded, the State University of New York at Buffalo continued forcing their faculty members to sign a similar certificate indicating that they had read the Regents' rules and:

1. that the rules and the statutes cited therein constituted terms of his employment;
2. that he was not now a member of the Communist Party; and
3. if he ever had been [a member of the Communist Party], he had communicated that fact to the president of the university.[39]

The year after the Feinberg Certificate had been rescinded (1966), several faculty members at the State University of New York at Buffalo were asked to sign the document; however, they refused to comply. Upon receiving word that these faculty members refused to sign the document, the university administration promptly informed them that if they refused to sign the document they would be terminated for insubordination.[40] Permitting the ones who refused to sign the Certificate one final opportunity, four individuals refused to sign. One of the four who did not sign was Harry Keyishian, a faculty member who had just completed his renewable yearly contract. Because of his refusal to sign the Certificate, Keyishian was informed that his yearly contract would not be renewed. Two of the remaining four faculty members, Hochfield and Garver, still had time remaining on their contracts and were threatened by the New York Board of Regents that, if they refused to sign the certificate, their contracts would not be renewed at the end of their service at the university. Keyishian and Hochfield (the plaintiffs) alleged that the university's requirement for employees to sign a certificate concerning their political affiliation, or lack thereof, with the Communist party violated the US Constitution which led them to bring action against the university to seek declaratory and injunctive relief designed to cease the "...enforcement of the civil statutes concerning employment of subversives and of the regulations and procedures used to implement those statutes."[41]

Their case was heard first before the US District Court for the Western District of New York. In their argument, the plaintiffs stated that the state laws and policies of the Board of Regents were not supported constitutionally and that such state legislation infringed upon their rights to freedom of expression.[42] In its determining if the state laws and the Board of Regents policies were constitutionally supported, the District Court referenced to *Adler v. Board of Education* (1952) in which the US Supreme Court ruled that:

> "A teacher works in a sensitive area in a schoolroom. There he shapes the attitude of young minds towards the society in which they live. In this, the state has a vital concern. It must preserve the integrity of the schools. That the school authorities have the right and the duty to screen the officials, teachers, and employees as to their fitness to maintain the integrity of the schools as a part of ordered society, cannot be doubted."[43]

In further support of the measures that had been taken by the state of New York, the District Court referenced *Barenblatt v. USA* (1959) in which the US Supreme Court upheld the termination of a teaching fellow at the University of Michigan. In this case, the instructor refused to answer questions concerning his past and (at that time) present evidence of his membership in the Communist Party. In its decision on that case, the US Supreme Court stated that "…questions as to the Communist Party affiliations of a witness before a subcommittee of the House Committee on Un-American Activities are pertinent to the subject which the subcommittee is authorized to investigate, namely, Communist infiltration into the field of education."[44] Furthermore, in *Barenblatt* the US Supreme Court stated that Congress had a legitimate interest in how the Communist party was "…infiltrating into our universities, or elsewhere, persons and groups committed to furthering the objective of overthrow."[45]

The plaintiffs' legal representative argued that the precedence established by the US Supreme Court in *Adler* was not pertinent to their case. They argued that in *Adler*, the teacher in question had been employed in a public school district whereas the plaintiffs in this case were employed as university faculty.[46] The focus of their argument rested on noting that the maturity level and level of intellectual development in university students was more developed than those of students in public school.[47] Furthermore, their attorneys noted that university students were more inclined to process conflicting political views and how they affect them individually at a higher level than students in high school. To counter this line of reasoning, citing the differences between public school students and university students, the District Court responded by stating that "…it would not be constitutional to prevent the teaching of Communist philosophy at the university level; but it would be dangerously anomalous to proscribe the advocacy of violent overthrow of government in all parts of the USA."[48]

The plaintiffs' second line of argument further claimed that the passage and enforcement of the Feinberg Law deprived them of their constitutional right of freedom of speech and due process. They argued that allowing such a law to determine an individual's ability to be hired by the state placed unjustifiable emphasis on criteria needed to safeguard the state from a violent political overthrow. However, the District Court disagreed with the plaintiffs' claim for the state's lack of justification in taking protective measures in safeguarding itself from political overthrow by referencing *Speiser v. Randall* (1958) in which the US Supreme Court stated that the state had a concerned interest in political overthrow when "…a limited class of persons in or aspiring to public positions by virtue of which they could, if evilly motivated, create serious danger to the public safety."[49]

The District Court responded to this claim by stating that the question related to the legality of the Feinberg Law was irrelevant in the case of *Keyishian* because the State University of New York at Buffalo had discontinued its use of the Feinberg Certificate in its hiring process on June 10, 1965. Likewise, the District Court explained that the process for determining employment eligibility at a state university allowed for the candidate to have an opportunity to address any accusations of subversive behavior. The District Court did, however, acknowledge that a candidate's refusal to answer questions asked of him were grounds for the state's refusal of employment.[50] On the plaintiffs' claims of a lack of due process, the District Court ruled that the dismissal of the plaintiffs' claims was not in response to an affirmation, or lack thereof, of affiliation with the Communist Party; rather, the non-renewal of their contract was based solely on their refusal to answer questions asked of them. If they had answered the questions posed them in the affirmative, they would have been allotted the right of procedural due process. However, because the plaintiffs' refused to respond to the questions presented them, they were non-renewed solely because of their insubordination.[51]

In response to the plaintiffs' claims of the Feinberg law's identification of membership within the Communist Party as being grounds for the disqualification for state employment infringing upon their right to due process, the District Court once again referred to the US Supreme Court's ruling in *Adler*. In *Adler* the Court stated that:

> Membership in a listed organization found to be within the statute and known by the member to be within the statute is a legislative finding that the member by his membership supports the thing the organization stands for, namely, the overthrow of government by unlawful means. We cannot say that such a finding is contrary to fact or that generality of experience points to a different conclusion. Disqualification follows therefore as a reasonable presumption from such membership and support. Nor is there here a problem of procedural due process. The presumption is not conclusive but arises only in a hearing where the person against whom it may arise has a full opportunity to rebut it. Where, as here, the relation between the fact found and the presumption is clear and direct and is not conclusive, the requirements of due process are satisfied.[52]

In the District Court's subjugation, it found that the Feinberg Law was constitutional and that the plaintiffs would have been awarded their right to due process had they answered the questions asked them in the affirmative. Weighing the evidence presented from both sides, the District Court ruled in favor of the defendant and denied any and all requests made by the plaintiffs.[53]

Shortly after learning of the District Court's decision, the plaintiffs filed an appeal and eventually their case found its way to the US Supreme Court. Before the Court, the appellants once again made their claim that the requiring of them to sign a certificate which questioned their affiliation with the Communist Party was unconstitutional. Furthermore, they argued that their refusal to sign the certificate should not have jeopardized their continued employment with the University of the State of New York at Buffalo.[54]

Upon hearing both sides of the argument, the US Supreme Court reached its decision in Keyishian's case. In arriving at its judgment, the Supreme Court referred to a case it had heard more than a decade before, namely *Sweezy*, where the Court ruled that teachers and students must always remain free to inquire, study, evaluate, and gain new maturity and understanding; otherwise, civilization will stagnate and die.[55] Reaching even further, the Supreme Court ruled that New York's Education Law, as well as its subdivisions which included the Feinberg Law, were unconstitutional.[56] In its opinion, the US Supreme Court stated that the state laws in question were unjustifiably vague in nature and unconstitutionally in violation of the First and Fourteenth Amendments.[57]

In the case presented here, *Keyishian*, the question of an instructor's right to the protections afforded him/her through the First and Fourteenth Amendments were raised based on the requirement of signing a state-supported document declaring that the individual has no political affiliation with the Communist Party. Although the District Court ruled in favor of the defense stating that the safeguards provided by the right to freedom of political affiliation and due process of the plaintiffs were never encroached upon by their employer, the termination of the plaintiffs was in response to their refusal to sign the document and, therefore, an act of insubordination. The District Court further explained that if the plaintiffs had answered the questions asked of them in the affirmative and then terminated, their claims for due process would have been judicially enforceable. However, because they refused to answer the questions asked by their employer, they forfeited their right to due process as their termination was in response to their act of insubordination. In its ruling, the Supreme Court demonstrated little support for the lower court when it ruled that requiring a state employee to sign a loyalty oath, one that is vague in nature, was unconstitutional and violated the plaintiffs' First and Fourteenth Amendment rights. Finally, as seen once again, the lack of tenure in this case did not hinder the professors' rights to the protections provided by the First and Fourteenth Amendment, rights to which every citizen is entitled.

Perry v. Sindermann (1972)

A third example of how academic freedom has been protected by constitutional rights guaranteed by the First and Fourteenth Amendments can be found in the case of *Perry v. Sindermann* (1972). In this landmark case, Robert Sindermann was employed by the state college system of Texas where he served as a member of the faculty and, on occasion, as one of the college's administrators from 1959 to 1969. After teaching at the University of Texas for 2 years and then at San Antonio Junior College for 4 years, Sindermann accepted a position as a professor in the Government and Social Science department at Odessa Junior College, a unit also within the state college system of Texas.[58] Throughout his entire employment in the Texas system, Sindermann served under renewable 1-year contracts.[59]

At Odessa he not only was a faculty member, but also served as the co-chairman of the Government and Social Science department during the 1968–1969 academic year. It was during his time as co-chair that Sindermann began to circulate documents to his colleagues criticizing the college and its board for their policies and regulations. As a result of his involvement with these documents, Sindermann was demoted from his position as co-chair and returned to a faculty position within the department.[60]

In spring, 1969, during the final year of his employment at Odessa Junior College, Sindermann was elected as President-Elect of the Texas Junior College Teachers Association.[61] Upon his election to the teacher's association, he requested that the college administration provide him with student clerical help, a reduction in his teaching load, and released time during the winter so that he could visit other junior colleges across the state.[62] In his capacity as the president-elect of the teachers association, Sindermann requested on several occasions that he be granted permission to miss several of his classes so he could testify before various committees of the state legislature on bills related to academic freedom and tenure; however, even though the college administration denied his requests to attend these state hearings, Sindermann decided nonetheless to attend them.[63]

Furthermore, during the 1968–1969 academic year Sindermann became involved in public disagreements with the policies established by Odessa Junior College's Board of Regents. The disagreements began when he aligned himself with *The Committee to Elevate Odessa College*, a committee that supported the advancement of the college from a 2-year institution to one that would be able to offer a 4-year degree. This position was strongly opposed by the college's board of regents.[64] In addition, during the 1968–1969 academic year Sindermann's name was associated with an article printed in a local newspaper that was highly critical of the college's board of regents, an article which supported the college's advancement to 4-year status.[65]

Then, several days prior to the official notice of Sindermann's letter of non-renewal, the college issued an 11-page document to the faculty body that described how the professional relationship between Sindermann and the college had deteriorated to a point where the relationship was non-salvageable.[66] In its press release the college's board of regents included a quote from a letter that Sindermann had sent to one of the state's legislators commenting that "[he had] been fired from Odessa College for attempting to testify on S.B. 512."[67] Although Sindermann indicated he would be fired from the college in the aforementioned communication to a state senator, he did not receive official notification of his non-renewal of employment until the end of his contract in May, 1969.[68] In its official notification of Sindermann's non-renewal, the college did not include any notification of the grounds for his dismissal.

When Sindermann was made aware of termination notice, he filed suit in the US District Court for the Western District of Texas. In his suit, he alleged that his non-renewal was based on three issues: (1) his affiliation with the Texas Junior College Teachers Association; (2) his public disagreement with the administration over college policies; and (3) his support of the advancement of the college to 4-year institution status. Furthermore, Sindermann claimed that his Fourteenth Amendment rights had been violated because he had not been provided the opportunity to receive a hearing before the Board of Regents to discover the reasons for his contractual non-renewal and to address any allegations made against him. Finally, Sindermann requested that he receive

"…compensatory and punitive damages and attorney's fees, a declaratory judgment adjudicating that the Regents' action violated his constitutional rights and that he was entitled to a hearing under suggested procedural guidelines, and a mandatory injunction requiring his reinstatement for the 1969–1970 college year at the same level of responsibility and function he had previously held."[69] After hearing the evidence presented before it, the Court granted summary judgment for the Board of Regents stating that since Sindermann worked on a year-to-year contract, he had no contractual right to continued employment at the college and thus was not awarded the opportunity to receive a hearing.

Upon receiving the District Court's decision, Sindermann appealed his case to the US Court of Appeals for the Fifth Circuit. In the ruling of the Fifth Circuit, the Court indicated that although Sindermann's request to attend a legislative hearing, which would inevitably lead to his absence from his classes, was a constitutionally protected right, the college administration did have the authority to deny his request for the absence. Additionally, the Court ruled that the Board's decision to refuse his contractual renewal, which was based on the Board's claim of Sindermann's insubordination, was based on the fact that the plaintiff disobeyed a directive provided him by the college administration which directed him to not attend the legislative hearing.[70] In its response to Sindermann's claims of violation of his right to due process, the Fifth Circuit stated that prior to the court ruling on what procedural rights should have been awarded to the plaintiff the Court had to first determine if a constitutionally protected right to re-employment was available to the plaintiff. According to its analysis of the hiring practices at the college as well as the established college policies for the re-employment of faculty members, the Court had to determine if the plaintiff had tenure within the university system or if he had been awarded continuous employment through college policy and past practices.[71] Upon its final review of the evidence presented, the Court stated that because there was no evidence to support the plaintiff's claim of continuous employment, therefore:

> …upon receipt of notice that a new contract will not be offered, the teacher must bear the burden both of initiating the proceedings and of proving that a wrong has been done by the collegiate action in not rehiring him. It is incumbent upon such a teacher, not the college, to shoulder these responsibilities because the college may base its decision not to reemploy a teacher without tenure or a contractual expectancy of reemployment upon any reason or upon no reason at all.[72]

In its support of the college and the college's ability to offer and renew faculty contracts, the Court stated that if it ruled in favor of the plaintiff, the ability of a college to have the contractual ability to employ personnel would be jeopardized. The Court further commented that by ruling in favor of the plaintiff, they would inevitably be granting tenure to every teacher within the state. However, the Court did indicate that a faculty member has the right to due process so he/she can hear the charges for termination brought against him/her and then provide evidence that addresses those allegations. Although Sindermann had claimed that he had not been awarded the right of due process, the US Court of Appeals for the Fifth Circuit indicated that the college administration informed the Court that prior to the Board receiving a request from the plaintiff for a hearing to address the reasons for his non-renewal of contract, the Board received a court subpoena addressing the charges submitted to the Court by Sindermann.

In the Court's opinion "School-constituted review bodies are the most appropriate forums for initially determining issues of this type, both for the convenience of the parties and in order to bring academic expertise to bear in resolving the nice issues of administrative discipline, teacher competence and school policy, which so frequently must be balanced in reaching a proper determination."[73] Furthermore, the Court explained that in cases dealing with academic matters, the courts should only be involved when either the institution or the employee fails to follow the procedures defined within school policy or when there is a disagreement between the parties with the outcome of a university hearing. In its verdict, the US Court of Appeals for the Fifth Circuit stated that when "...the court decided *Pred v. Bd. of Public Instruction* (1969), which classifies the rights of persons circumstanced such as [Sindermann] as constitutional rather than contractual...This new development in decisional law, coming as it did after the decision of the [district court], renders that court's summary judgment inappropriate and erroneous."[74] The Court reversed the District Court's decision for summary judgment for the defendant and remanded the case back for further review of the constitutional claims made by the defendant.

Upon the ruling of the US Court of Appeals for the Fifth Circuit, the defendants appealed the Court's decision to the US Supreme Court. In his defense, Sindermann showed that, although there was no formal tenure policy in place at Odessa Junior College, there was in fact a de facto tenure system in place that provided him the protection of tenure without tenure truly being evident. Likewise, the Court ruled that due process represents a wide range of interests that are secured by existing rules and policies and is not limited to a narrow scope which is defined by a haphazard conglomeration of forms and templates. Therefore, a person's interest in a benefit is considered to be a property interest for due process purposes if there are rules or mutually explicit understandings that support his/her claim of entitlement to that benefit. Likewise, the Court stated that, although there may not be an explicit contractual provision provided for tenure, that in itself may not always indicate that a professor has no property interest in re-employment. Therefore, the Supreme Court held that a professor within a state institution of higher learning who has the right of re-employment under state law which is defined from either an express or implied contract has a right guaranteed by the Fourteenth Amendment of the Constitution to some form of due process if his/her contract is not renewed.[75]

Additionally, the Court stated that no government, or agency of the government, may deny the benefit of employment to a person on a basis that infringes on that person's constitutionally protected rights. The Court further explained that an academic's freedom of speech cannot be denied because of his/her constitutionally protected speech or associations; otherwise, that person's protected rights would be jeopardized and inhibited. Furthermore, the Court described that in a similar case, *Keyishian*, the Court held that the non-renewal of a non-tenured university faculty member cannot be determined based on his/her actions which are protected by the First and Fourteenth Amendments of the US Constitution.[76] The Court concluded its ruling by citing *Pickering v. Board of Education* (1968), an earlier ruling of the Court, that a teacher's public criticism of his/her superiors on the topic of public matters of concern are constitutionally protected and may not be used as a reason for termination of that individual.[77] However, in *Perry*, the Court did indicate that the Constitution itself does not provide the right of a hearing for the non-renewal of a non-tenured faculty member unless that individual can show that the decision has deprived him/her of an interest in liberty or that he/she had a property of interest in continued employment.[78]

Several key concepts of academic tenure are apparent in this case of *Perry*. The first of these concepts is that in the Court's ruling it stated that in response to the defendant's claim that there was a lack of contractual right to continuous employment or a presence of academic tenure, which alone did not defeat Sindermann's claim, the college's decision to not continue his employment was based on reasons that were protected by the First and Fourteenth Amendment. Second, although there is no constitutionally protected right that safeguards the expectation of having continued employment, the policies and procedures followed at the college created a de facto tenure system that provided the individual with an opportunity for due process where the plaintiff could hear the charges against him and challenge their accuracy. In its judgment, the Court stated that it was evident that the plaintiff's non-retention was based on constitutionally protected rights (First and Fourteenth Amendment) and that the granting of summary judgment in favor of the defendant by the US District Court for the Western District of Texas was in error.

Cohen v. San Bernadino Valley College (1995)

The fourth case to illustrate the constitutional legality of academic freedom and its protection under the First and Fourteenth Amendments of the US Constitution is that of Dean Cohen, a tenured faculty member in the English Department at San Bernardino Valley College.[79] Cohen's employment at the college began in 1968 in the areas of English and Film Studies. In spring, 1992, Cohen taught English 015, a remedial English course which was a pre-requisite for various upper-level courses in the English Department at the college. Throughout his time at the institution, Cohen was known to use controversial teaching methods designed to shock his students as well as to have them write and research topics about which they typically would not be comfortable. During his spring 1992 section of English 015, Cohen introduced a new topic in his instruction that focused on pornography. In one of his lectures, Cohen took a controversial stance and indicated that he had written articles for *Playboy* and *Hustler* magazines. As part of his lecture, he read his articles out loud to the class from these publications. Upon the completion of his lecture, Cohen made an assignment for the whole class that they were to write an essay in which they defined pornography.

After making this assignment, a female student in the course, Anita Murillo, approached Cohen and indicated that she was uncomfortable with his lecture and was offended by the assigned topic. In addition, she requested that he provide her an alternative assignment. Cohen acknowledged the student's concern but insisted that she complete the assignment. According to Murillo, Cohen indicated that if she agreed, they could go to a bar to further discuss ways she could improve her course grade.[80]

Following this dialogue between the professor and the student, Murillo stopped attending the course and, due to the lack of her attendance and completed assignments, she received a failing grade. Being unhappy with the grade she received, she arranged a meeting with the chair of the English Department to complain about Cohen's teaching style and stated that Cohen had sexually harassed her and other female students during his lectures. She further indicated that on several occasions Cohen stared down her shirt as well as the shirt of other female students in the class. She also informed the chair that when she complained to the professor about his looking down her shirt, Cohen's response was that she was simply overreacting to the situation.[81] The chair of the department directed the student to file a formal grievance against Cohen based on her accusations.

Following the direction of the department chair, Murillo filed a formal student grievance with the San Bernardino Valley College Faculty Grievance Committee against Cohen on May 12. On May 26, 1993, the grievance committee held a hearing to investigate and verify the claims made by Murillo.[82] During the hearing, both Cohen and Murillo were provided an opportunity to present evidence to support their claims. Upon the completion of receiving testimony from Cohen and the student, the committee found that Cohen had violated the university's sexual harassment policy,[83] and had created a hostile learning environment in his classroom.[84] The committee submitted its findings to the President of the College District who agreed with the grievance committee in that Cohen had utilized inappropriate teaching methods and that he had sexually harassed his students by creating a hostile learning environment.[85]

Cohen appealed the decision of the grievance committee and the District President to the San Bernardino Valley College Board of Trustees. The Board heard the testimony of all those involved in the case on October 15, 1993, and November 11, 1993, and one week later, on November 17, 1993, handed down their decision siding with the District President. In their decision, the Trustees stated that Cohen had engaged in sexual harassment and, in so doing, had created an unsafe learning environment for his students.[86] Further, the Board of Trustees imposed restrictions on Cohen requiring that he:

1. Provide a syllabus concerning his teaching style, purpose, content, and method to his students at the beginning of class and to the department chair by certain deadlines;
 2. Attend a sexual harassment seminar within 90 days;
 3. Undergo a formal evaluation procedure in accordance with the collective bargaining agreement; and
 4. Become sensitive to the particular needs and backgrounds of his students, and to modify his teaching strategy when it becomes apparent that his techniques create a climate which impedes the students' ability to learn.[87]

Believing that the decision of the Board's was unjustified, Cohen filed suit with the US District Court for the Central District of California against the San Bernardino Valley College Board of Trustees and various other college officials on February 18, 1994. In his filing, Cohen alleged that the college's sexual harassment policy, and thus the sanctions that had been placed on him by the college, were an infringement on his First Amendment rights. To demonstrate support for his argument on how his First Amendment rights were violated by the college, Cohen identified several federal court cases to show that the First Amendment of the US Constitution provided support for faculty rights to academic freedom. According to Cohen (as supported by *Powell v. Gallentine* (1993)[88] and *Levin v. Harleston* (1992),[89]) his right to academic freedom, and thus freedom of speech, prevents the college from reprimanding him for in-class speech[90]. However, in the District Court's response to Cohen's claims concerning his First Amendment rights and its relationship to academic freedom, the Court indicated that although there were judicial rulings supporting academic freedom for faculty, the overall judicial consensus is that the concept of academic freedom is more clearly defined in academic literature than in the courts.[91] To support their opinion, the Court referred to an article by Byrne. In the article Byrne stated that:

> The First Amendment protects academic freedom. This simple proposition stands explicit or implicit in numerous judicial opinions, often proclaimed in fervid rhetoric. Attempts to understand the scope and foundation of a constitutional guarantee of academic freedom, however, generally result in a paradox or confusion. The cases, shorn of panegyrics, are inconclusive, the promise of their rhetoric reproached by the ambiguous realities of academic life.[92]

The District Court further defined how Cohen's claims had no legal backing when they discussed how the cases referenced by the plaintiff focused on non-classroom conduct and not in-class speech.[93]

The plaintiff further attempted to support his allegations of academic freedom within the classroom by referencing several court cases that dealt with a student's constitutional right of freedom of speech within the classroom. To make this point, Cohen referred to the classic case of *Tinker v. Des Moines Independent Community School District* (1969) in which several high school students decided to wear black armbands as a sign of protest against the Vietnam War. In the US Supreme Court's submission, the Court stated that "...[t]he wearing of armbands in circumstances that are entirely divorced from actually or potentially disruptive conduct by those participating in it is closely akin to pure speech which, the United States Supreme Court has repeatedly held, is entitled to comprehensive protection under the First Amendment."[94]

Referencing Cohen's use of a student's academic freedom within the classroom, the Court noted *Hazelwood School District v. Kuhlmeier* (1988). In this case, the US Supreme Court provided a school principal the ability to censor a school paper when the principal ascertained that articles written by student journalists were inappropriate for publication. According to the Hazelwood principal, the identity of students mentioned within the articles easily could be discovered by fellow classmates and the surrounding community.[95] In its ruling, the US Supreme Court stated that although "...[s]tudents in the public schools do not shed their constitutional rights to freedom of speech or expression at the schoolhouse gate; such students cannot be punished merely for expressing their personal views on the school premises—whether in the cafeteria, or on the playing field, or on the campus during the authorized hours—unless school authorities have reason to believe that such expression will substantially interfere with the work of the school or impinge upon the rights of other students."[96]

To provide additional support for its ruling in the case of *Cohen*, the US District Court for the Central District of California referenced *Connick v. Myers* (1983). This case was one in which the US Supreme Court ruled that the government has the right to restrict an employee's speech as long as that speech is not deemed a matter of public concern.[97] According to the District Court, because the plaintiff's speech was deemed as not being a matter of public concern, the defendant had the authority to "require Cohen to distribute a syllabus detailing his controversial teaching style, attend an anti-sexual harassment seminar, and to submit to a formal evaluation of his teaching methods."[98]

Upon receiving the decision from the District Court, Cohen filed an appeal with the US Court of Appeals for the Ninth Circuit, continuing on the grounds that his freedom of speech had been violated. In the Ninth Circuit's submission of Cohen's case, it referred to *NAACP v. Button* (1963) where the US Supreme Court ruled that, when a policy is vague in its understanding and that vagueness leads to an individual's First Amendment rights being threatened, a more precise policy needs to be created.[99] Furthermore, the Ninth Circuit further defined three objections to vague policies in reference to the First Amendment. These objections are: (1) such policies trap the innocent by not providing detailed meaning of the policy; (2) such policies rely on low-level administrators, or ad hoc committees, to interpret the policy; and (3) an unclear policy has the possibility of infringing on First Amendment rights.[100] In the Ninth Circuit's final ruling on Cohen's case, it reversed, in part, the District Court's ruling that held that Cohen's reprimand for his in-class speech did not violate his First Amendment rights; it remanded the case back to the District Court so that no further restrictions were to be placed on the professor; and stated that any indication of reprimand be removed from the plaintiff's personnel file.[101]

In the case described above, the question of a professor's right to academic freedom was raised when a student questioned an instructor's controversial teaching style by stating that the style utilized was in violation of the college's sexual harassment policy. However, when the Ninth Circuit handed down its ruling, it stated that "Cohen's speech did not fall within the core region of sexual harassment as defined by the Policy. Instead, officials of the College…applied the Policy's nebulous outer reaches to punish teaching methods that Cohen had used for many years."[102] The Court, in its decision, failed to rule on the issue of academic freedom because the legality of the college's policy on sexual harassment was vague in nature and unenforceable within a court of law. Furthermore, the Court of Appeals for the Ninth Circuit stated that "Regardless of what the intentions of the officials of the College may have been, the consequences of their actions can best be described as a legalistic ambush. Cohen was simply without any notice that the Policy would be applied in such a way as to punish his long-standing teaching style--a style which, until the College imposed punishment under the

Policy, had apparently been considered pedagogically sound and within the bounds of teaching methodology permitted at the College."[103]

Garcetti v. Ceballos (2006)

The fifth and final case to be examined related to the constitutional legality of academic freedom and its protection under the First Amendment of the US Constitution is that of *Garcetti v. Ceballos* (2006). Although this case does not deal directly with higher education, the implications of the US Supreme Court's decision have had an effect on academia. This effect has seen university administrations utilize the Court's ruling in determining a professor's right to academic freedom.

Richard Ceballos was employed by the Los Angeles County District Attorney's Office as a Deputy District Attorney in 1989.[104] Throughout his tenure with the District Attorney's Office, Ceballos performed his job to the satisfaction of his employer. In 1998 Ceballos was promoted to calendar deputy in the Pomona branch of the District Attorney's office.[105] While working at the branch office, Ceballos was approached by Richard Escobedo, a criminal defense attorney representing a defendant who was charged through the Pomona branch office (at the time, Ceballos was one of the deputy district attorney's working on *People v. Cuskey* [2000]). While in a conversation with Ceballos, Escobedo expressed his belief that one of the deputies that had arrested his client lied in the search warrant affidavit and requested that Ceballos review the case.[106] After reviewing the case file and visiting the scene of the crime, Ceballos determined that the deputy sheriff in question had grossly misconstrued the evidence in the case.

Upon arriving at his determination, Ceballos took his findings to his supervisor (Carol Najera) and the Head Deputy District Attorney for the county (Frank Sundstedt). After meeting with these individuals, it was agreed by all that the evidence presented by the sheriff was questionable. Therefore, on March 2, 2000, Ceballos submitted a formal memorandum to Sundstedt stating that the affidavit had been falsified and recommended that the case be dismissed.[107] When the memorandum from Ceballos was received by the Head Deputy District Attorney, Sundstedt contacted Ceballos and instructed him to reword his memorandum so that it was not overly critical of the arresting sheriff.[108] Following the direction of the Head Deputy District Attorney, Ceballos reworked his memorandum and resubmitted it to Sundstedt. On March 9, 2000, a meeting was called with several representatives from the sheriff's department, the Head Deputy District Attorney, Najera, and Ceballos to discuss the concerns identified by Ceballos in his memorandum. At the completion of this meeting, Sundstedt was still not convinced that the charges should be dismissed from Escobedo's client and decided to proceed with the case pending the outcome of a motion submitted by Escobedo challenging the search warrant.[109]

After being made aware of Sundstedt's decision to pursue the case, Ceballos contacted Escobedo and informed him that he believed the affidavit for the search warrant was falsified. Upon hearing Ceballos' expressions of doubt regarding the validity of the warrant, Escobedo decided to subpoena Ceballos to testify on the legality of the search warrant affidavit.[110]. When Ceballos received the subpoena, he approached his direct supervisor (Najera) and informed her that, in accordance with *Brady v. Maryland* (1963),[111] he would be making available to Escobedo all evidence in the case, including the memorandum he submitted to Najera and Sundstedt.[112] Najera instructed Ceballos to edit his memorandum to include only the statements made by one of the sheriffs present at the March 9th meeting, which Ceballos did.

Following his testimony at the hearing on the motion challenging the validity of the search warrant affidavit, Ceballos was removed from the prosecution team involved with the case against Escobedo's client. According to Ceballos, following his testimony in court regarding the facts behind the awarding of the search warrant, Garcetti (the District Attorney), Sundstedt and Najera retaliated against him. According to Ceballos, the following occurred as a direct result of his testimony:

1. ...they demoted him from his position of calendar deputy to that of trial deputy;
2. Najera 'threatened' him when he told her that he would testify truthfully at the hearing;
3. at the hearing itself Najera was 'rude and hostile' to him;
4. Sundstedt 'gave [him] the silent treatment';
5. Najera informed him that he could either transfer to the El Monte Branch, or, if he wanted to remain in the Pomona Branch, he would be re-assigned to filing misdemeanors, a position usually assigned to junior deputy district attorneys;
6. the one murder case he was handling at the time was reassigned to a deputy district attorney with no experience trying murder cases;

7. he was barred from handling any further murder cases; and
8. he was denied a promotion.[113]

Claiming that he had been subjected to adverse employment actions, Ceballos filed an employment grievance against Sundstedt, Najera, and Garcetti; however, after a brief investigation by the District Attorney's Office of Los Angeles County, he was informed that there was no evidence of retaliation against him. In response to the denial of his grievance, Ceballos filed a suit against Sundstedt and Najera in their individual capacities and against Garcetti in his individual and official capacities and requested the court for lost wages and injunctive relief.[114] Responding to the claims against them, the defendants petitioned the US District Court for the Central District of California for summary judgment based on their Eleventh Amendment rights. These rights were granted by the Court.[115] Furthermore, the defendants explained to the Court that the issues raised by the plaintiff resulted from a staffing shortage and in no way were in retaliation for the memorandum that he had sent. Upon being notified of the defendant's claims that there was no retaliation, Ceballos amended his complaint and resubmitted it to the Court noting that his First and Fourteenth Amendment rights were violated when the Los Angeles County District Attorney's Office retaliated against him for his use of speech that was protected by the First Amendment.[116]

The defendants responded to the plaintiff's claims alleging that they should be granted a summary judgment based on their qualified immunity. To support their claim, Garcetti, Sundstedt, and Najera argued that: "(1) ...[p]laintiff's speech (the March 2, 2000 memorandum) was not protected by the First Amendment; (2) even if the Court finds such speech was protected, the right violated was not 'clearly established'; and (3) the defendants' actions were reasonable under the circumstances."[117] In its ruling, the US District Court for the Central District of California stated that Ceballos's claim of First Amendment protection for his March 2, 2000 memorandum was unsupported by evidence and that because the speech in question was not a matter of public concern, as defined in *Connick*, the defendant's request for summary judgment was awarded.[118]

Upon receiving the verdict from the District Court, Ceballos decided to challenge the decision of the Court and submitted an appeal to the US Court of Appeals for the Ninth Circuit. In his appeal, Ceballos alleged that his use of protected speech in the March 2, 2000 memorandum that he wrote to his supervisor and the Head Deputy District Attorney resulted in him being subjected to adverse employment actions by Garcetti, Sundstedt, and Najera.[119] Additionally, in the plaintiff's submission of evidence, he argued that the District Court erred when it awarded the defendants the right to qualified immunity. Citing *Harlow v. Fitzgerald* (1982) in his defense, Ceballos stated that for a public official to receive qualified immunity, the person must have acted in a manner that did not violate "clearly established … constitutional rights of which a reasonable person would have known."[120]

During the Ninth Circuit's examination of the evidence, it identified that, for the purpose of summary judgment, qualified immunity was not available to the state or county officials because Ceballos's speech was considered a matter of public concern and, as such, was protected by the First Amendment. Furthermore, the Court identified that "… [because] the Eleventh Amendment does not apply to political subdivisions of the state, the county could ordinarily not assert sovereign immunity, although in this case it could do so if such immunity applied to the District Attorney."[121] However, regarding the District Attorney's ability to receive protection under sovereign immunity, the Court noted that because Garcetti's actions were not deemed as the function of the state or county, he was disqualified from receiving protection from the Eleventh Amendment.[123]

When the Court addressed Ceballos's claim of protected speech, it referenced *Coszalter v. City of Salem* (2003) where the Ninth Circuit stated that "…[s]peech that concerns issues about which information is needed or appropriate to enable the members of society to make informed decisions about the operation of their government merits the highest degree of [F]irst [A]mendment protection."[123] Likewise, the Ninth Circuit referred to the US Supreme Court's ruling in *Connick* where the Court noted that when an employee discusses matters of a personal nature in the workplace, such as soliciting an individual's colleagues to determine their perception of topics to promote a personal interest, the employee's speech is not protected by the First Amendment. Continuing, the Court referenced *Connick* when it addressed the matter of an employee's use of speech to discuss "the issue of whether assistant district attorneys are pressured to work in political campaigns is a matter of interest to the community upon which it is essential that public employees be able to speak out freely without fear of retaliatory dismissal."[124]

Reversing the lower court's decision, the US Court of Appeals for the Ninth Circuit remanded the case for further proceedings.

Upon learning of the Court of Appeals ruling, Garcetti submitted an appeal to the US Supreme Court. Following the conclusion of the arguments in the case, the US Supreme Court issued its ruling in which it stated that:

1. "When public employees make statements pursuant to their official duties, such employees are not speaking as private citizens for First Amendment purposes, and thus the First Amendment does not prohibit managerial discipline of such employees for such speech.
2. This result was consistent with the Supreme Court's precedents to the effect that government employees who make public statements outside the course of performing official duties retain some possibility of First Amendment protection.
3. This holding likewise was supported by the emphasis of the Supreme Court's precedents on affording government employer's sufficient discretion to manage their operations.
4. A contrary rule would commit state and federal courts to a new, permanent, and intrusive role involving judicial oversight of communications among government employees and their superiors in the course of official business.
5. The deputy's allegation of unconstitutional retaliation failed, for the deputy had spoken

    (a) not as a private citizen
    (b) pursuant to his official duties as a prosecutor fulfilling a responsibility to advise his supervisor about how best to proceed with a pending case."[125]

The Court further explained that similar to *Pickering*, the challenge that the Court faces is trying to provide a balance between an individual commenting upon a matter of public concern and the State, as an employer, providing a service to the public through its employees.[126] According to the Court, and referencing their decision in *Pickering*, it stated:

> In circumstances where a teacher has made erroneous public statements upon issues then currently the subject of public attention, which are critical of his ultimate employer but which are neither shown nor can be presumed

to have in any way either impeded the teacher's proper performance of his daily duties in the classroom or to have interfered with the regular operation of the schools generally, the interest of the school administration in limiting teachers' opportunities to contribute to public debate is not significantly greater than its interest in limiting a similar contribution by any member of the general public.[127]

As a result of the *Pickering* case, the Court developed a three-step approach for courts to use when determining what constitutional protections can be awarded to a public employee's speech. First, the court must determine if the individual's speech is considered a matter of public concern. If the answer to this question is yes, then the individual's speech is awarded the protection of the First Amendment; however, if the answer to the question is no, then the individual has no claim against his/her employer for the employer's reaction based on the individual's speech.[128] Similarly, in the case of *Garcetti*, the government as an employer has the discretion to restrict an employee's speech, but when doing so, the employing agency must be certain that the restrictions imposed on the individual's speech are in response to the individual's speech and how that speech could negatively affect the individual's work performance and, thus, the organization's ability to perform.[129]

The Court continued in its ruling by referencing *Waters v. Churchill* (1994). In that case, the Court stated that "[T]he government as employer indeed has far broader powers than does the government as sovereign"[130] and as such "...[g]overnment employers, like private employers, need a significant degree of control over their employees' words and actions; without it, there would be little chance for the efficient provision of public services."[131] Applying their statement from *Waters* to *Garcetti*, the Court stated that as a result of Ceballos's submitting a memorandum to his supervisor, an action that was identified as not being outside the realm of his responsibilities as a calendar deputy, the speech he used was not that of a citizen but rather of an employee and as such was classified as not being a matter of public concern; therefore, the protection of the First Amendment was not awarded. However, in the US Supreme Court's ruling in this case, the Justices indicated that the "...expression related to academic scholarship or classroom instruction implicates additional constitutional interests that are not fully accounted for by this Court's customary employee-speech jurisprudence. We need not, and for that reason do not, decide whether the analysis we conduct today would apply in the same manner to a case involving speech related to scholarship or teaching."[132] Furthermore, in support of the Court's indication that the rights awarded to an academic's freedom of speech in the classroom, the Court referred to *Keyishian* in which the United States Supreme Court stated that "...[o]ur Nation is deeply committed to safeguarding academic freedom, which is of transcendent value to all of us and not merely to the teachers concerned. That freedom is therefore a special concern of the First Amendment, which does not tolerate laws that cast a pall of orthodoxy over the classroom."[133] The decision handed down by the US Supreme Court reversed the Court of Appeals decision and remanded the case back to the lower court for further proceedings.

The question of an employee's speech and the protection it is guaranteed by the First Amendment is a key element raised within *Garcetti*. In the US Supreme Court's ruling, the Court reasoned that when an employee uses speech in his/her daily job, and to which that speech is considered to be within the realm of that individual's responsibility, his/her speech is not considered a matter of public concern and does not receive the protection of the First Amendment. However, even though the Court identified work-related speech as being outside the realm of the protection of the First Amendment, the Court did indicate that the decision reached in *Garcetti* did not imperil the First Amendment protection awarded to educators in public institutions of higher learning.[134]

Summary

In the preceding chapter, cases were examined that came through the lower courts and which provided support that faculty can be dismissed when the university can provide evidence that the dismissal is for financial exigency and that faculty were not deprived of their First or Fourteenth Amendment rights. This chapter moved the focus from the lower courts to the Appeals Courts and the US Supreme Court with an examination of five landmark rulings. In these cases, freedom of speech (academic freedom) and due process (academic tenure) were regarded as constitutionally protected rights awarded to faculty within the classroom and where academic freedom was viewed as a subset in the larger realm of freedom of expression.[135]

The key component of the decision in the case of *Sweezy* was that a state, while implementing measures to remove employees considered disloyal, cannot exclude an individual from state employment based solely on the individual's organizational membership. Furthermore, the US Supreme Court ruled that the nation's academic leaders cannot flourish in thought and deeds if their working atmosphere is one of suspicion and distrust. Finally, the Court stated that professors and students in higher education across the nation must have the ability to remain free to research, study, and learn new theories that broaden their way of thinking and the lives of all. It concluded that if these freedoms are repressed, our nation will become stagnate and die.[136]

Similarly, in its ruling in *Keyishian*, the US Supreme Court stated that even though a state has the right to implement safeguards to protect its educational system from subversion, it does not have the right to implement laws that will impede a person's individual rights, more specifically the right to due process and freedom of speech. The Court further explained that academic freedom is a safeguard that is not solely of interest to education, but a concern for the nation; that such a freedom is, therefore, a special concern of the First Amendment, which does not tolerate laws that cast a pall of orthodoxy over the classroom.[137] It was the US Court of Appeals for the Ninth Circuit in *Cohen*, however, that stated that although a college has the right to impose policies that affect someone's speech within the classroom, vague policies cannot be used to hold a faculty member accountable. The Appeals Court addressed Cohen's teaching style by stating that the instructor's speech did not fall under the definition of sexual harassment as identified by the policies of the school. It further stated that the college misused its policy to punish Cohen for teaching methods that he used for many years, thereby infringing on his freedom of speech within the classroom. In their conclusion, the Court stated that with the introduction of the new sexual harassment policy, the college applied the policies broadest interpretation to punish the instructor for his teaching style, one that he had used previously, which was considered pedagogically sound and was within the appropriate bounds of an accepted teaching style at the college.[138]

Although the Courts have set precedent where a professor's freedom of speech has been protected by the First Amendment of the US Constitution, several institutions (i.e., *Adams*) have tried to apply the US Supreme Court's ruling in *Garcetti* to a faculty member's academic freedom. As seen in the opinion of the Court in *Garcetti*, when a public employee functions within the realm of his/her official capacity, the individual is then no longer speaking as a private citizen, but as an employee and, in that capacity, relinquishes his/her protection of the First Amendment.[139] However, the Court further explained that the speech used by educators within their professional capacity, whether in their research or within the classroom, falls under the constitutional protection of the First Amendment which is not typically awarded to those outside the field of education when functioning within their official capacity.[140]

As demonstrated through all of the landmark cases discussed in this chapter, the higher courts have established a precedent through their opinions that the freedom to present unpopular topics in faculty research and in class lectures, as well as protection against termination without cause, are rights protected by the Constitution of the USA. Furthermore, the protections awarded to a faculty member through academic tenure and academic freedom are unrecognized within the court of law. However, as demonstrated in these landmark cases, the rights an educator receives regarding academic freedom and tenure are not acquired through the protections of the AAUP and its 1940 Statement of Principles, or the agreements of any other body, but are guaranteed through the First and Fourteenth Amendments of the US Constitution.

Notes

1. American Association of College Professors, "1940 Statement of Principles on Academic Freedom and Tenure," http://www.aaup.org/AAUP/pubsres/policydocs/contents/1940statement.htm (American Association of College Professors 1940).
2. American Association of College Professors, "1940 Statement of Principles on Academic Freedom and Tenure," http://www.aaup.org/AAUP/pubsres/policydocs/contents/1940statement.htm.
3. J. Peter Byrne, "Academic Freedom without Tenure?," *American Association for Higher Education* (1997) (Byrne 1997).
   U.S. Constitution, amend. 1.
   U.S. Constitution, amend. 14.
4. American Association of College Professors, "1940 Statement of Principles on Academic Freedom and Tenure," http://www.aaup.org/AAUP/pubsres/policydocs/contents/1940statement.htm.

5. J. Peter Byrne, "Academic Freedom without Tenure?," *American Association for Higher Education* (1997).
6. American Association of College Professors, "*1940* Statement of Principles on Academic Freedom and Tenure," http://www.aaup.org/AAUP/pubsres/policydocs/contents/1940statement.htm.
   J. Peter Byrne, "Academic Freedom without Tenure?," *American Association for Higher Education* (1997).
   Although an institution can remove tenured faculty for subpar performance, many choose not to do so because of the financial burdens this process places on an institution.
7. Richard Chait, "The Future of Academic Tenure," *Association of Governing Boards of Universities and Colleges*, no. 3 (Spring 1995) (Chait 1995).
   It is hard to defend to the American public why professors are safeguarded from dismissal during economic downturns, revenue shortfalls, and a reduction in market demand.
8. J. Peter Byrne, "Academic Freedom without Tenure?," American *Association for Higher Education* (1997).
   A system based on labor flexibility in higher education is similar to the one used by businesses who utilize temporary employment to meet market demand.
9. Richard Chait, "The Future of Academic Tenure," *Association of Governing Boards of Universities and Colleges*, no. 3 (Spring 1995).
10. Keyishian v. Board of Regents of the University of the State of New York, 385 U.S. 589 (1967).
    In the US Supreme Court case of Keyishian v. Board of Regents of the University of the State of New York, the Court stated that "Our Nation is deeply committed to safeguarding academic freedom, which is of transcendent value to all of us and not merely to the teachers concerned. That freedom is therefore a special concern of the First Amendment, which does not tolerate laws that cast a pall of orthodoxy over the classroom." This case is further discussed later in this chapter.
11. New Hampshire Subversive Activities Act of 1951, N.H. Rev. Stat. Ann., 1955, c. 588.
    Under this state act, any person was identified as a subversive person if they aided in any act intended to assist in the alteration of the constitutional form of government or overthrow the government by force or violence.
12. New Hampshire Subversive Activities Act of 1951, N.H. Rev. Stat. Ann., 1955, c. 588.
13. Sweezy v. New Hampshire, 354 U.S. 234 (1957).

The State Attorney General for the State of New Hampshire was authorized, by provisions awarded to him under the New Hampshire Subversive Activities Act of 1951, to conduct investigations of individuals who were alleged to have ties to the Communist Party.
14. Leo Huberman and Paul Sweezy, "*Introduction to Socialism*," Monthly Review Press: New York (1973) (Huberman and Sweezy 1973).
15. Sweezy v. New Hampshire, 354 U.S. 234 (1957).
16. Sweezy v. New Hampshire, 354 U.S. 234 (1957).
17. Sweezy v. New Hampshire, 354 U.S. 234 (1957).
18. Sweezy v. New Hampshire, 354 U.S. 234 (1957).
19. Sweezy v. New Hampshire, 354 U.S. 234 (1957).
20. Sweezy v. New Hampshire, 354 U.S. 234 (1957).
21. Sweezy v. New Hampshire, 354 U.S. 234 (1957).
22. Sweezy v. New Hampshire, 354 U.S. 234 (1957).
23. Sweezy v. New Hampshire, 354 U.S. 234 (1957).
24. Sweezy v. New Hampshire, 354 U.S. 234 (1957).
25. Sweezy v. New Hampshire, 354 U.S. 234 (1957).
26. Sweezy v. New Hampshire, 354 U.S. 234 (1957).
27. Sweezy v. New Hampshire, 354 U.S. 234 (1957).
28. Wieman v. Updegraff, 344 U.S. 183 (1952).
The Supreme Court ruled that a loyalty oath used by the State of Oklahoma violated the Fourteenth Amendment because it knowingly placed sanctions for membership in subversive organizations without the oath taker's knowledge.
29. Sweezy v. New Hampshire, 354 U.S. 234 (1957).
30. Sweezy v. New Hampshire, 354 U.S. 234 (1957).
31. Sweezy v. New Hampshire, 354 U.S. 234 (1957).
32. Keyishian v. Board of Regents of the University of the State of New York, 385 U.S. 589 (1967).
33. New York Education Law, section 3022 (1949).
According to Section 3022, "the board of regents shall adopt, promulgate, and enforce rules and regulations for the disqualification or removal of superintendents of schools, teachers or employees in the public schools in any city or school district of the state and the faculty members and all other personnel and employees of any college or other institution of higher education owned and operated by the state or any subdivision thereof who violate the provisions of section three thousand twenty-one of this article or who are ineligible for appointment to or retention in any office or position in such public schools or such institutions of higher education on any of the grounds set forth in section twelve-a of the civil service law and shall provide therein appropriate methods and procedure for the enforcement of such sections of this article and the civil service law."

34. Statutes Section 105 of the New York Civil Service Law and Section 244 of Article XVIII of the Rules of the Board of Regents of the State of New York had been previously passed and enabled the state to remove any state employee that had participated with any subversive organization.
35. New York Education Law, section 3022 (1949).
36. Keyishian v. Board of Regents of the University of the State of New York, 385 U.S. 589 (1967).
37. Keyishian v. Board of Regents of the University of the State of New York, 255 F. Supp 981 (1966).
38. Haig Bosmajian, "Freedom Not to Speak," (New York University Press: New York, 1999) (Bosmajian 1999).
39. Keyishian v. Board of Regents of the University of the State of New York, 255 F. Supp 981 (1966).
40. Keyishian v. Board of Regents of the University of the State of New York, 255 F. Supp 981 (1966).
41. Keyishian v. Board of Regents of the University of the State of New York, 255 F. Supp 981 (1966).
42. Keyishian v. Board of Regents of the University of the State of New York, 255 F. Supp 981 (1966).
43. Adler v. Board of Education, 342 U.S. 485, 493, 72 S. Ct. 380, 385, 96 L. Ed. 517 (1952).
44. *Barenblatt v. USA*, 360 U.S. 109 (*1959*).
    Barenblatt was a teaching fellow at the University of Michigan. He was called before the House of Representatives Committee on Un-American Activities to answer questions relating to his affiliation with the Communist Party. Barenblatt objected to the right of the Committee to question him on his political and religious beliefs. After refusing to answer questions posed to him by the Committee, Barenblatt was found to be in contempt of Congress and sentenced to six months in jail. The US Supreme Court upheld Barenblatt's conviction stating that the House of Representatives Committee on Un-American Activities had been given the authority to investigate Communist activities and that since the defendant didn't object to the questioning when originally posed to him there was no infringement on his Constitutionally protected rights.
45. *Barenblatt v. USA*, 360 U.S. 109 (*1959*).
46. Keyishian v. Board of Regents of the University of the State of New York, 255 F. Supp 981 (1966).
47. Keyishian v. Board of Regents of the University of the State of New York, 255 F. Supp 981 (1966).
48. Keyishian v. Board of Regents of the University of the State of New York, 255 F. Supp 981 (1966).

49. *Speiser v. Randall,* 357 U.S. 513 (1958).
    Plaintiff challenged the decision of the Tax Assessor of Contra Costa County, California when the tax assessor denied Speiser his claim for a veteran's property tax exemption. According to Randall (the tax assessor) the denial of the plaintiff's claim was based on the fact that Speiser had refused to sign an oath statement indicated that he did not support the overthrow of the government. The US Supreme Court ruled that a state's tax program could not suppress a person's freedom of speech.
50. Keyishian v. Board of Regents of the University of the State of New York, 255 F. Supp 981 (1966).
51. Keyishian v. Board of Regents of the University of the State of New York, 255 F. Supp 981 (1966).
52. Adler v. Board of Education, 342 U.S. 485, 493, 72 S. Ct. 380, 385, 96 L. Ed. 517 (1952).
53. Keyishian v. Board of Regents of the University of the State of New York, 255 F. Supp 981 (1966).
54. Keyishian v. Board of Regents of the University of the State of New York, 385 U.S. 589 (1967).
    Appellants refused to sign New York's teacher loyalty laws and regulations (§ 3021 of New York's Education Law) stating that such a requirement is unconstitutional.
55. Keyishian v. Board of Regents of the University of the State of New York, 385 U.S. 589 (1967).
56. Keyishian v. Board of Regents of the University of the State of New York, 385 U.S. 589 (1967).
57. Keyishian v. Board of Regents of the University of the State of New York, 385 U.S. 589 (1967).
    In its ruling, the US Supreme Court stated that the New York Education Laws, in particular New York Education Law, section 3022 (1949), were unconstitutional due to the fact that the state had defined that a person's association with the Communist party was justifiable reason for non-employment.
58. Perry v. Sindermann, 430 F.2d 939 (1970).
59. Perry v. Sindermann, 430 F.2d 939 (1970).
60. Perry v. Sindermann, 430 F.2d 939 (1970).
61. Perry v. Sindermann, 430 F.2d 939 (1970).
62. Perry v. Sindermann, 430 F.2d 939 (1970).
    Sindermann's request to receive paid time off to visit other state junior colleges was a request that had not been made by his predecessors.
63. Perry v. Sindermann, 430 F.2d 939 (1970).
64. Perry v. Sindermann, 430 F.2d 939 (1970).

65. Perry v. Sindermann, 430 F.2d 939 (1970).
66. Perry v. Sindermann, 430 F.2d 939 (1970).
67. Perry v. Sindermann, 430 F.2d 939 (1970).
68. Perry v. Sindermann, 408 U.S. 593 (1972).
69. Perry v. Sindermann, 430 F.2d 939 (1970).
70. Perry v. Sindermann, 430 F.2d 939 (1970).
71. Perry v. Sindermann, 430 F.2d 939 (1970).
72. Perry v. Sindermann, 430 F.2d 939 (1970).
73. Perry v. Sindermann, 430 F.2d 939 (1970).
74. Perry v. Sindermann, 430 F.2d 939 (1970).
75. Perry v. Sindermann, 408 U.S. 593 (1972).
76. Keyishian v. Board of Regents of the University of the State of New York, 385 U.S. 589 (1967).
77. Pickering v. Board of Education, 391 U.S. 563 (1968).
After a proposal was defeated to increase school taxes by local voters, Pickering, a local school teacher, wrote a scathing letter to the editor of the local newspaper chastising the board of education and the school system superintendent for the way they had supposedly mishandled past proposals in raising school funds. After the letter had been published in the newspaper, the school board determined that the article was detrimental to the efficient operation of the schools and that Pickering was to be terminated from employment. The Circuit Court of Will County, IL and then the Supreme Court of Illinois dismissed Pickering's claims of his letter being protected by the First Amendment. Upon hearing the case, the Supreme Court of the USA reversed the lower courts' decision and stated that since there was no proof that the statements made by Pickering were false and that since his remarks were of a public concern, his termination violated his First Amendment rights.
78. Perry v. Sindermann, 408 U.S. 593 (1972).
79. Cohen v. San Bernardino Valley College, 883 F. Supp. 1407 (C.D. Cal.. 1995).
80. Cohen v. San Bernardino Valley College, 883 F. Supp. 1407 (C.D. Cal.. 1995).
81. Cohen v. San Bernardino Valley College, 883 F. Supp. 1407 (C.D. Cal.. 1995).
82. Cohen v. San Bernardino Valley College, 883 F. Supp. 1407 (C.D. Cal.. 1995).
83. According to the San Bernardino Community College District Board Policies, sexual harassment is any "unwelcome sexual advances, requests for sexual favors, and other verbal, written, or physical conduct of a sexual nature...; 2) Such conduct has the purpose or effect of unreasonably interfering with an individual's academic performance or creating an intimidating, hostile, or offensive learning environment."

http://www.sbccd.org/~/media/Files/SBCCD/District/Board/Board%20Policies/5000/5510_Sexual%20Harrassment.ashx
84. Cohen v. San Bernardino Valley College, 883 F. Supp. 1407 (C.D. Cal.. 1995).
85. Cohen v. San Bernardino Valley College, 883 F. Supp. 1407 (C.D. Cal.. 1995).
86. Cohen v. San Bernardino Valley College, 883 F. Supp. 1407 (C.D. Cal.. 1995).
87. Cohen v. San Bernardino Valley College, 883 F. Supp. 1407 (C.D. Cal.. 1995).
88. Powell v. Gallentine, 992 F.2d 1088 (10th Cir. 1993).
Powell was a faculty member, as well as the head of the Humanities Department, at Western New Mexico University. He had made public allegations of grade fraud within a course taught by an adjunct instructor which was under his supervision. According to Powell, in response to his public allegations the university terminated his employment. In the court's opinion Powell's speech was classified as a matter of public concern and was protected by the First Amendment.
89. Levin v. Harleston, 966 F.2d 85, 88–89 (2d Cir. 1992).
Levin was employed as a philosophy instructor at The City College of The City University of New York. While the plaintiff had been employed at the university, he had written several papers that dealt with the intelligence and social characteristics of African Americans. After being assigned to teach a section of Philosophy 101, the Dean of the Humanities Department created a new section of the course for any of Levin's students who may want to transfer out of his class. The dean then wrote to the students enrolled in the plaintiff's class and informed them that a new section of the class had been added to the schedule and that they were free to transfer to it if they so desired. The department chair for the Philosophy Department and Professor Levin believed that the dean's actions were immoral and illegal and filed suit against the University President and the Dean of the Humanities Department. In the court's ruling, it stated that there had been a lack of evidence that supported the action of the defendants and that the threat of disciplinary action was a direct violation against the plaintiff's protected speech.
90. Cohen v. San Bernardino Valley College, 883 F. Supp. 1407 (C.D. Cal.. 1995).
91. Cohen v. San Bernardino Valley College, 883 F. Supp. 1407 (C.D. Cal.. 1995).
92. J. Peter Byrne, "Academic Freedom: A 'Special Concern of the First Amendment,'" (99 *Yale L.J.* 251, 1989) http://www.lexisnexis.com.proxy.lib.ilstu.edu/hottopics/lnacademic/ (Byrne 1989).

93. Cohen v. San Bernardino Valley College, 883 F. Supp. 1407 (C.D. Cal.. 1995).
94. *Tinker v. Des Moines Independent Community School District*, 393 U.S. 503 (1969).
95. *Hazelwood School District* et al. *v. Kuhlmeier* et al., 484 U.S. 260 (1988).
96. *Hazelwood School District* et al. *v. Kuhlmeier* et al., 484 U.S. 260 (1988).
97. *Connick v. Myers*, 461 U.S. 138 (1983).
    For a synopsis of this case, refer to Chap. 3.
98. Cohen v. San Bernardino Valley College, 883 F. Supp. 1407 (C.D. Cal.. 1995).
99. NAACP v. Buttons, 371 U.S. 415 (1963).
    On September 29, 1956, the Virginia General Assembly passed five statutes aimed to cripple the National Association for the Advancement of Colored People (NAACP) in Virginia so that the organization would not be able to submit integrationist lawsuits against the state. In the legislation, the state enabled itself to regulate the practices of barratry, champerty, and maintenance. Barratry is "the 'stirring up' of litigation by inducing individuals or organizations to sue when they otherwise would not." Champerty "occurs when a third party (neither the plaintiff nor their legal counsel) assumes the risks and financial costs of a lawsuit in return for a portion of the monetary award." Maintenance "occurs when a third party supports or promotes a litigant's suit in such a way as to prolong litigation when the parties would otherwise have brought an end to litigation or settled the suit." Later that year, the NAACP filed suit in federal court against the Attorney General of Virginia stating that the five statutes were unconstitutional and infringed on a person's 1st Amendment rights. The U.S. Supreme Court ruled that the statutes were unconstitutional.
100. *Cohen v. San Bernardino Valley College*, 92 F.3d 968 (9th Cir. 1996)
101. *Cohen v. San Bernardino Valley College*, 92 F.3d 968 (9th Cir. 1996)
102. Adams v. Trustees of the University of North Carolina-Wilmington, 640 F.3d 550 (4th Cir. 2011).
103. Adams v. Trustees of the University of North Carolina-Wilmington, 640 F.3d 550 (4th Cir. 2011).
104. *Ceballos v. Garcetti*, 361 F.3d 1168, 1170 (9th Cir. 2004).
105. A Calendar Deputy is a supervisory position that oversees other deputy district attorneys.
106. *Ceballos v. Garcetti*, 361 F.3d 1168, 1170 (9th Cir. 2004).
107. *Ceballos v. Garcetti*, 361 F.3d 1168, 1170 (9th Cir. 2004).
108. *Ceballos v. Garcetti*, 361 F.3d 1168, 1170 (9th Cir. 2004).
109. *Ceballos v. Garcetti*, 361 F.3d 1168, 1170 (9th Cir. 2004).
110. *Ceballos v. Garcetti*, 361 F.3d 1168, 1170 (9th Cir. 2004).

111. Brady v. Maryland, 373 U.S. 83 (1963).
    Brady had been accused of murder. During the trial, the defendant had indicated that he had been involved in the murder but had not been the one that did the actual killing. Prior to the hearing, the prosecution had received a written statement from Brady's accomplice indicating that the accomplice had been the one that had actually committed the killing; however, the prosecution withheld the fact that they had received such a letter from the defense. In the USA Supreme Court's ruling, it stated that withholding evidence from the defense had violated Brady's right to due process.
112. *Ceballos v. Garcetti*, 361 F.3d 1168, 1170 (9th Cir. 2004).
113. *Ceballos v. Garcetti*, 361 F.3d 1168, 1170 (9th Cir. 2004).
114. *Ceballos v. Garcetti*, 361 F.3d 1168, 1170 (9th Cir. 2004).
115. *Ceballos v. Garcetti*, 361 F.3d 1168, 1170 (9th Cir. 2004).
116. *Ceballos v. Garcetti*, CASE NO. CV 00-11106 AHM (C.D. Cal. 2002).
117. *Ceballos v. Garcetti*, CASE NO. CV 00-11106 AHM (C.D. Cal. 2002).
118. *Ceballos v. Garcetti*, CASE NO. CV 00-11106 AHM (C.D. Cal. 2002).
119. *Ceballos v. Garcetti*, 361 F.3d 1168, 1170 (9th Cir. 2004).
120. *Harlow v. Fitzgerald*, 457 U.S. 800 (1982).
121. *Ceballos v. Garcetti*, 361 F.3d 1168, 1170 (9th Cir. 2004).
122. *Ceballos v. Garcetti*, 361 F.3d 1168, 1170 (9th Cir. 2004).
123. Coszalter v. City of Salem, 320 F.3d 968 (9th Cir. 2003).
124. *Connick v. Myers*, 461 U.S. 138 (1983).
125. *Garcetti* v. Ceballos, 547 U.S. 410 (2006).
126. *Garcetti* v. Ceballos, 547 U.S. 410 (2006).
127. *Pickering v. Board of Education*, 391 U.S. 563 (1968).
128. *Pickering v. Board of Education*, 391 U.S. 563 (1968).
129. *Garcetti* v. Ceballos, 547 U.S. 410 (2006).
130. *Waters v. Churchill*, 511 U.S. 661 (1994).
131. *Garcetti* v. Ceballos, 547 U.S. 410 (2006).
132. *Garcetti* v. Ceballos, 547 U.S. 410 (2006).
133. *Keyishian v. Board of Regents*, 385 U.S. 589 (1967).
134. *Garcetti* v. Ceballos, 547 U.S. 410 (2006).
135. Warren Sandmann, "Current Cases on Academic Freedom," annual meeting of the National Communication Association, New York City, NY, November 19–24, 1998 (Sandmann 1998).
136. Sweezy v. New Hampshire, 354 U.S. 234 (1954).
137. Keyishian v. Board of Regents of the University of the State of New York, 385 U.S. 589 (1967).
138. Cohen v. San Bernardino Valley College, 92 F.3d 968 (9th cir. 1997).
139. *Garcetti* v. Ceballos, 547 U.S. 410 (2006).
140. *Garcetti* v. Ceballos, 547 U.S. 410 (2006).

References

American Association of College Professors. 1940. *Statement of Principles on Academic Freedom and Tenure*. http://www.aaup.org/AAUP/pubsres/policydocs/contents/1940statement.htm.

Bosmajian, Haig. 1999. *Freedom Not to Speak*. New York: New York University Press.

Byrne, J. Peter. 1989. Academic Freedom: A 'Special Concern of the First Amendment'. *Yale Law Journal* 99: 251.

Byrne, J. Peter. 1997. *Academic Freedom without Tenure?* American Association for Higher Education.

Chait, Richard. 1995. The Future of Academic Tenure. *Association of Governing Boards of Universities and Colleges* 3 (Spring): 1–12.

Huberman, Leo, and Paul Sweezy. 1973. *Introduction to Socialism*. New York: Monthly Review Press.

Sandmann, Warren. 1998. Current Cases on Academic Freedom. Paper Presented at the Annual meeting of the National Communication Association, November 19–24, in New York City.

CHAPTER 5

Conclusion: Summary and Recommendations

As noted in Chap. 2 of this book, the concept of tenure as a vehicle to provide job security for faculty in higher education can be traced back to the early part of the twentieth century although other venues to provide faculty job security can be seen as far back as the twelfth century. Prior to the arrival of tenure in American universities, faculty in higher education were retained in their positions on informal yearly contracts which were sometimes referred to as "gentlemen's agreements" because they were between gentlemen, namely the university administration and the professor. Contracts such as these were seen as placing a faculty member's continuation of employment at the whim of the university administration or wealthy donors who funded various aspects of the university with large sums of money. This collegial arrangement changed, however, in the early part of the twentieth century when Ross, a Stanford University professor (see Chaps. 1, 2), was summarily terminated for taking stands on issues deemed unacceptable by the wife of Stanford's founder. Ross's termination is seen as a catalyst for the formation of the American Association of University Professors (AAUP), an organization which was formed having as one of its tenets the formalization of tenure and academic freedom among faculty in higher education.

With ever increasing demands for increased productivity and scholarship from moneyed and external political forces being placed on higher education faculty, as well as university administrators terminating faculty for not adhering to university religious or political beliefs, the AAUP sought to codify its position on job security/tenure during its initial meeting in 1915.[1] The original position taken by this association on tenure and academic freedom (as described in Chaps. 1, 2) included a 10-year probationary period during which time new faculty were to have annual reviews to determine their fit with university life. Areas considered essential to university life for faculty, and therefore under yearly review, included a person's proficiency in three distinct components related to academic life. These areas, established in 1915, continue to remain the foundation for tenure decisions to this day and are: teaching/providing quality instruction; service to the university and community as a whole; and scholarly research/publications which, in many instances today, have been further delineated into sub-categories depending on the discipline.[2]

Although these three components are widely accepted within today's higher education environment, no uniform rubric across the higher education spectrum has been developed to assess them. Nonetheless, the concept of quality instruction is generally determined from periodic peer reviews, student evaluations, and administrative reviews of the professor. Similarly, the service caption is generally viewed as the individual's service to the department, college/university through such efforts as committee and accreditation work and the community at large. The research component to faculty reviews is perhaps the most difficult of the three areas to assess as, depending on the individual's area of expertise, a performance or exhibit may be considered comparable to a publication. However, in most disciplines, the research/publication caption encompasses peer-reviewed publications, peer-reviewed presentations, competitive grants, and/or research in one's field of expertise.[3] Then, upon receiving satisfactory evaluations in the three areas cited, and following the recommended probationary period, the faculty member is granted tenure and, therefore, unable to be terminated at the whim of the administration or a wealthy donor.

At the outset of the AAUP's recommendations, many higher education institutions did not comply with the association's recommendations on tenure; however, in 1940, the association revised its tenure position and recommended that the probationary period be reduced from 10 to 7 years (Metzger—Chap. 1). Then, following the end of World War II, as university enrollments began to swell with returning veterans entering higher education with financial assistance provided through the Montgomery GI Bill, universities looked for incentives to retain existing faculty as well as inducements to use when searching for new faculty to accommodate the increasing demand for classes. It was at this point that institutions of higher education began to view tenure as a benefit of employment and implemented the AAUP's recommendation for acquiring tenure following a 7-year probationary period combined with satisfactory reviews of the three components.

As universities moved forward offering their faculties the opportunity to attain tenure based on the AAUP recommendations, they found that the probationary period prior to the awarding of tenure gave them an opportunity to observe how the faculty member interacted with students and peers and provided the administration time to evaluate the value of the individual to the university. In addition, when the probationary period was combined with the three components of the tenure review process, university administrators found that the termination of non-tenured faculty members was less problematic provided that they did not violate the individual's constitutional rights. Even though newly hired faculty were given the opportunity for tenure, university administrators found that non-tenured faculty continued to seek legal recourse to gain tenure as seen in Chaps. 3 and 4. However, for the most part, these attempts to have the courts provide tenure proved unsuccessful because of the policies states and universities had adopted for the acquisition of tenure.

While the path to tenure has a professor undergo periodic review of three components deemed essential for success in university life as well as a probationary period of 7 years, universities have found it difficult and costly to dismiss an instructor once tenure has been granted. Today, with tenure and academic freedom firmly in place at most institutions of higher education, questions concerning the legal relevance of these concepts within the court system have been raised as faculty bring legal proceedings against their institutions for their dismissal regardless of whether they are tenured or not. Therefore, as dismissals of faculty regardless of their tenure status have increased, the following questions are then raised:

What is the definition the courts have provided for the concept of academic tenure?

In answering this question, one must first identify issues related to faculty being terminated because of reasons related to their instructional methods and who filed lawsuits to be awarded injunctive and declaratory relief. With the promise of job security provided through tenure, those who are seeking tenure as well as those already with tenure are still able to seek legal recourse in the event they are denied tenure or terminated after acquiring tenure. Although some individuals may argue that tenure is necessary for the safeguarding of academic freedom, the following case summaries address the legal stance within the court system related to academic tenure.

A landmark case of how due process, or more specifically freedom of speech, was upheld in the courts is found in the case of *Perry v. Sindermann* (1972).

This case, heard before the US Supreme Court, identified tenure as being synonymous with property loss. In this case, Sindermann was employed at several units within the University of Texas system over a period of 10 years on a year-to-year contractual basis. During his last year in the system, he was elected by his peers to be the president of the Texas Junior College Teachers Association. In this role, he publicly supported the concept of Odessa Junior College moving to a 4 year senior institution within the system, a change in status for the college that was in direct opposition to the college's governing board. When his statements were made known to Odessa's administration, he was denied a contract for the coming year and was publicly labeled as being insubordinate by the college's governing board.

Sindermann's case was heard through the lower courts before eventually making its way to the US Supreme Court. In its ruling, the Court found that the college's decision to non-renew his yearly contract was based on the instructor's public opposition to policies passed by the governing board and not his performance in the classroom or as a contributing faculty member of the institution. Furthermore, the Court found that the Texas University System had violated the instructor's First Amendment rights. As can be seen in *Perry*, an instructor's right of freedom of speech was protected by the First Amendment. Furthermore, even though the Court defined Sindermann as having de facto tenure, it established that it was the guarantee of due process (the Fourteenth Amendment) and not tenure that had provided the safeguard of the instructor's employment within the college system.

A second example of a case that establishes tenure as a right to due process is found in *Katz v. Georgetown University* (2001). In this case, the university identified that it had a fiscal exigency which required it to transfer control of its hospital and clinical practices to a private organization while still maintaining control over its medical school. During the transition of the hospital and clinical practices from Georgetown University to MedStar Health, Inc., Katz, who was employed as a tenured clinical professor at the university's hospital, was informed that he could apply for a position at the hospital, now under new management. In addition, the university informed Katz that he also could pursue a non-tenure-track position at the medical school. Finally, as part of the tender related to the transfer of control, Katz was offered a severance package and a monthly installment for 1 year designed to equalize his salary at the now corporate-run hospital with his previous salary at the university. After some consideration, however, he refused the offer and filed a suit against the university insisting that, by university policy, it was required to give him at least a 1 year notice prior to his termination.

This case eventually found its way to the US Court of Appeals for the District of Columbia Circuit. In its ruling, the Court stated that there was no requirement of the university to give Katz a 1 year notice prior to termination. Moreover, the Court found that, according to the faculty handbook, an economic exigency was a just cause for termination of a faculty member (a cause supported by the AAUP in its *1940 Statement of Principles on Academic Freedom and Tenure*). As seen in *Katz*, the right to due process was upheld even though the professor was ultimately dismissed for reasons of financial exigency.

A third example of judicial actions that supports the claim that university faculty have the protection of their Fourteenth Amendment rights regardless of their tenure status is found in the case of *Bignall v. North Idaho College* (1976). In this case, Bignall was employed by North Idaho College for 12 years. During her last year of employment, the college experienced a reduction in enrollment and, therefore, a reduction in student supported income for the college. In a meeting with the college's board of trustees, the college president was instructed to reduce the faculty complement by two full-time positions due to the cutback in funding. Because of the board's directive, the president informed Bignall that her employment would not continue for the upcoming academic year; however, in her notice of termination, the president provided her no reason for his decision.

Upon receiving her letter of termination, Bignall requested a hearing before the board of trustees to discuss the reasons for her termination. In response to her request, the board's attorney informed Bignall that her request was denied because her employment was considered probationary and being such, she was considered a probational employee with no contractual right for due process. Furthermore, the board's attorney indicated that if she provided evidence supporting her claim that she was a tenured faculty member, her request for a hearing would be granted. In response to the trustee's attorney, Bignall filed suit against the college noting that her Fourteenth Amendment rights had been violated and that the college's decision to terminate her was in retaliation for her husband's legal representation of minority students who had filed a lawsuit against the college.

Initially, this case was heard in a district court where the court ordered the college to provide Bignall with a hearing, which it did. However, when the college refused to provide Bignall's attorney with confidential employment records of other faculty members, she withdrew from the hearing and resubmitted her lawsuit to the District Court. Her case was eventually heard by the US Court of Appeals for the Ninth Circuit. In its ruling, the Ninth Circuit identified that Bignall had been provided access to due process, but, on her own volition, decided to withdraw from the process. The Court also referred to the AAUP's *1940 Statement on Academic Freedom and Tenure* (as it did in Katz) when it cited that a faculty member can be released from employment in cases of financial exigency. As seen in this case, although a professor was not tenured, she, nonetheless, was awarded the right to due process, and her withdrawal from the due process hearing became the turning point of the Court's decision to support the board's decision for her termination.

Finally, a noteworthy case related to this question and one that was adjudicated recently within the Federal Court System and which was discussed in this book, is that of *Adams v. Trustees of the University of North Carolina-Wilmington* (2011). In this case, Adams was employed as an assistant professor of criminology by the University of North Carolina, Wilmington Campus. Several years after being awarded tenure, Adams became an evangelical Christian and began publicly expressing issues related to the political state of the university and nation. Several months after publishing a book entitled *Welcome to the Ivory Tower of Babel: Confessions of a Conservative College Professor*, Adams submitted his application for promotion from associate to full professor. After being informed that his request for promotion was denied, he requested to know the reason(s) for the denial in a communication to the chair of the department. In the chair's response to his request, Adams was informed that his promotion was denied due to a lack of scholarly work included in his promotion application.

Upon receiving the notification of his denial of promotion, Adams filed a claim with the US District Court for the Eastern District of North Carolina against the university alleging that the university had violated his First and Fourteenth Amendment rights. According to Adams, the reason for his denial of promotion was in response to his religious beliefs and his lack of support for the political state of the university and nation. Responding to his claims, the university requested and received a summary judgment. Additionally, in its ruling, the District Court referenced the US Supreme Court's decision in *Garcetti v. Ceballos* (2006) where the Supreme Court stated that when public employees function within the realm of their official capacity, they no longer are acting as private citizens and, therefore, are not protected by the First Amendment.

Not accepting this lower court's decision, Adams appealed his case to the US Court of Appeals for the Fourth Circuit. After hearing the case, the Fourth Circuit ruled that, although he failed to prove that the university discriminated against him for his religious convictions, the lower court, in fact, had misinterpreted *Garcetti's* application to this case. It was here that the Fourth Circuit noted that the US Supreme Court, in its summation of *Garcetti*, stated that the freedom of speech issue noted in its case (*Garcetti*) was not applicable to an educator's speech within the classroom. Furthermore, in utilizing the McVey test the Court ruled that Adam's freedom of speech had been violated and referred Adams' case back to the US District Court for the Eastern District of North Carolina for further proceedings.

As seen in these cases, the court system did not recognize the protections awarded to a professor through academic tenure. Instead, the courts insisted that the individual be granted his/her right to due process in each case through the protections awarded by the Fourteenth Amendment. The constitutional right to due process was applied to the plaintiff's claims against their employers and upheld where applicable. Therefore, the answer to the first question of this book, what is the definition the courts have provided for the concept of academic tenure can be summed up as follows: Where the concept of tenure interacts with the Fourteenth Amendment, it provides the expectation of continued employment unless specific conditions subsequent occur. That expectation is what ultimately triggers protection under the Due Process Clause of the Fourteenth Amendment, which is the actual safeguard against arbitrary and capricious termination.

What is the definition the courts have provided for the concept of academic freedom?

The answer to this question is based on the finding that the courts do not recognize academic freedom, but rather consider such cases as a question focusing on a person's right to freedom of speech, a right that is guaranteed to every US citizen by the First Amendment of the Constitution of the US. In each of the cases presented in this book that have focused on academic freedom, and thus freedom of speech, the courts have identified that the matter of academic freedom/freedom of speech within higher education is a constitutionally protected right that is awarded to both adjunct and full-time professors alike. However, when determining the relevancy of the speech in question, the courts have stated that for speech to be protected by the First Amendment the speech must be classified as a matter of public concern. Therefore, the definition of academic freedom, as defined by the courts, is synonymous with freedom of speech and in those cases where this freedom has been contested, the issue of due process (Fourteenth Amendment) has been raised. This relationship will be elaborated upon in Question 3.

Citing the First and Fourteenth Amendment of the Constitution of the USA, what impact have the courts had on academic freedom/tenure?

As noted above, the previous two questions are integrally related as when issues of academic freedom and academic tenure are adjudicated, the courts look at not only legal cases dealing with a professor's right to freedom of speech, but also those cases which address an instructors' constitutionally protected right to due process. As seen in the cases reviewed in this book, the courts do not legally recognize either academic tenure or academic freedom; however, when presented with cases related to these two topics the courts have applied the standards of the constitutionally protected rights of due process and freedom of speech when passing down their verdicts. Within this book, relevant cases were used to address these issues.

The first of these cases related to academic freedom, or as the court identified it, freedom of speech, without the individual possessing tenure which was addressed in this book was that of *Hardy v. Jefferson Community College* (2001). In this case, Hardy was employed as an adjunct instructor in the Communication Department at Jefferson Community College. In the summer semester, 1998,

Hardy was teaching a course entitled the Introduction to Interpersonal Communication. During one of his in-class activities in the course, his students used offensive terms such as "nigger," "faggot," and "bitch" to demonstrate how society uses language to demoralize minority groups. Some students who were in attendance when these words were used were offended by such language. Although the instructor apologized to the students being offended, several African-American students did not accept his apology and contacted a local community leader. This community leader, along with the students, approached the college president and threatened the college's enrollment if action was not taken against the instructor. Following that meeting, the college president met with the assistant dean of students and instructed her to notify Hardy that the issue had been resolved; however, the assistant dean made no mention of the action taken.

Shortly after his meeting with the assistant dean of students, Hardy was contacted by the dean of the communication program and informed that there were no classes available for him to teach the coming semester. At this point, Hardy requested a meeting with the assistant dean of students and the dean of the communication program to discuss the measures being taken. The case eventually found its way to the US Court of Appeals for the Sixth Circuit. In its ruling, the Sixth Circuit found that there was evidence supporting Hardy's First Amendment claims and that his termination was in retaliation to his method of instruction; a clear violation of his First Amendment rights. Therefore, as seen in *Hardy*, the protection of the professor's First Amendment rights were upheld without the instructor having the protection of tenure.

A similar case emphasizing how tenure and academic freedom have been questioned as to their legal relevance within the courts can be found in *Cohen v. San Bernardino Valley College* (1997). In this case, Cohen was a tenured faculty member in the English Department at San Bernardino Valley College. An assignment in one of his courses was for the students to define the topic of pornography. After class a female student informed Cohen that she was offended by the topic of the assignment and asked if she could be given an alternative assignment. Cohen explained to the female student that the assignment was designed to have the students conduct research in an area that was viewed as controversial. The student did not accept his response and filed a complaint with the Chair of the English Department in which she claimed that the instructor sexually harassed female students and that his lecture created a hostile learning environment. In addition to filing her claim with the department chair, the student stopped attending class and followed her departmental complaint with the filing of a formal grievance against Cohen.

The formal grievance filed by the student was heard by the faculty grievance committee, a committee of Cohen's peers. This committee found that Cohen violated the college's sexual harassment policy and that, through the use of his language and assignments, he had created a hostile learning environment. Upon learning of the grievance committee's decision, Cohen appealed his case to the District President and the Board of Trustees. After conferring with the Board, the District President imposed sanctions on Cohen which, according to Cohen, infringed on his First Amendment rights.

Cohen's case finally reached the US Court of Appeals for the Ninth Circuit. In its decision, the Ninth Circuit ruled that the college's sexual harassment policy was unclear and that Cohen's First Amendment rights, indeed, were violated. The issue addressed within *Cohen* focuses on a professor's right to due process and freedom of speech. In the Court's opinion, and thus an example of the protections awarded an academic, when an institutional policy is established that is vague in nature and which impedes a professor's First and/or Fourteenth Amendment rights, that policy is deemed an unlawful encroachment upon the individual's constitutionally protected rights.

A final landmark case that lends support to the claim that a professor's right to freedom of speech is safeguarded with or without the presence of tenure can be found in *Sweezy v. New Hampshire* (1957), a case which took place during the heightened tension of the Red Scare of the late 1940s/early 1950s. In this case, the Attorney General for the State of New Hampshire was directed by the state legislature to seek out public employees who were sympathetic to the Communist Party. Sweezy, a guest lecturer at the University of New Hampshire, was subpoenaed to testify before the State Legislature. During his testimony, Sweezy was asked and answered questions about his political affiliations; however, he refused to answer questions centered on his political affiliation with the Progressive Party and the contents of a lecture that he had provided to course at the University of New Hampshire earlier that year. This refusal prompted the attorney general to petition the Superior Court of Merrimack County, New Hampshire to require Sweezy to answer the attorney general's questions related to his political affiliations and the in-class lecture. When Sweezy continued his refusal to answer these questions, the Court found him in contempt. Following several appeals of lower court decisions, the case eventually wound its way to the US Supreme Court. In its ruling, the Supreme Court stated that when the government exercises its power during the investigative process it cannot infringe upon a person's freedom of speech, freedom of political association, or political affiliation. The Court further noted the right of an individual working within academia to his/her freedom of speech and, more specifically in *Sweezy*'s case, to the right of political affiliation, was constitutionally safeguarded when challenged by his/her employer, or in this case a state government.

The answer then is that the impact that the courts have had on academic freedom and academic tenure derives from the protections awarded to citizens through the Constitution of the USA and its Bill of Rights. In each of the cases presented within this book, the courts have identified that the matters of higher education are best decided upon by educators. The courts, however, have also stated that when a policy encroaches upon an individual's constitutionally protected rights, specifically the right to freedom of speech under the First Amendment and the right to not be deprived of property without the due process of law under the Fourteenth Amendment, those policies then are subject to the court's ruling on the legality of those policies. As witnessed within the cases presented and as an example in *Hardy*, a professor in higher education does not lose his/her First Amendment rights when teaching/lecturing within a classroom and any such claim to the contrary are legally unsupported. Furthermore, as stated previously, although the court system does not legally recognize either academic tenure or academic freedom, the matter of due process (Fourteenth Amendment) and freedom of speech (First Amendment) are protections that have been provided to all citizens, academics included, by the court system.

SUMMATION

Throughout this book, legal cases have been presented to emphasize that there are certain rights awarded to all American citizens of which faculty in higher education are a subset. Moreover, because of these rights granted to American citizens, the protection of tenure sought by faculty members is, in reality, a relic of the past which is no longer required as a safeguard to protect academic freedom within the classroom. It must be noted that tenure in itself does not induce or allay fears of faculty members; the well-developed conversations faculty attempt to pull from their students, as well as among their peers, are not tied to tenure, but rather to the continuing desire to challenge, unbind, and cultivate learning for students as well as the faculty.[4]

Today, public opinion against tenure continues on the rise and legislative measures similar to Oklahoma's House Bill 2598,[5] an attempt to abolish tenure at the state level, will likely become increasingly popular. This public resentment to tenure comes from a view that tenure protects faculty who are outdated and who no longer provide academic value to the university. Such measures and opinions are calling for the tenure's elimination which, in turn, has caused higher education faculty to question how their right to academic freedom will be safeguarded from wrongful termination. Evidence suggests that a good number of professors subscribe to the belief that if tenure is abolished, their right to academic freedom will be minimized.[6] However, in reality, the very rights that tenure awards to each academic professional are already protected by the First and Fourteenth Amendments of the US Constitution. This then raises an unspoken question of this book: What then is the need for tenure in academia?

A postulate to this question is that an alternative to tenure could be the implementation of long-term contracts with periodic reviews prior to renewal as well as built-in grievance procedures to be followed prior to a faculty member's termination. Furthermore, with the increasing frequency of court cases related to tenure, it appears that tenure is an expensive way to protect academic freedom, especially since law and contracts are already in place to prevent institutions of higher education from dismissing professors for exercising their First Amendment rights. Colleges with contract systems have formally endorsed and codified the concept of academic freedom within their faculty handbooks. Therefore, based on the cases cited, it appears that tenure is not needed to protect a professor's freedom of speech.

Recommendations

According to the American Association of University Professors' (AAUP) *1940 Statement of Principles on Academic Freedom and Tenure*, academic freedom cannot exist without the presence of tenure (American Association of College Professors, 1940). Byrne raised the question of whether tenure is really necessary to protect academic freedom when he noted that faculty members who do not possess tenure receive the same protection provided by academic freedom as their colleagues who possess tenure.[7] Likewise, the need for a system within academia which protects a faculty member's freedom to deliver course materials in the classroom is unwarranted because the individual's freedom of speech, and thus academic freedom, is protected by the First Amendment of the USA.[8]

Most recently, White stated that tenure lays no claim to the guarantee of lifetime employment with a university; rather, it only provides that no person retained as a full-time faculty member beyond a probationary period may be dismissed without adequate cause.[9] Incorporating these ideas then into a position on the topic of tenure, it can be stated that tenure as a safeguard to protect an employee's right to due process is a right that is already protected by the Fourteenth Amendment of the USA. Therefore, it is essential that when considering the relevance of concepts such as tenure and academic freedom, one must examine federal and state laws. already in place.

Throughout this book, the relevance of the First Amendment of the US Constitution (Freedom of Speech) and the Fourteenth Amendment (right to due process) were referenced by the courts in termination and denial of tenure cases. The cases cited here, by no means, are meant to be the totality of the cases that exist related to the issue of faculty rights protected by the US Constitution. These cases (*Sweezy*, *Perry*, *Keyishian*; *Adams*; and *Hardy*) were chosen because of the scope of their decisions, their reference to the two Amendments and the impact they have had in the area. Furthermore, in all of the cases cited in this study, the courts ruled that the freedom of speech and the right to due process for the individual are guaranteed and protected rights afforded all citizens of the USA and that instructors in higher education do not relinquish these rights and privileges when accepting employment at institutions that receive federal and/or state funding. Therefore, given the evidence presented through these cases and the ensuing discussion, it is the recommendation offered in this work that tenure, as currently considered and implemented in higher education, is not essential for the protection of instructors as they fulfill their educational obligations to their students, peers, and institutions.

Finally, to provide some semblance of security and continuity to all professional employees in higher education, it is recommended that renewable multi-year contracts which utilize a review process by peers, students, and administration be implemented. This multi-year contractual process, if utilized, must include guarantees to the faculty that their First and Fourteenth Amendment rights will be protected if this route is to become a viable alternative to the current practice of granting tenure as a measure of job security for higher education faculty without the trappings tenure entails. The terms of a multi-year contract system typically operate like those of a tenure system; however, this system must also include wording for an end-of-contract review to provide the requisite information needed to make well-informed decisions regarding the renewal or non-renewal of continuing employment for the individual at the end of the contract term. A renewable multi-year contract system as outlined above provides the individual job security similar to that of a tenure-based system, but also provides the university with flexibility in the event of unforeseen circumstances, either on the part of the university or on the part of the individual. Successful implementation of this type of contractual employment system requires that all professional employees at the institution remain involved with their students, university, and community throughout their careers and addresses the concerns identified by external constituents related to tenure.

NOTES

1. American Association of University Professors, supra, 235.
2. Illinois State University, "Faculty Appointment, Salary, Promotion, and Tenure Policies," http://provost.illinoisstate.edu/downloads/aspt/ASPTmasterAugust2011.pdf (Illinois State University 2011).
3. Id.

This reference is being used as an example due to the fact that it is fairly representative of typical policies at similar universities. However, it is not referenced because there is a uniform policy at all institutions of higher learning.

4. Jonathan Palmer, interview with the Chronicle of Higher Education. Quoted in Robin Wilson, "Tenure, RIP: What the Vanishing Status Means for the Future of Education," (*Chronicle of Higher Education*, July 4, 2010), http://chronicle.com/article/Tenure-RIP/66114/ (Wilson 2010).
5. Oklahoma House of Representatives, "House Bill 2598," Oklahoma City, 2012, http://legiscan.com/gaits/view/372624.

6. Kurt Hochenauer, "Measure Could Abolish Tenure in Oklahoma," (*Blue Oklahoma*, January 29, 2012), http://www.blueoklahoma.org/diary/2554/measuire-could-abolish-tenureTenure-in-oklahoma (Hochenauer 2012).
7. J.P. Byrne, "Academic freedom without tenure?" Washington, DC: American Association for Higher Education (1997) (Byrne 1997).
8. Id.
9. L. White, "Academic tenure: Its historical and legal meanings in the United States and Its relationship to the compensation of medical school faculty members," http://www.lexisnexis.com.proxy.lib.ilstu.edu/us/lnacademic/results/docview/docview.do?docLinkInd=true&risb=21_T9769 416595&format=GNBFI&sort=BOOLEAN&startDocNo=1&resultsUrl Key=29_T9769416598&cisb=22_T9769416597&treeMax=true&treeW idth=0&csi=139118&docNo=5 (White 2000).

References

Byrne, J.P. 1997. *Academic Freedom Without Tenure?*. Washington, DC: American Association for Higher Education.

Hochenauer, Kurt. 2012. Measure Could Abolish Tenure in Oklahoma. *Blue Oklahoma*, January 29. http://www.blueoklahoma.org/diary/2554/measuire-could-abolish-tenure-in-oklahoma.

Illinois State University. 2011. *Faculty Appointment, Salary, Promotion, and Tenure Policies.* http://provost.illinoisstate.edu/downloads/aspt/ASPTmasterAugust2011.pdf.

White, Lawrence. 2000. Academic Tenure: Its Historical and Legal Meanings in the United States and Its Relationship to the Compensation of Medical School Faculty Members. *Saint Louis University Law Journal* 44 (1): 51–80.

Wilson, Robin. 2010. Tenure, RIP: What the Vanishing Status Means for the Future of Education. *Chronicle of Higher Education.* http://chronicle.com/article/Tenure-RIP/66114/.

GLOSSARY

Academic Freedom This term is used to refer to the ability of students and university professors to learn, conduct research, and provide instruction without a professor's or student's fear of reprimand from university or community officials for investigating and addressing controversial topics and issues

Academic Tenure This term is used to refer to an employment standard which follows the expiration of a probationary period. As defined by the American Association of University Professors, individuals who hold tenure enjoy permanent or continuous job security and should only be terminated for just cause or financial exigencies. Academic tenure also provides faculty members a safeguard for academic freedom. The term is also referred to in this paper as tenure

Probationary Period This term is used to refer to a period of time in higher education during which a faculty member is required to display his/her abilities related to various criteria as set forth by the state, the institution, or both prior to being awarded tenure. The time span of this period ranges from 5 to 7 years depending on the state and/or institutional policy

Summary Judgment This term is used to refer to a court ruling where sufficient facts have been provided to the court allowing it to make a ruling without the case having to go to trial

Index

A
Academic freedom, 2–5, 11, 13, 15, 16, 20, 29, 32, 38, 39, 50, 52–54, 61, 74, 75, 84, 87, 88, 91, 93, 94, 99–101, 104, 106, 111, 123, 124, 126, 127, 132, 139–142, 146, 152, 157, 159–162, 168–171, 181–184, 188, 189, 191–193
Adams v. Trustees of the University of North Carolina-Wilmington, 101, 177, 186
American Association of University Professors (AAUP), 2, 4, 11, 23, 37, 51, 61, 74, 75, 79, 80, 83, 87, 140, 181, 192, 194
Authentica Habita, 24, 62
Avignon, 27

B
Barbarossa, 23, 24, 62
Bignall v. North Idaho College, 131–133, 185

Board of Community College Trustees for Baltimore County—Essex Community College v. Jane Adams, 112, 116, 133, 134
Board of Regents of State Colleges v. Roth, 8, 18
Board of Regents of the Kansas State Agricultural College v. B. F. Mudge, 40, 69
Bracken, 32, 33, 65, 66
Bracken v Board of Visitors and Governors of the College of William and Mary, 33

C
Churchill v. The University of Colorado at Boulder, 94, 127–129
Civil Rights, 6, 7, 57, 59, 79, 96, 103, 104, 110
Cohen v. San Bernadino Valley College, 157
Communism, 5, 17, 61, 77

D

Declaration of Principles of Academic Freedom and Tenure, 4, 52, 67, 74
Dewey, 4, 13, 16, 51, 53
Dube v. The State University of New York, 8, 18
Dunster, 14, 31, 69

E

Ely, Richard, 4, 50
European, 3, 4, 23, 24, 28, 30, 31, 37, 39, 62, 63

F

Fairchild vs. Vermont State Colleges, 9
First Amendment, 8, 19, 55, 56, 61, 78, 87, 91–97, 99–101, 103–106, 108, 124, 126, 127, 129, 130, 139, 143, 144, 146, 159–162, 164–169, 171, 175, 176, 184, 187–193
Fourteenth Amendment, 8, 12, 19, 79, 83, 87, 91, 104, 109, 112, 121, 124, 132, 139, 145, 152, 153, 156, 157, 164, 168, 172, 184–188, 190, 191, 193, 194
Freedom of speech, 1, 6, 9, 13, 38, 56–58, 77, 78, 87, 91, 94, 101, 105, 106, 121, 126, 127, 132, 139–141, 145, 149, 156, 159–161, 168, 169, 174, 184, 187, 188, 190–193

G

Garcetti v. Ceballos, 103, 130, 162, 178, 187
Governing board of trustees, 2
Great Western Schism, 23, 27, 63

H

Hardy v. Jefferson Community College, 88, 125–127, 188
Harvard College, 30, 31, 35, 65, 69
Harvard, John, 30, 65
Hatch Act, 48, 61, 71
Homestead Act, 42, 43, 45, 46, 70, 71
Humboldt, 29, 64

K

Katz vs. Georgetown University, 117
Keyishian v. Board of Regents of the University of the State of New York, 146, 171–175, 178

L

Land Ordinance of 1785, 43–45, 70
Lehrfreiheit, 1, 29, 38, 68
Licentia docendi, 25, 26, 62
Lovejoy, 4, 13, 16, 51, 53, 74, 75, 123

M

Mather, Increase, 35
McCarthy, Joseph, 6, 17, 56, 77, 142
McVey test, 105, 130, 187
Middle Ages, 23, 62, 63, 68
Montgomery GI Bill, 5, 17, 182
Morrill Act, 3, 14, 37, 42, 43, 45, 48, 49, 61, 67, 70–72
Morrill, Justin, 46

N

Northwest Ordinance, 43, 45, 70

O

Omosegbon v. Wells, 10, 19

P

Perry v. Sindermann, 7, 17, 58, 79, 92, 124, 126, 131, 132, 152, 174, 175, 184
Pickering balancing test, 92, 126
Pickering v. Board of Education, 92, 100, 125, 126, 129, 156, 175, 178
Plato, 1, 13
Prussian Constitution, 38

R

Ross, Edward, 4, 13, 50, 67, 83, 86, 123

S

Said, Edward, 87, 124
Statement of Principles on Academic Freedom and Tenure, 5, 16, 17, 54, 55, 87, 106, 116, 123, 135, 140, 170, 171, 185, 192
Studium generale, 24–26
Sweezy v. New Hampshire, 142, 171, 172, 178, 190

T

Tenure, 1–20, 23, 24, 36, 37, 39, 40, 50–58, 60, 61, 64, 66, 67, 74, 75, 78, 79, 83–88, 93, 94, 100–102, 106, 109, 111, 115–124, 126, 131, 132, 134, 136, 139–141, 146, 152–156, 162, 168, 170, 181–195
Term of employment, 34, 35, 39, 88, 119
Title VII, 7, 58, 103, 104, 106, 130
Triennial Act, 35
Turner, Jonathan Baldwin, 46, 71

U

Universitas facultatum, 24–26
University of Heidelberg, 27, 28, 63

W

Westward expansion, 23, 41, 42, 45, 46, 60, 72
William and Mary, 14, 30–34, 36, 64, 65
Wisconsin, 4, 7, 8, 17, 18, 50, 72, 73

The manufacturer's authorised representative in the EU is Springer Nature Customer Service Centre GmbH, Europaplatz 3, 69115 Heidelberg, Germany. If you have any concerns regarding our products, please contact ProductSafety@springernature.com

Printed and bound by CPI Group (UK) Ltd, Croydon, CR0 4YY

23/03/2026

02076735-0003